THE CITIZEN'S GUIDE TO CLIMATE SUCCESS

Humanity has failed for three decades to decarbonize our energy system to address the climate threat, yet average citizens still don't know what to do personally or what to demand from their politicians. For climate success, we need to understand the combined role of self-interested and wishful thinking biases that prevent us from acting effectively and strategically. Fossil fuel and other interests delude us about climate science or try to convince us that every new fossil fuel investment is beneficial. But even climate-concerned people propagate myths that hinder progress, holding to beliefs that all countries will agree voluntarily on sharing the cost of global decarbonization; that carbon offsets are effective; that behavioral change is critical; that energy efficiency and renewable energy are cheap; and that carbon taxes are absolutely essential. For success with the climate-energy challenge, we must strategically focus our efforts as citizens on a few key domestic sectors (especially electricity and transportation), a few key policies (regulations and/or carbon pricing); and the identification and election of climate-sincere politicians. As leading countries decarbonize their domestic electricity and transportation sectors, they must use various measures, including carbon tariffs, to ensure that their efforts spill over to affect the efforts of all countries. This book offers a clear and simple strategic path for climate-concerned citizens to drive climate success by acting locally while thinking globally.

A PDF version of this title is also available as Open Access on Cambridge Core at doi.org/10.1017/9781108783453.

A professor of sustainable energy at Simon Fraser University in Vancouver, Jaccard has a PhD in economics from the University of Grenoble. He has helped many governments with climate-energy policy, including serving on the China Council for International Cooperation on Environment and Development and the Intergovernmental Panel on Climate Change. In the 1990s, he chaired British Columbia's utilities commission and in the 2000s he helped design its famous carbon tax, clean electricity standard and other climate-energy policies. He is a member of the Royal Society of Canada in recognition of his research, and a frequent media presence in Canada and the US. His book, *Sustainable Fossil Fuels* (Cambridge, 2005), won the Donner Prize. His efforts on the climate challenge range from testifying before the US Congress and the European Commission to being arrested for blocking a coal train, as he explains in this book.

Advance Praise for *The Citizen's Guide To Climate Success*

"I cannot think of another book that covers this ground. Mark Jaccard has done a huge service, helping to lay out the vexed ground of climate information, disinformation, and conflicting conclusions. In doing so, he helps pave the way for a meaningful conversation on effective solutions to the climate crisis. This is a must-read and must-teach book."
Naomi Oreskes, Professor, Harvard University, and author of Why Trust Science?

"There could not be a more timely guide to taking effective climate action."
Tim Flannery, author of The Weather Makers

"If you're looking for a book that cuts through the contention and cant surrounding our climate crisis, this is the place to start. Renowned economist Mark Jaccard identifies and demolishes ten common myths about climate change and humanity's transition to a low-carbon future. Then he shows what steps we should take, as individuals and societies, to address this critical problem effectively. Fearless in challenging received wisdom, and bold in his prescriptions, Jaccard speaks with a clear, brilliantly informed voice about the greatest challenge of our time."
Thomas Homer-Dixon, Professor, University of Waterloo, and author of
The Ingenuity Gap

"At a time when all too many have given up hope in the battle to avert catastrophic climate change, Mark Jaccard's important new book *The Citizen's Guide to Climate Success* provides a roadmap for success. Jaccard details a viable strategy for citizens working together, placing collective pressure on politicians, to adopt policies that will lead to rapid decarbonization of our economy and the avoidance of truly dangerous planetary warming."
Michael E. Mann, Director, Penn State Earth System Science Center, and co-author of The Madhouse Effect: How Climate Change Denial is Threatening Our Planet, Destroying Our Politics, and Driving Us Crazy

"Mark Jaccard's new book is essential reading for the concerned citizen. Some of the described 'myths' were deliberate lies, but, armed with this deeply thoughtful book, bringing science and human bias and political foibles together, the engaged voter can find the path to meaningful climate action."
Elizabeth May, Canadian Member of Parliament and Leader of the Green Party of
Canada

"Besides taking an axe to the clichés that dominate the current climate change debate, Mark Jaccard tackles head-on the challenge of creating climate change policies that can achieve sustained political support. This is the book to read if you want a realistic, attainable, and sustainable climate change agenda. It's also a master class in teaching about climate science."

Michael Ignatieff, President, Central European University

"Mark Jaccard draws on three decades of extensive expertise and experience from the forefront of academic, national, and international energy policy to dismantle the common myths and skewer the sacred cows that hold us back from the clean energy transition. He doesn't shy away from discussing the difficult, thorny issues of justice and equality, the dirty politics behind policies, and the risks of putting all our eggs in one basket, whether it's nuclear power or carbon pricing. If you've ever wondered what it will take to fix climate change, this book offers the facts, the analysis, and, ultimately, the clarity we need to understand fully the challenges that confront us and the solutions that will lead us to a better future."

Katharine Hayhoe, climate scientist and Professor, Texas Tech University

"A gem. Jaccard welds an activist's passion to a bullshit detector honed by decades of practical experience in the muck of energy policy. Mark has forged a uniquely personal voice out of decades of academic work tempered by hard-won experience in the energy–climate wars. It's smart and relevant yet also fun – finding time to explore the carbon footprint of our sex lives. A bucket of ice water to the face after too many soporific climate books. An impassioned yet dispassionate call to action."

David Keith, Professor, Harvard University, and author of A Case for Climate Engineering

"What is effective climate leadership and how do we overcome political inertia and our biases to ensure swift action? If that's a question that haunts you, Mark Jaccard's *The Citizen's Guide to Climate Success* is the book for you. With the benefit of decades of experience, research, and designing policy, Mark shares his insights and explores some of the myths and delusions that are holding us back in this well-written and exhaustively researched book. I have more hope for our collective success on climate action after reading Mark's clear, uncompromising analysis. Whether you are a concerned citizen, a journalist, an academic, a student, or an elected politician, you should read this book."

Tzeporah Berman, International Program Director, Stand.Earth

"Mark Jaccard gives us very direct, practical steps to make a real difference in the climate crisis – both in our daily lives and with our political powers. This is a potent, smart book that draws on Mark's decades of leadership on climate change, economics, and politics. A crucial read to learn what actions will effectively transform our world from climate crisis to a bright livable future."

Gregor Robertson, Mayor of Vancouver (2008–2018), and Global Ambassador for the Global Covenant of Mayors for Climate and Energy

THE CITIZEN'S GUIDE
TO CLIMATE SUCCESS

Overcoming Myths That Hinder Progress

Mark Jaccard

CAMBRIDGE
UNIVERSITY PRESS

University Printing House, Cambridge CB2 8BS, United Kingdom

One Liberty Plaza, 20th Floor, New York, NY 10006, USA

477 Williamstown Road, Port Melbourne, VIC 3207, Australia

314–321, 3rd Floor, Plot 3, Splendor Forum, Jasola District Centre,
New Delhi – 110025, India

79 Anson Road, #06–04/06, Singapore 079906

Cambridge University Press is part of the University of Cambridge.

It furthers the University's mission by disseminating knowledge in the pursuit of
education, learning, and research at the highest international levels of excellence.

www.cambridge.org
Information on this title: www.cambridge.org/9781108479370
DOI: 10.1017/9781108783453

First published 2020

Printed in the United Kingdom by TJ International Ltd. Padstow Cornwall

A catalogue record for this publication is available from the British Library.

Library of Congress Cataloging-in-Publication Data
Names: Jaccard, Mark Kenneth, author.
Title: The citizen's guide to climate success : overcoming myths that hinder progress / Mark Jaccard,
Simon Fraser University, British Columbia.
Description: Cambridge, United Kingdom ; New York, NY : Cambridge University Press, 2020. | Includes
bibliographical references and index.
Identifiers: LCCN 2019029336 (print) | LCCN 2019029337 (ebook) | ISBN 9781108479370 (hardback) |
ISBN 9781108742665 (paperback) | ISBN 9781108783453 (epub)
Subjects: LCSH: Energy policy. | Climatic changes – Government policy. | Environmental policy. |
Environmental responsibility. | Sustainable development.
Classification: LCC HD9502.A2 J328 2020 (print) | LCC HD9502.A2 (ebook) | DDC 363.738/74–dc23
LC record available at https://lccn.loc.gov/2019029336
LC ebook record available at https://lccn.loc.gov/2019029337

ISBN 978-1-108-47937-0 Hardback
ISBN 978-1-108-74266-5 Paperback

To Esther

Contents

Figures

Acknowledgments

This book has had a long gestation. I apologize to anyone whose early contribution I've now forgotten.

I thank above all my partner, Esther Verheyen, who would drop everything on short notice to review a chapter, even while she effortlessly directed her genetics research lab, wrote and reviewed academic papers, taught university courses, and parented her two teenagers. I also thank my children, Ingram, Kjartan, Torsten, and Sigbrit, for their feedback on my work and continuous help in finding the humorous and fun side of life.

Many others contributed suggestions and provided help along the way, including Brad Griffin, John Nyboer, Noori Meghji, Bruce Mohun, James Glave, Lally Grauer, Thomas Homer-Dixon, John Pearce, and Naomi Oreskes. In particular, I thank Chris Harrison, my editor at Cambridge University Press, for his friendly combination of intellectual rigor and creative encouragement.

I have benefited enormously through the years from the talented and committed grad students in my Energy and Materials Research Group, and the students who take my graduate interdisciplinary course in sustainable energy. Former students who especially contributed to this book include Jacob Fox (for editing and providing the cartoons), Adam Baylin-Stern, Sally Rudd, Aaron Pardy, Rose Murphy, and Thomas Budd.

CHAPTER 1

The Role of Myths in Our Climate-Energy Challenge

We are all capable of believing things we know to be untrue ... the only check on it is that sooner or later a false belief bumps up against solid reality, usually on a battlefield.

George Orwell

I N THE SUMMER OF 1990, AS HE ANNOUNCED HIS ARMY'S SURPRISE invasion of Kuwait, the Iraqi dictator Saddam Hussein told his people that the neighboring oil-rich country was rightfully theirs. Many believed him. When he announced Kuwait's annexation, as Iraq's 19th province, they celebrated with patriotic fervor.

Several months later, a US-led military coalition, which included Arab states, threatened to expel the Iraqi occupiers. Undaunted, Hussein assured his people that their army would annihilate its foes in the "mother of all battles."[1] By this time, some Iraqis were probably questioning, at least to themselves, the veracity of Saddam's claims. But under his brutal dictatorship there was little they could do. In early 1991, they watched in horror as coalition forces destroyed the fleeing Iraqi army. Thousands of their sons, brothers, and husbands were helplessly slaughtered in the desert by the massive firepower of the coalition.

As George Orwell said, a battlefield provides a solid reality check on false beliefs.

The US president who led the coalition was George H. W. Bush. His forces could easily have taken Baghdad and overthrown Hussein. Instead, they halted their advance in southern Iraq and then withdrew. They had achieved their objective of liberating Kuwait – not to mention ensuring that this country would remain a reliable US oil supplier.

Twelve years later, however, Bush's son, following his father's footsteps in the presidency, told Americans that Saddam Hussein was developing weapons of mass destruction that could be used against the US homeland, threatening a repeat of attacks like those of September 11, 2001. Most Americans trusted the second President George Bush and supported his 2003 invasion of Iraq. They believed that overthrowing Hussein would ultimately save American lives by establishing a peaceful, democratic Iraqi government allied with the US.

Six weeks after the attack, under a banner that read Mission Accomplished, Bush declared the end of the conflict. By this time, many Americans were questioning the veracity of his claims. They could no longer overlook daily news of a growing insurgency against the occupying forces and intensified sectarian violence. In the ensuing chaos, most came to realize that the second President Bush and key members of his executive had overstated the threat Hussein posed to their security, and in the process deluded themselves and fellow Americans about the ability of military intervention to transform Iraq into a stable ally. Eventually, the government quietly acknowledged that it had found no weapons of mass destruction in Iraq.

In 1991, many Americans were amused at the blatant self-delusion of Saddam Hussein and his followers in the first Iraq war. The term "mother of all (fill in any word)" became a popular joke.

By 2003, however, the tables had turned. Although few were initially willing to admit it, many came to realize that in the second Iraq war it was the US government and most of its citizens who were delusional. Apparently, even a democratic country like the US, with its educated populace, independent media, separate judiciary, professional intelligence service, and established tradition of political opposition, is vulnerable to collective self-delusion.[2] George Orwell's comment about war's role in correcting delusion can apply to anyone, not just a people under the heel of a despot.

These contrasting histories of the first and second Iraq wars under the first and second George Bush presidents are a reminder that being selective with the facts cannot be dismissed as a temporary phenomenon that only began in 2016 with the US election campaign and presidency of Donald Trump. Certainly, many of Trump's followers seem especially prone to ignore or disbelieve inconvenient evidence, preferring to accept his 'fake news' response to media reports of his falsehoods. But were the enthusiastic supporters of the second Iraq war really so different in their eagerness to see a threat, despite independent UN weapons inspectors saying otherwise?

Indeed, to all but the extremely naïve, it should be obvious that we humans have a propensity to delude ourselves and others. And though we can sometimes detect the delusions of others, we're less good at detecting our own, even when faced with contradictory evidence.

But that seems strange. Surely being incorrect about reality is a detriment to survival, and this must have always been the case. Or was it?

My dictionary defines delusion as "believing a falsehood to be true." This sounds like a fault we would want to correct. If we didn't correct it, surely nature would teach us some hard lessons.

Where survival is at stake, evolution would have forced our ancestors to develop critical thinking skills, to be vigilant for evidence that contradicted their beliefs about the real world in order to correct those beliefs. Otherwise, they might believe a shaman who prophesied that the prey they were stalking would migrate in one direction when evidence suggested otherwise. Or, they might succumb to the wishful belief that the neighboring tribe had peaceful intentions despite strong evidence to the contrary.

But as I read further in my dictionary, the story gets complicated. For the word delusion is akin to the word myth, which is defined as "a commonly held view about the world that may lack factual basis or historical accuracy." Anthropologists tell us that myths have played an important role in social evolution. Commonly held views about our origins, and the religious and social rules that govern our obligations to our families and tribes, ensured the social cohesion with which our prehistoric ancestors survived in nature and outcompeted other humans. Myths about the special powers and authority of individuals and groups among us fostered increasingly effective societal coordination and control, whether for making food or making war.

Thus, myths are stories about the world that can bind and strengthen us collectively in our competition with others. We are more likely to believe them when told by people we trust. And the people we trust are more likely to belong to our family or to groups with whose survival interests we most closely associate – whether tribal, ethnic, religious, socio-economic, or national. This combination of trust and shared belief enables people to coordinate their actions to mutual benefit.[3]

Even so, this strength from shared myths does not negate the fact that trusting a deluded leader is risky. Iraqis paid dearly for Saddam Hussein's delusion about the resolve and capability of countries that would oppose his occupation of Kuwait. Americans paid dearly for the second George Bush's delusion about the resolve and capability of groups that would oppose his occupation of Iraq.

* * *

In the 30 years that I have led a graduate seminar in sustainable energy at my university in Vancouver, a mainstay of the first week of class is an exercise in which I ask the students to give their opinion on one of the controversial options to address climate-changing greenhouse gas (GHG) emissions. These options include massive expansion of nuclear power, greater use of biofuels like ethanol, widespread deployment of carbon capture and storage at coal-fired power plants, major development of large hydropower dams, and geoengineering of the earth's climate. Most of the students have strongly negative views of these options, and explain why with detailed, passionate arguments. Being in an environmental program, they usually argue that the only valid options are energy efficiency and renewable energy. And since their views are similar, I watch them nodding in approval as each presents his or her arguments.

Then comes part two of the exercise. I make them reverse their positions. I make them each provide the best possible evidence and argument for an option they don't like.

At least, that's what they're supposed to do. Most of them do a terrible job. They present feeble, easily countered arguments in support of nuclear power, geoengineering, and so on. So I make them do it again. And again. Eventually, some of them progress. Some even embrace the

4

exercise, keenly probing for the most convincing evidence and arguments in favor of a position they initially opposed.

Others, however, continue to perform poorly. As Chris Mooney noted in a 2011 essay in *Mother Jones*, they can't shift from "thinking like a lawyer to thinking like a scientist."[4] A lawyer is a hired gun, who must focus only on evidence and clever arguments to support the interests of those who hire him or her. In contrast, a scientist can change sides. Indeed, ideal scientists are alert to the best evidence and arguments that counter their current view, and are willing to embrace these. And there is no better way to understand a contrary position than by earnestly presenting it in its best light.

Note that I said 'ideal scientists.' I'm not suggesting all scientists behave this way all the time. But the ideal scientific model is to apply critical skepticism to positions one currently accepts, an open mind to positions one currently rejects, and a willingness to change one's mind after an unbiased assessment of previously unconsidered evidence and arguments. As I tell these graduate students, if they are to do well as academic researchers, they need to be excellent critical thinkers, and they need to apply that talent to their own currently held views.

In my career, I have tried to follow this model. I have pushed myself and research collaborators to know intimately the best evidence and counter-arguments to positions we hold, to even be excited at the prospect of changing our views in the face of new evidence.

This approach has led me to change my mind during the course of my career, sometimes rejecting arguments I once thought irrefutable. One example is the profitability of energy efficiency. In my early days as an academic, I believed we would make money acquiring energy-efficient vehicles, furnaces, appliances, building insulation, light bulbs, industrial equipment, and so on. The higher up-front cost of home insulation, a more efficient furnace, or a high-efficiency light bulb would be compensated by lower energy bills over time. But evidence from leading researchers in top academic journals kept poking holes in this assumption, so I focused my reading on carefully designed research making this case, and even applied some of my research to the topic. Eventually, the evidence compelled me to shift position. For a number of reasons, the unbiased evidence – rather than evidence produced by efficiency advocates – shows that energy efficiency investments are often far less profitable than they initially appear. Researchers conducting hindsight studies find, for example, that insulating an older house often costs more than expected, while the energy savings are often less than expected. My own experiences over three decades of investing in efficiency in seven different houses, with careful recording of all costs and bill savings, provided supporting anecdotal evidence.

Maybe my position on the profitability of energy efficiency will change again. That would be fine. What matters is that my ideas are consistent with evidence and logic from leading independent research. If not, I should be conducting quality research that slowly compels other researchers to reconsider their views.

Another of my early assumptions was that we were rapidly exhausting our fossil fuel reserves, which would result in continuously rising prices of oil, natural gas, and coal. But contrary evidence undermined that assumption. Leading researchers kept demonstrating that the planet's fossil fuel resources are plentiful, especially if our estimates include unconventional forms of oil and natural gas, such as the huge quantities of these resources contained in shale rocks. And evidence from periods of high fossil fuel prices showed how quickly the improved potential for profits can trigger innovations and intensified exploration that increases global estimates of the reserves that are economical to exploit. Certainly, on a finite planet, fossil fuels are finite. But their exploitable quantity is enormous compared to what humans have thus far consumed. This means that innovations might at any time drive their cost of production, and therefore their price, down rather than up.

The emerging evidence two decades ago on the higher cost of energy efficiency and the abundance of fossil fuels changed my assumptions on these two issues. But some of my other early assumptions about energy have survived because the research of leading scholars continues to support them.

Many researchers, including me, have long shown how we have the technological capability to transform the global energy system to one with much lower GHG emissions. Although some people with a vested interest in the fossil fuel status quo have questioned this finding, researchers continue to demonstrate that at a moderate cost we can transition the growing global energy system over several decades. This low-GHG energy system would be dominated by renewable energy, likely in combination with some nuclear power as well as natural gas and coal, where these latter two were used with carbon capture and storage technologies.

This transformation is popularly referred to as 'deep decarboniza-tion,' since carbon dioxide is the most significant greenhouse gas.[5] Estimates of the cost of this energy transition have changed little since calculations by me and many other researchers decades ago. If realized gradually over several decades, it would cost just a few percentage points of Gross Domestic Product (GDP), which is equivalent to losing one year of economic growth over a 30-year period of sustained growth. This modest cost should be compared to the far greater cost and planetary chaos from instead continuing on our rising GHG path.

We have known this for some time. Ongoing research helps refine the numbers but does not affect the validity of this widely held view of the net benefit of an energy transition that would dramatically reduce GHG emissions. Thus, while climate scientists have long agreed on the funda-mentals of GHG emissions and their effects, most energy-climate econo-mists have held fairly similar views on the costs of deep decarbonization of the global energy system. Their views have a somewhat wider range when it comes to the monetary value of the damages from GHG emis-sions. But that is to be expected, given the difficulty of estimating the probabilities and impacts of catastrophic events (hurricanes, relentless droughts and wildfires, fast melting of permafrost and ice sheets, reversal of ocean currents), likely monetary values for biodiversity losses (such as the extinction of polar bears), and the relative weighting of far-distant versus near-term costs (what economists call 'the choice of discount rate').

Given this general consensus among climate scientists and near-consensus among climate-energy economists, our political leaders should have been implementing serious policies at least three decades ago to cause the energy transition, and by now global GHG emissions should be falling. But this did not happen. Instead, while some jurisdic-tions have recently stabilized and even slowly decreased their emissions, global emissions are still rising.[6] Many researchers now admit it is virtually impossible to prevent global temperatures from rising by at least 2°C; there is too much inertia in the energy system for the rapid transformation required to stay within this limit.

But why did it come to this? Why were we unable to act on the climate-energy challenge three decades ago? Why are we still not acting today at anywhere near the required effort? And what can we learn about our past failures to rapidly reduce GHG emissions?

The longer I have worked on this issue, the more my focus has been drawn from my traditional field of expertise – the modeling of energy-economy systems – to the disciplines of political science, public policy, behavioral economics, sociology, psychology, and global diplomacy. It seems almost pointless for experts like me to produce yet another study showing how deep decarbonization is achievable and affordable if that finding continues to have negligible effect on the decisions made by individuals, firms, and governments.

I now believe that people with my expertise must learn from these other disciplines so that we might integrate our knowledge of the energy-economy system with their knowledge of how people make personal and collective decisions, including how they respond to challenges to their worldviews. From this perspective, the psychological research on our all-too-human propensity to delude is critical.

* * *

The recent history of the two Iraq–US wars illustrates delusion operating at the level of countries. Sociologists, psychologists, and other social scientists also focus on delusion among individuals and groups. At the individual level, perhaps it's a friend who denies he has a drinking problem, or a relative who ignores her financially ruinous gambling addiction, or neighbors who insist that their son is an angel when he is a well-known bully. We have all encountered someone who refuses to accept an inconvenient truth that is obvious to those around them.

While we want to help people who are seriously deluded, many false personal views are not easily shed. And it can seem like meddling if we challenge the dearly held illusions of our friends, family, and neighbors.

Sometimes, however, we are forced to meddle. If someone's behavior threatens not just themselves, but others, we may have no alternative.

What if the drinker is poisoning his liver, but also jeopardizing innocent people by driving under the influence? What if the gambler is falling deep into debt, but also stealing from you to support her habit? What if the bully's threats, initially verbal, escalate to physical abuse of your children?

In some cases, events force individuals to acknowledge reality. The threat of divorce motivates the drinker to acknowledge his problem and act to save his marriage. Bankruptcy proceedings lead the gambler to admit her addiction and seek help. The bully's suspension from school motivates his parents to address his behavior. Indeed, our societies have developed legal and institutional mechanisms to protect people when the delusions of some could harm others. Drunk driving is illegal. Bankruptcy leads to loss of credit. Physical abuse incurs criminal assault charges.

In the case of individuals, perhaps a trusted friend, relative, or neighbor will intervene before our delusion gets crushed by reality. Because of that trust, we might be willing to listen. But when it comes to groups, the people we trust often harbor the same delusion.

In an oft-cited 1950s psychology experiment, students from two Ivy League schools, Dartmouth and Princeton, were separately shown the film of a previous game between their football teams.[7] This had been a controversial match, after which the Princeton team had accused Dartmouth of numerous flagrant fouls. But when each movie viewer was asked to record the number of Dartmouth fouls, Dartmouth students noticed only half as many as Princeton students. Depending on their group allegiance, the students saw different realities.

According to Yale professor Dan Kahan, who today conducts similar experiments, 'group ties' are responsible.[8] Just as our perception of reality is biased by our individual self-interest, so too is that perception biased by our group self-interest. In the football game, the students' school loyalty led to a cognitive bias toward evidence that supported the self-interests of their school. And this bias existed not just during the intense emotions of watching the game live in the stadium, but also in the dispassionate setting of a film screening room months later. And it didn't matter that these students attended elite institutions with reputations for promoting objectivity.

Watch any sporting event, professional or amateur, and you will see ample evidence of group cognitive bias. Fortunately, with sports the stakes are not high – although don't try saying that to the parents screaming at the umpire of a Little League baseball game. Unfortunately, group cognitive bias is strongly evident even when the stakes are high.

During his presidential campaign, many of Donald Trump's unfounded claims in speeches and on Twitter presented a textbook case of cognitive bias. He treated as factual unfounded insinuations about his political opponents, whether it was the true birthplace of Barack Obama or the US security threat from Hillary Clinton's use of a private e-mail server. What is interesting from the perspective of group delusion, however, is the striking difference in how those who voted for and against Trump dealt with evidence about him. He promised transparent and corruption-free government yet would not disclose his income taxes. He said he respected women, yet a video of his confidential comments and testimonials from several women indicated the opposite. He claimed he was an honest and sincere person, yet repeatedly made statements that were blatantly false.

Opponents of Trump have a long list of these indictments. Yet almost half of American voters opted for Trump on election day. When pollsters asked why, some explained that they didn't trust Hillary Clinton, so Trump was the lesser of two evils. But many of his supporters said they could not believe bad news about him once they had decided that, as the Republican nominee, he best represented their interests and views. Getting specific facts right didn't matter.

Salena Zito, writing in 2016 in the *Atlantic Monthly*, noted that "Trump's supporters took him seriously but not literally, while the press (and his opponents) took him literally, but not seriously."[9] In other words, the people who ultimately supported Trump came to feel he was more likely than Hillary Clinton to be a member of their group, more likely to be someone who shared their values, faith, views on government, and aspirations for resurrecting American dominance of the world's economy and politics. And, as they came to recognize their group affiliation with Trump, these supporters took his intentions seriously, while becoming selective and dismissive of negative evidence about him. This was easier when one's friends and fellow supporters did the same. And with today's ideologically segregated media and the echo-chamber effect of social media, it was easy for his supporters to downplay and avoid evidence about Trump. Members of the group reinforced each other's cognitive biases.

But while Trump's supporters provide an obvious example, it would be a mistake to think that only one side in the US election campaign was prone to self-delusion. Hillary Clinton's supporters had theirs, as did supporters of her Democratic rival Bernie Sanders. Many of his supporters believed that, if elected president, he would be able to implement left-of-center policies, like tuition-free university, nationalized universal health care, and massive tax increases on the wealthy, in spite of the need to garner majority support for such policies from senators and representatives with far different views.

Such manifestations of group cognitive bias in the US 2016 election should not come as a surprise. The election might have been more extreme than usual in US politics (who knows what the future holds?), but the phenomenon is ubiquitous. In politics and elsewhere we favor evidence and arguments that are consistent with the worldview, self-interest and convenience of groups with which we identify, and we put greater trust in people who have a similar worldview and interests.

But being too far out of sync with reality, whether as individuals, countries, or groups, is risky. For, like Saddam Hussein and the second George Bush, we may one day bump up against that reality, causing great harm to ourselves and others. In the case of GHG emissions and climate change, the independent experts agree, and have agreed for a long time, that the reality we are heading toward is an increasingly harsh one of heat waves, hurricanes, floods, forest fires, rising sea levels, species extinctions, acidifying oceans, and mass migrations of people fleeing devastated areas.

"Thankfully, doctor, I don't suffer from delusion."

Figure 1.1 Cartoon by Jacob Fox

* * *

In 2005, I published a book that summarized the state of research about our energy system and its environmental impacts. I titled the book *Sustainable Fossil Fuels: The Unusual Suspect in the Quest for Clean and Enduring Energy*.[10] I chose this provocative title in hopes that it might stir experts and non-experts to reconsider some of their firmly held beliefs about energy and the climate change threat.

I was already familiar with our human propensity to delude. After all, by 2005 I had been advising governments for over a decade on climate-energy policy. I had seen the challenges for climate-sincere politicians when it came to implementing policies that would reduce our reliance on burning fossil fuels. Nonetheless, I was still surprised at the book's reception from some people. On the one hand, many leading scholars endorsed the book. On the other, the reaction of some people revealed our ability to be selective with evidence.

Those who want to believe that climate change is not caused by humans quickly dismissed my recap of the leading climate science.

Many of the same people, however, accepted my summary of the research confirming that fossil fuels are plentiful. The latter was consistent with their preferences; the former was not.

Those who want to believe we will soon exhaust fossil fuels rejected the research from leading academics showing the abundance of these resources. (When I published the book, the 'peak oil' myth was popular, as it tends to be when oil prices are high.) Yet many of the same people were favorable to my evidence showing we can reduce GHG emissions at a reasonable cost.

Those holding the simplistic view that fossil fuels are evil and renewables good were unwilling to accept evidence that in some locations it might be cheaper and even better for the environment to continue using fossil fuels, albeit while capturing and storing most of the carbon emissions. But they readily accepted the evidence showing that renewables could one day, if we so desired, replace all uses of fossil fuels at an acceptable cost.

As I noted above, these selective interpretations of the book's evidence in conjunction with my growing experience as a climate-energy policy advisor in several jurisdictions gradually shifted my interest from the technical and economic analysis of our energy options to the political, psychological, and sociological challenges of the much-needed energy transition. A special motivator was the ongoing failure of most jurisdictions to implement effective policies, even when experts agreed on the best policies.

My reading of the research was reinforced by these years of real-world personal experiences of policy and political frustrations. As early as 1989, as a novice professor, I was sent by the Canadian government to an expert meeting at the International Energy Agency in Paris to discuss policy options for GHG reduction. We participants were mostly energy economists. We easily agreed that the governments of industrialized countries should immediately implement modest, gradually rising carbon taxes. I helped get the word back to my government. In response, it said the right things, but ultimately didn't act.

From 1992 to 1997, I served as chair of my province's energy regulatory agency, the British Columbia Utilities Commission. In that role, I learned about the challenges of motivating energy utilities to implement energy efficiency and energy substitution programs to reduce GHG emissions. I also served on the Intergovernmental Panel on Climate Change (IPCC), working with other academics to propose and assess climate-energy policies. The disconnect was striking between our policy prognoses in the IPCC reports and what most governments were willing to do. Their initiatives were usually confined to non-compulsory policies, like information programs and subsidies, with negligible effect on fossil fuel burning, and thus GHG emissions.

After Canada signed the Kyoto Protocol in 1997, the university research team I direct was selected by the Canadian government to do the modeling of alternative policy portfolios in a major national policy design process. Later, the government ignored the policy proposals issuing from this multi-year negotiation, and instead trotted out a long list of ineffective policies. In frustration, I co-authored a couple of additional books in the 2000s. *The Cost of Climate Policy* explained the compulsory policies the Canadian government should have implemented to reach its Kyoto commitment.[11] *Hot Air* explored the real-world political calculations behind the government's failure to implement effective climate-energy policies. It helped that one of my co-authors was Jeffrey Simpson, Canada's leading political columnist at the time.[12]

Societal interest in climate change is cyclical, thus so too is political interest. In the period between Hurricane Katrina in 2005 and the global financial crisis in 2008, climate change was a major concern in industrialized countries and increasingly the rest of the world. Al Gore's book and movie, *An Inconvenient Truth*[13] appeared in 2006, as did Nicholas Stern's high-profile report for the UK government, *The Economics of Climate Change*.[14]

As a non-partisan advisor to several Canadian political leaders (our federal government, ten provincial governments, and three territorial governments all expressed interest in GHG reduction), I again experienced first-hand the challenge of enacting policies to cause a major energy transition. I helped design British Columbia's carbon tax of 2007, quickly recognized as the leading climate policy in North America. But during the exhausting and frustrating period of defending the tax against severe misinformation campaigns, I learned the importance of understanding the myths that can confound and defeat the efforts of sincere politicians.

I needed no more hard lessons in real-world policy-making. Unfortunately, it seems that others did. When Stephane Dion, the leader of Canada's federal Liberal party, contemplated a national carbon tax as the central plank of his 2009 election platform, he first asked my advice. In suggesting he consider less politically risky policies, such as the regulations being adopted in California at the time, I said "while the carbon tax might be good policy, it doesn't appear to be good politics." He responded with "I think good policy *is* good politics!" I seem to recall mumbling, "We live on different planets," but perhaps I said that to myself on the bus ride home.

It was obvious to me that his carbon tax proposal would cost him the election, which it did. Prime Minister Stephen Harper, leader of the Conservative Party, focused his campaign on saving Canadians from "job-killing carbon taxes." His victory helped sustain almost a decade of faking-it federal climate policies, along with the aggressive GHG-increasing development of Alberta's oil sands. Thanks to Dion's carbon tax campaign, Canada's emissions went up rather than down.

There is a saying that we should not let perfection be the enemy of good. The carbon tax is, from an economic efficiency perspective, the perfect policy, which is why lots of people, especially economists, keep saying *we must price carbon emissions.* But this statement is factually incorrect; even 100% decarbonization can be achieved by regulations alone. And, in the real world of politics and policy, the selection of GHG-reducing policies involves a trade-off between cost-effectiveness and the likelihood of implementation. Single-mindedly pursue carbon pricing and we could end up with nothing, which is exactly what happened in Canada in the 2000s. I have used this experience, and observations from policy struggles in Australia, France, the US, and other countries, to motivate my research into the trade-offs between academically ideal policies and politically achievable policies. If the latter get implemented and the former don't, which are the better climate-energy policies?

As a university student, I witnessed steady progress in addressing several energy-related environmental challenges, including smog, acid rain, and lead emissions. Early in my academic career, I assumed we would soon achieve similar success with GHG emissions. At one time, I even wondered if we might solve the climate threat too quickly for my intended career as a sustainable energy economist. How's that for delusional thinking?

Instead, the climate-energy issue has emerged as the 'mother of all environmental challenges.' We may reduce other emissions and effluents, restore wetlands, preserve soils, protect threatened ecosystems, but all of this environmental progress will be fruitless if we don't also dramatically reduce GHG emissions, because these impact *everything*. Each decade a new multi-country agreement raises hopes of a serious global effort, only to prove ineffective with the passage of time. In the Toronto agreement of 1988, G7 countries committed to reducing their GHG emissions, but afterwards failed to implement the necessary policies. In the Kyoto Protocol of 1997, all industrialized countries promised to reduce their emissions, but in the ensuing decade the US withdrew and other countries like Canada failed to implement effective policies. In the Copenhagen commitment of 2009, industrialized countries set 2050 targets as a face-saving gesture, after failing to achieve a global agreement requiring immediate action.

A fully global agreement was finally signed in Paris in 2015, but this was only possible by allowing each country to set its own emissions targets, which collectively are far too high for the 2 degrees Celsius limit, and by again avoiding a mandatory compliance mechanism.[15] In sum, after three decades of acknowledged concern by world political leaders, the global effort to reduce GHG emissions is still feeble and sporadic, while fossil fuel-based economic growth, especially in the developing world, increases emissions. Initially, the seemingly achievable goal was to prevent any temperature increase beyond what had happened since the start of industrialization around 1800. But with no action and increasing emissions, the goal has shifted to preventing more than a 2°C increase by 2100, which itself is seriously in doubt.

Our inability to reverse the upward trajectory of GHG emissions is explained in the first instance by our lack of a global governance system combined with the long-standing assumption in international negotiations that voluntarily *all countries will agree on climate fairness*. And while we wait for this impossible agreement to materialize, the effect on national governments is paralyzing. Since none can solve the problem on their own, there are strong incentives to delay a serious effort.

And if climate-sincere politicians in individual jurisdictions wish to show global climate-energy leadership, they must overcome conscious and unconscious myths that hinder their efforts. People who feel committed to fossil fuels, whether for financial benefit or fear of wasteful government policies, deny or obfuscate the climate science, and some of them foster the outlandish claim that *climate scientists are conspirators.* Even people who accept climate science may advance deliberate or inadvertent myths that delay national efforts. Those whose wealth or income is still tied to fossil fuels justify ongoing expansion by fabricating the myth that *this fossil fuel project is essential* – claiming that we must have its jobs and tax revenues, while its share of global emissions is inconsequential. Other people, ignoring the huge quantities of oil in the earth's crust, worry that oil depletion is an imminent threat to sustainability. But the myth that *peak oil will get us first anyway* only helps fossil fuel interests convince governments that regulatory and carbon pricing policies are not needed, since GHG emissions will soon decline as we exhaust fossil fuels.

People who sincerely want rapid decarbonization are also not free of myths that can hinder progress. Those who believe *we must change our behavior* make the solution more difficult than it is by suggesting that climate success requires everyone to live as transit-riding, airplane-avoiding vegetarians. Others believe that instead of changing behavior *we can be carbon neutral* by buying offsets as we continue to drive in cars, fly in planes, eat meat, and so on. Unfortunately, the evidence is clear that many offsets don't reduce GHG emissions.

Some people argue that *energy efficiency is profitable,* because the extra costs of the most efficient appliances, vehicles, buildings, and equipment is repaid many times over from energy bill savings. Unfortunately, inde-pendent research shows this to rarely be true. This wishful thinking bias seems innocent enough, but it inadvertently reduces the pressure on politicians to enact regulations and carbon pricing. If firms and house-holds save money by making energy efficiency investments that also reduce GHG emissions, there is no compelling argument for stringent climate-energy policies.

A similar problem arises from the belief that the costs of solar, wind, and other low-emission energy sources have fallen below that of fossil fuels, suggesting to some people that *renewables have won* the economic contest. Unfortunately, this too is a myth. While the costs of some renewables like solar and wind have fallen dramatically in the past two decades, which is a wonderful development, fossil fuels are still the best option for developing countries to access energy and this won't change any time soon. Renewable advocates and hopeful environmentalists must not allow their wishful thinking bias to inadvertently enable procrastinating politicians to argue that market forces will inevitably reduce GHG emissions because a field of solar panels is cheaper than a coal plant. The accurate and essential message is that renewables, and other zero-emission options like nuclear, won't outcompete fossil fuels until governments regulate or price carbon emissions.

These beliefs that I presented in italics in the above paragraphs, and which are the titles of this book's chapters, are the most salient myths that hinder our progress on climate. Unfortunately, our ongoing failure on the climate-energy challenge has provided the opportunity for many other people to attach additional myths. One prominent example is the belief that *we must abolish capitalism* for climate success. But there are many others.

Trying to make sense of this cacophony of barriers, distractions, and seemingly essential solutions is a nightmare for the climate-concerned citizen. They hear about breakthrough global agreements to save the planet. But in the succeeding months and years they see these agreements unravel while emissions keep rising.

They elect politicians who profess sincerity. But eventually the media confirms their suspicions that little is happening. Even the sincere politicians seem constrained by powerful corporate interests fighting to sustain fossil fuels until the next political or economic crisis shifts everyone's attention, and the climate-energy effort once again dissipates.

They hear inspiring accounts of people taking individual initiatives – abstaining from driving, flying, eating meat, using plastics. But eventually they notice that these people remain a small minority, with little effect on a global problem whose solution requires transformation of the entire global energy system, and a set of compulsory policies in every country to cause the essential decarbonization.

The concerned citizen wants effective action from the global community and their own government, and they want to act now along with fellow citizens. But how do they make governments act effectively? And what can they do individually?

I wrote *The Citizen's Guide to Climate Success* to answer these questions.

By presenting the key takeaways from three decades of experiences and social science research, and by identifying and separating deliberate and inadvertent myths from the evidence on which most leading researchers can agree, my goal is to help concerned citizens become effective as change agents in the face of our daunting climate-energy challenge, strategically recognizing the few tasks on which we must focus our efforts.

I conclude this opening chapter with a synopsis of the book's evidence and arguments. The titles of Chapters 3 through 12 are statements reflecting beliefs that are widely held, but range from blatantly wrong to questionable, once we probe the evidence. Some of these, like the idea that climate scientists are conspirators, are the fabrication of powerful economic interests trying to slow humanity's response to the climate threat in order to continue earning personal wealth from fossil fuels. Some are beliefs of sincere climate-concerned people, like the assumption that renewables are cheaper than fossil fuels, that may inadvertently retard our efforts to reduce GHG emissions. Fortunately, the challenge is simpler than most people realize. We need to quickly decarbonize a few key sectors of our economy, and there are only a couple of policies that can do that. We need to make sure that our politicians understand that a global effort requires realism about international politics, and always act on this understanding. We need to strategically focus ourselves, our friends, our fellow citizens, and our political leaders on these few sectors, actions, domestic policies, and international mechanisms on *the simple path to success with our climate-energy challenge.*

* * *

The combustion of fossil fuels is the primary cause of rising global GHG emissions. Because the global energy system is more than 80%

dominated by fossil fuels, the transformation to reduce emissions is a major undertaking. It is especially challenging because fossil fuels are wonderful sources of energy that have provided great benefits to humanity over the last two centuries, and still do. The rapid improvement in human material well-being in China from 1985 to 2015 is the latest testament to how fossil fuels can enable a tremendous increase in human welfare, albeit while also rapidly increasing GHG emissions. And because fossil fuels are the incumbent energy source in our global energy system, many people associate their personal self-interest either with the fossil fuel supply industry or with the consumption of fossil fuels, as coal in their power plants, gasoline in their cars, and natural gas in their homes. These people have difficulty accepting the idea that we must quickly phase out fossil fuel extraction and the technologies that combust fossil fuels, and some have worked hard to prevent or slow this development by deluding themselves and others about the problem and its possible solutions.

The reduction of GHG emissions is a 'global collective action problem' in that all countries must act together for success. Otherwise, the GHG reduction efforts of some countries will be defeated by increasing emissions from other countries that continue to benefit from developing and consuming fossil fuels. Because we do not have a global government, we must agree on effective global mechanisms that incentivize and enforce the GHG-reducing efforts of all countries. Unfortunately, the global community of nations has had only limited success in developing such mechanisms.

One success was the voluntary global agreement, the Montreal Protocol of 1987, that quickly phased-out emissions of chemicals that were destroying the ozone layer. For some, this agreement is a sign for optimism for negotiating a voluntary global agreement on GHG emissions.

However, the dominance of fossil fuels in the global energy system, and the enormous benefits they provide, make GHG reduction a challenge of far greater magnitude. In particular, the interests of different countries diverge dramatically. Some countries that are endowed with valuable fossil fuel reserves are less enthusiastic about a global agreement, and some are downright obstructionist. Most poorer countries, even if they have no fossil fuels, are not willing to forgo the economic development benefits of importing and consuming fossil fuels, just as China did, unless wealthier countries will help them with the higher costs of restricting themselves to low-emission energy alternatives.

Yet, in spite of these strong incentives against an effective global agreement, and 30 years of demonstrated failure, international negotiations are still dominated by the assumption that countries will somehow agree *voluntarily* on a fair allocation of the burden. This assumption must change, but this requires individual countries to accept sooner rather than later the role that unilaterally imposed carbon tariffs must play in assembling a true global effort.

These two constraints – the global dominance of fossil fuels as a valuable commodity and the global governance nature of the GHG reduction challenge – make it extremely difficult to motivate effective domestic GHG-reducing efforts by national and sub-national levels of government. If one government alone forces its industries to reduce emissions, these will accuse it of foolishly destroying the domestic economy for no global benefit, since competing industries in laggard countries will gain market share, the result being a loss of jobs and wealth with no net reduction in global emissions. In fossil fuel endowed countries, the same argument applies. Why constrain one's extraction and export of coal, oil, or gas if this domestic restriction will inevitably be offset by expanded fossil fuel production elsewhere?

These constraints help explain the wide gap between the promises of national political leaders when making long-term GHG commitments, and their short-term enactment of feeble policies with negligible effect. If individual governments are to make headway, they must realize, as some now are, that their domestic decarbonization efforts should focus on sectors of their economy and energy systems that are less vulnerable to international competition. Significantly decarbonizing the electricity system and energy used in transportation, buildings, and low energy-intensity economic sectors, including agriculture and forestry, is possible without detrimentally affecting the competitive position of most countries. Electricity and transportation stand out because these two sectors count for more than 50% of expected global emissions growth over the next two decades, with most of this occurring in developing countries.

And when climate-leading countries finally recognize the necessity of carbon tariffs, they should join forces with like-minded countries to form 'climate clubs' that establish consistent carbon tariffs on the imports from laggard countries. This will incentivize these latter to take their own domestic GHG-reducing actions to avoid the imposition of tariffs. This hard-nosed approach to GHG emissions offers the best prospects for finally forging an effective global climate effort.

It also improves the prospects for aggressive domestic action. It is easier to convince people to support such actions in one jurisdiction when they can see that their efforts are not futile, but instead part of a successful global strategy to address the global collective action problem.

Unfortunately, our prolonged failure in implementing a successful global strategy has bought time for defenders of the fossil fuel status quo to hone their techniques for deluding people that the climate science is still uncertain or that this particular fossil fuel project is essential or that policies are unnecessary because we'll soon run out of fossil fuels thanks to peak oil.

Faced with this desperate situation, the citizen has two options. One is to avoid thinking about climate change. Since one person is powerless in the face of such an enormous problem, it does no good to keep worrying about it. Understandably, many people have consciously or unconsciously taken this approach.

The other option is to think strategically about how to apply one's efforts to greatest effect. This book is for these people. Drawing on leading independent research, I provide guidance for citizens seeking to act more effectively as consumers, neighbors, investors, participants in social and conventional media, voters, and political and social activists. We must improve at distinguishing efforts that are strategically effective from the many distractions that reduce our chance of success. If, for example, we are personally focused on energy efficiency or behavioral change or carbon neutrality, we need to incorporate lessons from leading research to guide us in integrating these efforts with strategic political pressure to attain climate-energy policies that will amplify our efforts. We need to understand which policies and individual actions are more effective and, of these, which have a better chance at political acceptance and collective success.

Citizens should understand that while the situation is dire, it is not hopeless. Several converging developments may soon help humanity reach a tipping point beyond which our global deep decarbonization efforts will accelerate. One of these developments, albeit not a happy one, is that GHG impacts are intensifying, making it increasingly difficult to delude people about the climate science. Scientists predicted rising temperatures and an increasing intensity and quantity of hurricanes, droughts, wildfires, heat waves, and other extreme events, and these are now appearing on cue. Just like the previous shift in public beliefs about the cancer threat from smoking, several decades of evidence are gradually shifting public views, and thus the public's readiness to accept more serious government efforts to cause an energy transition.

Another encouraging development is the falling cost of key low-emission alternatives to burning fossil fuels. Electricity from wind power and solar power, when matched with reliable backup such as natural gas turbines, pumped hydro, or batteries, costs much less than just a decade ago, and costs are still falling. As several jurisdictions are demonstrating, rapid reduction in GHG emissions in the electricity sector can be achieved without dramatic increases in electricity prices – a possibility that seemed fanciful just two decades ago. Likewise, electric vehicles are now rapidly penetrating the market, allowing leading jurisdictions to target the complete phase-out of gasoline vehicle sales within a decade. Electric cars still cost more to purchase, but their operating costs can be one quarter that of an equivalent gasoline or diesel vehicle. And their initially high purchase price is rapidly falling.

A third positive development is the growing recognition in developing countries of the co-benefits of deep decarbonization, especially in the electricity and transportation sectors. The choking smog caused in large part by coal-fired power plants and fuel-burning vehicles threatens the health of urban elites in developing countries. National political leaders in capital cities like Beijing, Delhi, Jakarta, and Mexico City are concerned about the impacts of urban air pollution on their fellow citizens and their own families, and are starting to pursue energy transformation without waiting for financial support from wealthier countries. With a strong set of policies, China now leads the world in generating electricity from wind and solar and in the production and consumption of electric cars. The benefit from decarbonizing electricity generation and urban transportation presents an attractive model for all developing countries, even if they do not yet feel financially able to pursue GHG reduction as a stand-alone objective.

A decade ago, middle-class citizens, whether in well-off or less well-off countries, were severely limited in their ability to voluntarily reduce their individual emissions. Since the energy system was completely structured around fossil fuels, they would have had to stop using electricity, stop driving, and stop heating and cooling their homes to reduce emissions. Today, however, electricity generation emissions in most developed countries are falling as the output of coal-fired power plants declines, which in turn dramatically increases the GHG impact of switching from a gasoline to an electric car, and from switching to electric heating and cooling. These changes are not always cheap. But they are also not exorbitant, increasing the cost of household energy services by 5 to 15% in a typical jurisdiction. And since energy services normally account for only 5 to 8% of typical household budgets in developed countries, and in the middle-class urban areas of developing countries, this is a small cost to prevent climate change. Thus, anyone with a middle-class income can today become zero-emission in their home energy use and personal mobility. Imagine the effect as more people pursue this path and demonstrate for neighbors, friends, and family the ease of achieving zero-emission daily living through their technological choices.

As individual consumers, we still have no way to avoid the fossil fuels used by airplanes, steel plants, cement plants, and plastic manufacturers. But as we decarbonize electricity, transportation, and buildings, the pressure on these other sectors intensifies. Yes, policy implementation is more difficult in these sectors because of their exposure to international competition. But we now have commercialized bio-jet fuels, steel plants that can include carbon capture and storage, and cement plants that can use biofuels and bio-rich municipal solid wastes while capturing and storing their process emissions. In all cases, the cost of near-zero-emission plane travel and producing commodities like steel, plastic, and cement would increase, but not enough to significantly increase the cost of final manufactured goods, like houses, cars, wind turbines, and solar panels.

Thus, we can now take actions as consumers that directly reduce emissions from our homes and vehicles, and this increases the chance that our friends, family, and neighbors will follow our lead. We can also be more focused in our social, political, and civil efforts by distinguishing faking-it policies from real policies. We now know that politicians in well-off countries should have already implemented regulations that phase out coal plants and required their replacement by low-GHG electricity generating alternatives, mostly renewables. We now know that these politicians must immediately implement carbon pricing or regulations that phase out gasoline and diesel in transportation, triggering the wholesale shift to electric, hydrogen, and biofuel vehicles. We also know that domestic efforts to decarbonize electricity and transportation must be combined with international efforts to develop carbon tariffs with other climate-leading countries. Otherwise, our domestic efforts will be inconsequential against a global challenge, and opponents of GHG reduction are experts at convincing many people of this futility.

The good news, if we can call it that, is that effective actions and policies are easier to detect because, as the situation becomes urgent, we know they must cause a clear and rapid decarbonization of electricity and transport. Actions and policies that are tangential or even working at cross-purposes should be viewed with skepticism.

But my goal is not to convince people to abandon strategies they support in the decarbonization effort. Rather, I suggest how they might integrate their advocacy of behavioral change, carbon neutrality, energy efficiency, renewable energy, and political change, with the few key actions and policies that are essential for the energy transition. Challenging people's perceptions and priorities is never easy. My hope is that by showing what leading scholars agree on, I might nudge people toward a more effective individual and collective effort by integrating their pursuits with those that are clearly essential. And by being more open to options they had previously rejected for some reason.

Thus, I challenge readers in the same way that I challenge the new graduate students each year in my sustainable energy course. If you have firm views on some aspect of the climate threat, I ask you to find the best possible counter-arguments to your view. If you believe that nuclear power must be phased out, force yourself to develop an argument that nuclear power could be sustained where plants already exist, and perhaps in other jurisdictions, especially if safer technologies and radioactive waste disposal are developed. If you believe nuclear power must be expanded, ask yourself why that might not be necessary, and why it will be so difficult to convince a sufficient number of people to support the location of new nuclear plants near their homes.

If you believe no amount of biofuels should be allowed because this option would inevitably destroy rainforests and raise food prices, force yourself to design a regulatory regime in which some amount of biofuels could be produced in environmentally benign methods to replace only a segment of oil demand, such as jet fuel or diesel for long-distance trucking. If you are certain that energy efficiency is important, challenge yourself to think about how a singular policy focus on energy efficiency is endorsed by the fossil fuel industry if this helps delay implementation of the essential fuel-switching policies. And if you believe that carbon pricing is essential, force yourself to argue for equally effective policies that have a greater chance of political success in the drive to deep decarbonization.

The goal of this exercise in critical thinking and reverse argumentation is not to cause people to completely abandon their beliefs and strategies. Rather, the exercise is of value if it prompts some to explore ways of integrating their favored action or action-motivating policy with that small subset of actions and policies that is absolutely essential. The text box summarizes these essential elements of the path to success with the climate-energy challenge.

Decarbonizing the global energy system is a global collective action problem, but humanity lacks global governance mechanisms for allocating costs among countries and enforcing universal compliance.

A 'voluntary' global agreement is unattainable because country interests differ greatly.

1. Poorer countries want substantial support to forgo fossil fuels in favor of low-emission energy, which wealthier countries will only partly provide.
2. Fossil fuel-rich jurisdictions are resistant to rapid decarbonization.

The simple path to climate success requires leader countries to pursue three strategies.

1. Apply regulations and/or carbon pricing to decarbonize domestic electricity and transportation, and work with other leader countries to globalize this effort.
2. Apply carbon tariffs on imports from climate-laggard countries and work with other leader countries to form climate clubs that globalize this effort.
3. Assist poorer countries in adopting low-emission energy, especially where this meets air quality and other co-benefit objectives.

Citizens must focus their governments on the strategic path, which requires overcoming deliberate and inadvertent myths that deflect us from these strategies.

This task of focusing our political leaders on the simple path sounds simple. But it isn't. The lack of global governance, the delusional tactics of vested interests, and our widespread propensity for wishful thinking combine to produce climate-insincere governments. This leads to the critical question: What should climate-concerned citizens do when their compatriots elect such governments?

The range of options for the concerned citizen is wider than most people are willing to consider. But if ever there was a time to recognize the full extent of that range, this is it. Thus, if unwilling or insincere politicians succeed electorally in a given jurisdiction, concerned individuals and groups should be willing to frequently, loudly, and non-violently express the strength of their conviction about the need to address this threat. Demonstrations and other acts of civil expression, perhaps even passive civil disobedience, may be required. Citizens concerned about the climate-energy threat need to understand the instrumental role that a relatively small number of committed people can play in driving change. As Margaret Mead is purported to have said, "Never doubt that a small group of thoughtful, committed citizens can change the world. Indeed, it's the only thing that ever has."[16]

We have to be honest with ourselves about our responsibilities with this daunting global challenge. For if we cannot quickly focus on this strategic path, including on our efforts as individual and groups of citizens, we are, as George Orwell might have suggested, destined to bump up against hard reality – on a planet that looks increasingly like a battlefield.

CHAPTER 2

The Art of Deluding Ourselves and Others

A man with a conviction is a hard man to change. Tell him you disagree and he turns away. Show him facts or figures and he questions your sources. Appeal to logic and he fails to see your point.

Leon Festinger

I N JULY 1992, THE MARLBORO MAN DIED OF LUNG CANCER. IN October 1995, he died of lung cancer again. And in October of 1999, he did it yet again. I remember being confused by the news of these deaths. Having grown up in the sixties, I had naïvely assumed that the Marlboro Man was a real person, some cowboy who begrudgingly tolerated a rare photo-shoot at the ranch. But now there were several of them, and they were dying. Why?

The history of Marlboro cigarettes is a marketing case study in business schools. In the 1920s, Marlboros captured only a niche market as one of the first filtered cigarettes. Targeting women with the slogan "mild as May," their advertisements promised that the filters protected teeth from smoke-stains. But in the 1950s, researchers started claiming that cigarettes caused lung cancer, as well as heart disease, bronchitis, emphysema, and diabetes.

In response, tobacco companies downplayed and discredited the research, while each angled for a competitive edge by promoting its brand as less risky thanks to special tobacco, special filters, special production processes, and reassuring new slogans like "more doctors smoke Camels."[1] Philip Morris and Company, the maker of Marlboros, hired Leo Burnett's advertising agency to concoct a new ad campaign.

(If you've watched the Madmen TV series, you can picture the era and its characters.) Although their research showed that men were interested in switching to filters because of health concerns, it also showed they wouldn't switch to Marlboros because of the feminine image. Burnett's rebranding brainwave was to sidestep the health issue when targeting men by creating a masculine image of the male Marlboro smoker as a rugged, uncompromising cowboy. The risk of lung cancer wouldn't concern this hombre.

Right from the start of its 1955 advertising launch, the company noticed a strong response. In two years, Marlboro sales jumped from $5 billion to $20 billion. They sold well with every male profession except cowboys, who were presumably not so keen to emulate some modeler dude. In 1962, Marlboro incorporated its famous theme song (from the movie *The Magnificent Seven*) to complete the image of a mythical land of self-reliant cowboys enjoying a good-tasting cigarette, that just happened to be filtered, with the slogan "Come to where the flavor is, come to Marlboro Country." In my generation of city-slickers, this music and slogan still evokes visions of cowboys on dusty cattle drives. Allan Brandt, in *The Cigarette Century*, accurately described me and my friends in writing "children of the 1960s can sing the Marlboro jingle on cue."[2] By the time the US banned tobacco advertising on television and radio in 1971, Marlboro had climbed from number six in the US to number one in the world. Marlboro country had become Marlboro planet.

Some people don't know that mass consumption of cigarettes is a 20th-century phenomenon. In 1900, less than 5% of adult males smoked them (pipe and cigar use was higher). Male cigarette smoking started rising in World War I and continued to climb for 50 years, peaking at 60% in 1958. Female use rates were much lower, but then rose during and after World War II to peak at 35% in the late 1960s. With smoking rates of both genders finally declining, they converged in the 1980s and have continued down to below 15% today. While at one time almost all celebrities and politicians openly smoked, today most are discrete about their addiction.

Prior to the cigarette fad, lung cancer was a rare disease. But by the 1950s, health researchers detected a dramatic increase, especially in men. In fact, with disturbing precision, the growth of the disease tracked the cigarette adoption rate with a two-and-a-half decade lag: rising first for males, and then for females, after a delay that perfectly matched the delay in female uptake of smoking.

As for the identity of the Marlboro Man in the ads, there had been several, some of them actual cowboys. Darrell Winfield had the longest run. A rancher before being discovered by advertisers in 1968, he appeared in Marlboro ads for the next two decades. Besieged by news of dying Marlboro men in the 1990s, Philip Morris maintained that Winfield was the only true Marlboro Man.

But this was not true. Wayne McLaren modeled briefly for Philip Morris in 1976. A lifelong smoker, he was diagnosed in 1989, at age 50, with lung cancer. He devoted the last two years of his life to a high-profile anti-smoking campaign that directly targeted the Marlboro Man. This included a TV ad showing him wasting away in a hospital bed with a commentator saying, "Lying there with all those tubes in you, how independent can you really be?" Removal of a lung couldn't stop the cancer from spreading to his brain. His death was followed by the lung cancer-related deaths of former Marlboro men David McLean in 1995 and Richard Hammer in 1999, prompting an anti-smoking campaign that branded Marlboros as "cowboy killers."

Thus, the Marlboro Man is famous and infamous: a symbol of the triumph of creative advertising, but also of the ability of clever corporations, using enormous financial resources, to convince people to ignore risk. The experience with cigarettes, and especially Marlboros, has important lessons that go beyond the risks from smoking.

* * *

In the 1950s, the tobacco industry created the Tobacco Institute and the Tobacco Industry Research Committee. These entities played a prominent role in the 'smoking war' of the 1950s and 60s, as industry tried to sustain sales by thwarting challenges from scientists first, then activists, then the media, and then government regulators. The standard technique was to publicly downplay the scientific findings while privately funding research to create doubt about its validity. A key strategy, as Richard Kluger noted in *Ashes to Ashes*, was to present scientific findings as "just a theory."[3]

By 1959, with its 'alternative' research churning out diversionary studies, the Tobacco Institute was able to release press statements claiming that scientific evidence conflicted with the tobacco-smoking theories of lung cancer. It wasn't necessary to completely refute the scientific evidence. Creating doubt was sufficient. Surveys showed widespread public uncertainty on the issue, even though independent scientific research was by then consistently verifying the strong link of smoking to lung cancer. Scientists had reached a consensus on the causal relationship, although there remained lots of uncertainties on specific aspects of the risk.

The surveys also showed how some people's propensity to believe independent scientific research depends on their financial self-interest or their personal convenience. Those professionally involved in the tobacco industry were less likely to accept that cigarettes cause cancer, even if they accepted scientific evidence in most other aspects of their lives. Smokers were also biased. If you were addicted to smoking, if your self-image involved smoking, you were less likely to believe the science. It was too inconvenient.

A 1954 survey found that while 49% of non-smokers believed smoking caused lung cancer, only 31% of smokers did. Remarkably, this pattern was found even among doctors, a profession that relies directly on scientific health research. While 65% of non-smoking doctors accepted that smoking caused lung cancer, only 31% of smoking doctors did – the same percentage as smokers among the general public.

But while the tobacco industry continued its doubt-sustaining campaign, health advocacy groups made steady progress in pushing the policy agenda. In 1964, the US Surgeon General officially accepted the scientific evidence that smoking can cause lung cancer. New US regulations prohibited sales to minors and banned advertising on TV and radio. Cigarette taxes were increased to deter consumption. Governments introduced educational programs in schools, public service ads on TV and radio, and danger labels on cigarette packages, some in horrifically graphic detail. Over time, views about the science gradually shifted.

Figure 2.1 summarizes several decades of Gallup polls asking people if they believe smoking causes cancer. It suggests that the government regulatory and educational policies of the 1960s had a significant effect.

	Believe smoking causes cancer (%)		
Year	Smokers	Non-smokers	All
1954	31	49	41
1958	33	54	45
1969	59	78	71
1981	69	91	83
1998	88	93	92

Figure 2.1 Smoking and cancer beliefs

In the 11 years from 1958 to 1969, Americans making the connection vaulted from 45% to 71%. Since 1998, more than 90% of Americans accept that smoking causes lung cancer, which is probably as good as can be hoped given the percentage of die-hard contrarians in any population.

Notice the longevity of the gap between the left and center columns. Smokers and non-smokers heard the same evidence from scientists, government, and anti-smoking advocates since the 1950s. But they also heard from the science-denial campaign of the tobacco industry. As psychologists explain, the health risk information was disquieting for smokers, so more of them were willing to disbelieve the legitimate science. A gap of 20 points between the beliefs of smokers and non-smokers continued for four decades as the US government and anti-smoking advocates tried to counter the campaign of the tobacco industry. The gap only closed to 5 points in the 1990s, by which time almost everyone had accepted the science.

That it took four decades to overcome the science-denying campaign is alarming news for those who hope to see our society accept and act upon scientific information about climate change. But there is some good news in this story. We didn't have to wait for everyone to accept the science before government acted in the 1960s and 70s. Although there were still a lot of skeptics, a growing coalition of scientists, anti-smoking advocates, and smoking-concerned politicians stood up to the tobacco industry and finally implemented effective policies. Gradually, these efforts helped bring public views into alignment with scientific views.

Today, the inconvenience of quitting is counter-balanced by the inconvenience of finding a comfortable place to smoke, often huddling outside in a cold alcove trying to avoid rain and snow. This reversal of inconvenience occurred because governments finally acted on a second volley of scientific research showing that non-smokers face a health risk from second-hand smoke. Governments were helped in this effort by the growing militancy of non-smokers in their demands to work, play, travel, and reside in smoke-free environments. Once again, these efforts were resisted by the tobacco industry.

This second smoking war emerged in 1986 when a report by the US Surgeon General concluded that second-hand smoke also caused lung cancer. The tobacco industry replicated its earlier tactics, this time with even greater financial resources and sophistication. As explained by Naomi Oreskes and Erik Conway in *Merchants of Doubt*, the Reynolds Tobacco Company hired Fred Seitz, a physicist who had helped build the first atomic bomb, to distribute $45 million in the 1980s to biomedical research that might reveal the many other factors besides second-hand smoke that could cause lung cancer and other lung-related illnesses for non-smokers. The public relations departments of tobacco companies used this research to cast doubt on statements by scientists, doctors, and the US Surgeon General. It provided ammunition for what Oreskes and Conway describe as "successful strategies for undermining science, and a list of experts with scientific credentials available to comment on any issue about which a think tank or corporation needed a negative sound bite."[4] These tactics helped to delay action on the legitimate scientific findings until 1992, when the US Environmental Protection Agency finally ruled that second-hand smoke causes lung cancer.

The smoking wars reveal a lot about the connection between self-interest, delusion, and risk. Thanks to the tobacco industry's determined, well-funded efforts, public acceptance of the scientific consensus on the health risks of first- and second-hand smoke took decades longer than it should have, delaying policies that would have saved millions of lives. The 'undermine-the-science-to-delay-policy' strategy of the tobacco companies ensured massive profits for decades.

As David Michaels notes in *Doubt Is Their Product*, the lessons for other industries facing similar threats would not go unnoticed.[5] People's willingness to be deluded for reasons of self-interest and convenience is an exploitable trait for those seeking to protect the profits of an industry engaged in harmful activities.

* * *

Researchers try to determine when and why humans delude themselves, and when and why they don't. In *Brain and Culture*, Yale psychologist, Bruce Wexler, detailed how the brain's neurological development is partly determined by genetics and partly by our social-environmental experiences, especially those occurring early in our lives.[6] Once our neural structures are developed, mature individuals increasingly pursue and create experiences that reinforce the way their brain sees the world, while rejecting, downplaying, or ignoring information that is at odds with this vision. In short, we get stuck in our ways.

This doesn't mean, however, that humans are incapable of adapting their vision of the world, especially when experience shows us that this may be necessary for survival. While the initial responses to the plagues sweeping Europe in the Middle Ages emphasized prayer in hopes of being spared God's wrath, some townspeople augmented their prayers with campaigns to eradicate rats and quarantine the sick. When this seemed to help, people adapted their views and their practices. They did not stop praying to God and giving thanks when spared from the plague. They simply integrated an effective harm prevention practice with their existing spiritual beliefs because these latter served additional purposes. History is replete with such examples.

Thus, we shouldn't assume that our views about the world, and especially our behaviors, can never change in response to counter-evidence. Rather, we should think about our brains as balancing what they experience with what they want to see. As D. Gilbert said in *Stumbling on Happiness*, "To ensure our views are credible, our brain accepts what our eyes see. To ensure that our views are positive, our eyes look for what our brain wants. The conspiracy between these two servants allows us to live at the fulcrum of stark reality and comforting illusion."[7]

This is how self-help authors and motivational speakers earn a living. They try to help people modify their views to better accord with reality. The consumer lifestyle of many people far exceeds their income, leading to unsustainable levels of personal debt. With help, some overcome their unrealistic views about what they can afford to buy, and develop restrained consumer habits. Many people want to accomplish more, but lack motivation. With help, some become more realistic in linking daily activities to personal and career goals.

While psychologists work on individual misperceptions, social psychologists, sociologists, and anthropologists study collective delusions. In the 1950s, Leon Festinger and colleagues studied the Seekers, a cult that believed it was communicating with aliens, one of whom was the reincarnation of Jesus Christ.[8] Channeling through one of the Seekers, the aliens set a precise date for the end of the Earth – December 21, 1954. The Seekers believed that they alone would be rescued by a space ship. When the date passed uneventfully, Festinger observed that instead of abandoning their beliefs in the face of this refuting evidence, the group soon constructed an explanation to sustain their delusion: the planet had been spared because of their devotion. They became more convinced than ever in the validity of their beliefs, and the reinforcing effect of like-minded thinkers made denial and delusion that much easier. It was from observations like these that Festinger developed the theory of cognitive dissonance, which explains ways that people deal with evidence that contradicts what they believe.

Indeed, how we perceive reality as a group can be scarier than our perceptions as individuals. Having the people we trust reinforcing our distorted view of reality makes it even more difficult for us to recognize and accept contradictory evidence. But wasn't the advance of science supposed to change all of this? Are we not now living in an evidence-based society in which we modify our collective worldviews according to the latest understanding generated by scientific inquiry? Isn't collective delusion diminishing thanks to science?

There is no doubt that critical thinking and scientific processes have unleashed an amazing dynamic of human comprehension and mastery of the physical world. Think of the risks to human health from first- and second-hand smoke. Independent scientists began to detect a causal relationship. Soon other scientists were trying to verify or refute this interpretation of the world. Their work reinforced the emerging understanding that smoking is indeed a cause of lung cancer. Critical thinking, research, and scientific processes lead to an advance in human knowledge that could improve health, if acted upon.

But then what happened? Those whose financial self-interest would be harmed by this new understanding – the tobacco industry – raised doubts about the science, or at least its perception by the public and government. And those whose lives would be inconvenienced by this new understanding – smokers – became less likely to accept the findings from independent scientists and more likely to embrace information that undermined it. And like the Seekers, these interest groups reinforced each other's skepticism, inoculating themselves against the external threat from science.

This is how the collective human propensity to delude plays out repeatedly in a world that otherwise appears to accept the validity of independent scientific inquiry. People are generally open to the findings of science, but less so when those findings conflict with their financial interests or lifestyle. Those whose financial self-interest depends on fostering delusions that disagree with the findings of science are well aware of this all-too-human propensity, and increasingly adept at exploiting it. And as investigations of the smoking wars showed, this new field of creating and sustaining delusion became as sophisticated as the disinterested scientific processes it sought to subvert.

A key tactic is to find scientists who for some reason reject the emerging consensus on a given issue. Some of these individuals may be contrarians by disposition or may hold their convictions deeply based on their unique interpretation of evidence. Some may be enticed by research funding or personal income from the corporations that finance them. Some may be high-profile scientists with expertise in a different field, who nonetheless enjoy presenting themselves as experts in other fields. Oreskes and Conway chronicled in *The Merchants of Doubt* how the same few scientists brazenly presented themselves to the US media and policymakers as experts on smoking and cancer, then the ozone layer, then acid rain, and then climate change.

A second tactic is to focus on areas of scientific disagreement and present these as critical to the whole enterprise. Even in areas of broad agreement, the nature of science is to focus on uncertainties, no matter how trivial. The resulting scientific debates and uncertainties can appear to the public and media, if presented in the right light, as fundamental problems. Scientists agree that tobacco smoke contains chemicals that can damage DNA to trigger cancerous cell growth, and that smoking spreads these toxins into your lungs and then through your body. But they continue to research and debate the details of this process. The trick is to present this ongoing research and debate as proof that scientists are still uncertain about the underlying causal link between smoking and cancer.

A third tactic is a well-known technique in debate called 'poisoning the well.' This involves finding some reason to question the credentials of the scientists whose research confirms the harmful causal relationship. This happened during the tobacco wars. As we shall see in the next chapter, the practitioners of science confusion also applied this technique with climate change.

I conclude this brief chapter by reiterating that while I have only an amateur reader's understanding of research on human bias, I believe that we natural scientists, engineers, and economists who work on the climate-energy challenge need to better understand research by the disciplines that probe this subject and we must integrate its lessons into our work. We cannot afford to stay in our silos. We know why society must act. We know the few actions which are absolutely essential. But we don't think enough about how we make those actions happen. A critical task is to help our fellow citizens see through the delusionary techniques of those who don't want action.

CHAPTER 3

Climate Scientists Are Conspirators

We run carelessly to the precipice, after we have put something before us to prevent us from seeing it.

Blaise Pascal

O N TUESDAY, AUGUST 23, 2005 THE US NATIONAL HURRICANE Center detected a low-pressure system southeast of the Bahamas and quickly classified it as tropical depression 12. Initially, there was nothing noteworthy about this storm. But by mid-morning the next day, as the depression traveled northwest toward the Bahamas, data from Doppler radar, satellite, and aircraft reconnaissance indicated winds reaching tropical storm speed. The National Weather Service promptly christened it in accordance with the alphabetized naming system for tropical storms and hurricanes. The next name had been used twice previously, once for a 1999 hurricane that swept Central America and once for a 1981 hurricane that hammered Cuba. But this would be the last run for the name Katrina. After 2005, it would be officially retired, just as professional sports teams retire the numbers of memorable players.

With its winds accelerating, Katrina turned west, heading straight for the Florida coast near Miami. The weather service issued a hurricane warning. With winds reaching 130 kilometers (80 miles) per hour on the 25th, Katrina passed the threshold to Category 1 hurricane status. Soon after, it made landfall, battering southern Florida over the next 20 hours as it crossed the peninsula, inflicting modest structural damage and 14 fatalities. Since hurricanes weaken over land, Katrina's winds abated, and when they fell below 110 kilometers per hour, the National Hurricane Center demoted it back to tropical storm status.

In satellite photos, hurricanes look like galaxies, with arcs of clouds spiraling from the center. At ground level, moist air is racing in toward the low-pressure eye. Dragged in by the rapidly rising warm air near the center, the inward-spiraling air picks up evaporating ocean moisture as water vapor, which heats from friction as it races over the ocean. As this moist warm air rises up the sides of the eye, it cools with altitude and its water vapor starts condensing into heavy rain. At heights above 12 kilometers it deflects away from the center, continuing to cool and condense. At this height, the air in the hurricane eye can be 15 degrees Celsius (30 degrees Fahrenheit) warmer than the surrounding air at that altitude. This temperature differential is the powerful 'heat engine' that produces the whirling clouds seen from above, and the torrential rains and screaming winds experienced below.

The warmer the ocean, the more powerful the hurricane. Warm ocean water more readily evaporates, which increases the moisture content of the air, the speed at which air rises near the hurricane's eye, the speed of air sucked in over the ocean, and the amount of energy released from condensation at higher altitudes. As Kerry Emanuel of MIT described in his book, *Divine Wind*, ocean temperatures of at least 30 degrees Celsius (85 degrees Fahrenheit) can produce powerful hurricanes.[1]

When Katrina entered the Gulf of Mexico on August 26, its eye passed directly over the Loop Current, a warm water current that originates between Cuba and the Yucatan, heads north into the Gulf, and then loops back down the west coast of Florida before passing out into the Atlantic. In August 2005, the current's surface water temperature was an abnormally hot 30 degrees Celsius. On contact, Katrina's heat engine throttled into super-charger mode.

Realizing what was happening, the National Hurricane Center reinstated Katrina as Category 1, issuing a warning that it would reach Category 3 or higher given the very warm sea. On Saturday morning, August 27, Katrina was upgraded to Category 3, with winds of 200 kilometers (120 miles) per hour. It was heading straight to New Orleans.

That afternoon, New Orleans Mayor Ray Nagin announced a state of emergency and called for voluntary evacuation. New Orleans captured the attention of the nation, for once not because of Mardi Gras. Still, it is the Big Easy, which might explain a government bulletin noting that bars in the French Quarter were rocking on that Saturday night before the storm, and witnesses later claimed that patrons on Bourbon Street showed a preference for a powerful cocktail called 'the Hurricane.'

After midnight, Katrina revved up to 230 kilometers per hour (145 mph) with gusts over 300. With winds extending 200 kilometers from its eye, Katrina was now one of the five strongest Atlantic hurricanes ever recorded: a heat engine poised to unleash its tremendous force on a vulnerable, ill-prepared US metropolis.

The rest of the story is well known. On Sunday, the mayor mandated evacuation of the city and offered the Superdome stadium as a refuge-of-last-resort. This was critical since 100,000 residents had neither personal vehicles nor the financial means to afford transportation and accommodation away from the hurricane's path. By Sunday evening, 20,000 people had entered the Superdome. Others found the safest place they could think of and hunkered down.

In a hurricane, one might assume that the safest place is the cellar. In low-lying coastal areas like New Orleans it's not. Onshore winds raise water levels, and low air pressure near the eye enables the water to rise even higher. This 'storm surge' can reach 7 meters (20 feet) as the hurricane's eye crosses the coastline. Statistics for the last century show that drowning causes 90% of hurricane-related fatalities.

If the shoreline is steep, the spatial impact is limited. But on a flat coastal plain, extensive flooding can occur as the surge combines with heavy rains to inundate lowlands. If the coastline is also a delta, it must contend with water from three sources – a storm surge from the sea, torrential rain from the sky, and the inflow of the river whose run-off is blocked by the rising sea. The Mississippi River carries the greatest water volume of any river in North America, and New Orleans lies in the middle of its delta. The sediments on which the city was built have compacted during 300 years of settlement, leaving most districts more than 2 meters (6 feet) below the river and nearby Pontchartrain Lake, which are at sea level. Tucked in a bowl below sea level, New Orleans' survival depends on the performance of its levees.

Katrina made landfall southeast of New Orleans early Monday, August 29. Fortunately, its wind speeds had ebbed to about 200 kilometers per hour, back to Category 3. The hurricane's eye missed the city, passing to the east. Even so, its winds battered buildings and structures, ripping off part of the Superdome roof to the terror of the drenched people below. Major media reported that New Orleans had dodged the bullet yet again, just as with Andrew in 1992, George in 1998, and Ivan in 2004. But over the next 12 hours, 80% of New Orleans flooded as storm surges breached its levees, causing 3 meters of flooding on average, double that in some wards.

In the following days, Coast Guard, National Guard, federal troops, city police, state police, and rescue services extricated tens of thousands of survivors stranded by the flood. The death toll reached 1,500, mostly from drowning.

Then the blame-game started. Federal, state, and municipal politicians pointed at each other, initially for why it took so long to rescue people, then for who was at fault for the flooding, and then for who would pay for clean-up, repairs, and reconstruction. About 80% of buildings in the city's low-lying wards were destroyed or severely damaged from the flood. Total damages were estimated at $80 billion.

Today, the debate still rages over who to blame for what has been called the worst civil engineering disaster in US history. Is it the fault of the Army Corps of Engineers, who built the city's levee system? Is it the rapid loss of delta wetlands of the last few decades, increasing the exposure to storm surges? Or, is the city simply unsustainable, given rising ocean temperatures and sea levels, both of which scientists attribute to climate change?

Of the books written about Katrina, I've read Jed Horne's *Breach of Faith*[2] and Douglas Brinkley's *The Great Deluge*.[3] These are substantial, engaging works. Both devote considerable space to assessing and allocating blame for the disaster. But neither book explores the contribution of climate change to this and future hurricane disasters. To climate scientists, this oversight is incomprehensible.

* * *

In 1824, Jean-Baptiste Fourier (1768–1830), a French mathematician and physicist, published an essay on the earth's temperature with the French Royal Academy of Sciences.[4] He had been trying to explain why incoming solar radiation didn't make the earth inhospitably hot, and why it wasn't immediately reflected back into space, which would make the earth inhospitably cold. He speculated that the atmosphere's gases allow solar radiation to reach the earth more easily than they allow it to reflect back into space. This delay in the dissipation of heat sustains the earth's surface air temperature at an average of 14 degrees Celsius (52 degrees Fahrenheit) instead of minus 20 degrees Celsius. For this insight two centuries ago, Fourier is recognized as one of the discoverers of the atmosphere's greenhouse effect.

While other scientists were receptive to Fourier's idea, it attracted only minor attention for three decades. Then, in 1859, Irish scientist John Tyndall (1820–1893), working in his laboratory at the Royal Institute in London, calculated the heat-absorptive properties of the individual GHGs in the earth's atmosphere, these being water vapor, carbon dioxide, nitrous oxide, methane, and ozone.[5] Tyndall's findings supported Fourier's hypothesis. Some of the incoming solar energy that penetrates our atmosphere as ultraviolet radiation is reflected back from the earth as infrared radiation. This latter is more easily absorbed by GHGs, and while it is eventually reflected back into space, the delay raises the temperature in the atmosphere and on the earth's surface to higher levels than if there were no GHGs.

Ironically, Tyndall's curiosity was piqued by fears that the earth might enter another ice age, given the contemporary discovery by geologists that the earth's climate had oscillated between ice ages and warm periods. Tyndall suspected that millennial changes in the atmospheric concentrations of GHGs were somehow linked to the temperature changes that caused the ice ages. Thanks to his work in measuring the effect of each GHG, it became possible to associate these gases with their differing contributions to the earth's greenhouse effect. But the numerical equation linking the atmosphere's GHG concentration and a specific temperature on earth was still unknown.

It would be 36 years before the Swedish scientist, Svante Arrhenius (1859–1927), tried to estimate this relationship. He focused on carbon dioxide (CO_2) because this was the GHG whose atmospheric concentration humans were changing by burning coal in ever-greater amounts. In 1896, he used Fourier's greenhouse theory and Tyndall's measurements of the heating effect of each GHG to hypothesize that doubling the CO_2 concentration in the atmosphere would increase the earth's surface air temperatures by an average of 4 to 6 degrees Celsius (8 to 11 degrees Fahrenheit).[6]

This relationship is now known as 'climate sensitivity,' the estimated temperature change caused by a change in the atmospheric concentration of GHGs, especially CO_2. Amazingly, Arrhenius' somewhat crude calculation of climate sensitivity is still within the range of current estimates, these latter produced by climate models with thousands of equations running on powerful computers grinding through huge quantities of data.

The first researcher to test Arrhenius' climate sensitivity estimate against temperature data was Guy Callendar (1898–1964), a British mechanical engineer. By the 1930s, meteorological records were sufficient in some locations to statistically detect 100-year temperature trends, which on average were found to be rising. Callendar related the temperature trend data to the rising rate of human-generated CO_2 emissions from burning coal and increasingly oil. In 1938, he presented a paper to the Royal Meteorological Society which integrated CO_2 from burning fossil fuels, the resulting rise in CO_2 atmospheric concentrations, and historical temperature records to estimate climate sensitivity.[7] His synthesis is the basis of modern climate science and the consensus that combustion of fossil fuels increases global temperatures by an amount we can roughly predict.

This consensus is as solid as the scientific consensus that we can predict lung cancer rates from smoking. And it materialized from the same process of scientific inquiry. Independent researchers kept finding evidence that supported rather than refuted the theories of Fourier, Tyndall, Arrhenius, Callendar, and other climate science pioneers. Some researchers tracked the rising concentrations of CO_2 in the atmosphere since the start of industrialization and compared these to past periods of high CO_2 concentrations by using ice cores to develop prehistoric records going back hundreds of thousands of years. Others developed protocols for combining multiple spot temperature readings to estimate an average temperature for the surface of the earth. Some developed techniques for estimating temperature records covering thousands of years from fossilized plants.

As always, there were scientists who disputed certain aspects of the emerging consensus. They developed alternative interpretations and tested these by collecting and analyzing data. In the case of climate science, this normal skepticism and the research it triggered has caused minor adjustments, but nothing that undermines the central conclusions of Fourier, Tyndall, Arrhenius, and Callendar.

As scientists informed the popular media and political leaders about the risks of climate change, governments began to respond as they had with the emerging scientific consensus on smoking. They established scientific panels and multi-author assessments, asking leading scientists to collaborate on reports that explained areas of agreement and areas of remaining dispute or uncertainty. In the United States, the *National Academy of Sciences* produced several reports on climate change, the first in 1979.[8]

Moreover, since preventing further climate change requires a global effort, political leaders and international agencies recognized the importance of international cooperation in assessing the state of scientific knowledge. Getting every country to act together is easier if every country's experts agree on the evidence. In 1988, the World Meteorological Organization and the United Nations Environment Programme established the Intergovernmental Panel on Climate Change (IPCC) to produce periodic assessments of climate change science. The IPCC produced assessments in 1990, 1995, 2001, 2007, and 2014.[9] The next is scheduled for 2022.

Each of these assessments summarizes the state of the science. With the accumulation of evidence over the past two decades, the IPCC's consensus conclusions have become more definitive with each report. The early reports explained why scientists agree that human GHG emissions would cause temperature rise and ocean acidification, thus justifying GHG-reducing actions. But with our ongoing failure to act effectively since the first report in 1990, more recent reports focus on what it was hoped could be prevented. They show how much climate change is now happening, including the human, biological, and earth system impacts. The language has gradually shifted from urging preventative action that would avoid impacts to explaining what is actually now happening because of our failure to act – rising average temperatures, ocean acidification, destruction of coral reefs, accelerated melting of ice caps and glaciers, rising sea levels, pest infestations, increased malaria, and rising instances of extreme events like droughts, heat waves, floods, wildfires, and powerful hurricanes.

The IPCC assessments also forecast the atmospheric GHG concentrations and global temperatures in 50 and 100 years if humanity continues on its current trajectory of burning fossil fuels, reducing forest cover (which means less carbon stored in plants and in the soil), and other activities. The latest estimates suggest that by 2100, global average surface temperatures will increase between 1.5 and 4.5 degrees Celsius (3 and 12 degrees Fahrenheit). And once this increase approaches 2 degrees Celsius, we may pass tipping points after which global warming may accelerate.[10] For example, melting permafrost in the Arctic could release more methane, which, as a potent GHG, would raise arctic temperatures faster, thus melting permafrost faster and releasing even more methane in a self-propelling cycle. As the science progresses, the IPCC reports have become more confident in predicting a rising rate of extreme events like hurricanes. With powerful computer models that simulate hurricane development under different ocean temperatures and other factors, scientists now simulate the mechanisms which drove Katrina's quick acceleration to a Category 5 hurricane. Thus, scientists can now confirm that many extreme weather events have been made worse by rising GHG emissions.

The strange-sounding discipline of paleo-tempestology studies coastline soils to measure the hurricane-revealing sediments left by storm surges over the past millennia. Not surprisingly, warmer periods are associated with more hurricanes, especially more intensive ones. In other words, evidence from the past confirms what scientists know about the physics of hurricane intensity. Warmer ocean water increases the likelihood of more ferocious hurricanes. From this knowledge, scientists predict that 40 years from now, if we continue to increase global emissions, an ocean that is 1.5 degrees Celsius warmer than at the time of

Katrina would, with all other conditions similar, produce a hurricane with peak winds 25 kilometers per hour (15 mph) faster than Katrina and a storm surge several meters higher. In explaining the future effects of global warming, commentator Bill Maher depicted future hurricanes as "Katrina on steroids."[11] It is difficult to imagine the scene if a hurricane of this intensity scores a bullseye on New Orleans.

The steroids analogy is a good one for explaining the probabilistic relationship between rising GHG emissions and hurricanes like Katrina. We know that a baseball slugger on steroids will hit more home runs, but we cannot attribute any particular home run to the steroids. Sluggers who don't take steroids also hit home runs, just less. Likewise, we know that more GHGs in the atmosphere will heat the ocean and a warmer ocean increases the likelihood of hurricanes of the intensity of Katrina. Scientists are extremely confident of this relationship, as the climate scientist James Hansen explained in his aptly titled 2009 book, *Storms of My Grandchildren.*[12] And people who do not have a self-interest motive to reject this science easily understand this probabilistic relationship between global warming and extreme hurricanes, just as they eventually recognized the relationship between smoking and lung cancer. It's a question of the willingness to accept inconvenient evidence, not the mental capacity to understand changing probabilities.

* * *

The IPCC reports explain how rising atmospheric concentrations of GHGs impact the earth's geophysical and biological systems, and what this means for humans. The reports also explain what is needed to reduce GHG emissions, thus also involving researchers in engineering, economics, and other social sciences.[13] This might seem complicated, but it doesn't need to be. If we focus on the global energy system, which produces over 70% of GHG emissions, and an even higher percentage of the emissions we have the best political means of reducing, our options can be understood with the following relationship. It says that energy-related GHG emissions result from the GHG intensity of the energy we use (GHG/Energy), multiplied by the energy intensity of our economy (Energy/$ of Income), multiplied by our per capita income (Income/Person), multiplied by the population.

$$\text{GHGs} = \text{GHG/Energy} \times \text{Energy/\$Income} \times \text{Income/Person} \times \text{\#People}$$

Scanning from right to left, if the number of people increases, while everything else stays the same, GHG emissions rise. Thus, one way to reduce emissions is to reduce population. But except for China's one-child policy in the 1990s and 2000s, no governments have been willing to push this agenda, and certainly not as a means of tackling climate change. Thankfully, demographers note that increased education for women is strongly linked to falling birthrates, suggesting that the total global population will stop growing later this century. While growth may stop, a dramatic reduction of the global population won't happen any time soon, at least not for peaceful reasons.

If income per person grows while everything else stays the same, emissions also increase. But convincing governments to stop economic growth to reduce emissions is just as difficult as getting them to reduce population. Certainly, it won't be easy to convince over one billion people who have negligible access to electricity and modern fuels that we should forgo the economic growth that offers them a means to access valuable services that most of us take for granted.

Continuing to the left in the equation, another possibility is to reduce energy use per dollar of income (the energy intensity of the economy). For the last two centuries, energy intensity has declined in industrialized countries. But this trend has been offset by economic growth, such that total energy use has grown. Over the last several decades, however, wealthy countries with stable populations, such as western Europe and Japan, have seen stable or declining energy consumption, which has not been the case for wealthier countries with growing populations, such as the US, Canada, and Australia.

In most developing countries, energy use is rising rapidly, where growing populations and incomes outstrip reductions in energy intensity. And since much of the industrial output from developing countries like China is destined for rich countries, one could argue that energy use in these latter has also risen if we count energy embodied in the goods we import.

The final option shown on the left of the equation is to reduce the GHG emissions intensity of our energy system. This means substituting away from fossil fuels and, wherever we still use them, capturing and storing GHGs to prevent them from reaching the atmosphere. In switching from burning coal, oil, and natural gas to renewables, and possibly some nuclear and fossil fuels with carbon capture, we would transform the global energy system to one dominated by technologies and fuels with low or zero carbon emissions.

These last two categories – reducing energy intensity and reducing energy-related emissions – are widely recognized as critical for addressing climate change. The good news, as we shall see, is that we already have the technologies and energy alternatives to make this happen. So even though this will not be easy, it is much easier than stopping population and economic growth in just a couple of decades.

I should add a qualification to the equation. It focuses on GHG emissions from the global energy system. But there are also CO_2, methane, nitrous oxide, and other GHG emissions from a variety of activities including forestry, agriculture, the treatment of municipal solid wastes, and some industrial processes, like the production of aluminum and cement. The IPCC investigates all of these GHGs and all options for reducing them. But we must not forget that CO_2 from coal, oil, and natural gas accounts for over 70% of human-produced GHG emissions. If we don't reduce these dramatically, we won't succeed with the climate-energy challenge.

But just as the scientific consensus on the risks of burning tobacco threatened the profits of the tobacco industry, the scientific consensus on the risks of burning fossil fuels threatened the profits of the fossil fuel industry. What has ensued is predictable and disturbing.

As with tobacco, people and organizations associated with the fossil fuel industry devote time and money to manufacture the delusion that climate scientists are in a conspiracy to fabricate the climate change threat. Some of these people propagate this delusion for self-interest, as recipients of fossil fuel industry revenues. These include executives and investors, politicians receiving political donations from the industry, paid lobbyists, and advertisers. Others align themselves with these direct beneficiaries for various ideological reasons, such as the fear that reducing emissions will increase the size of government, constrain individual freedom, and slow economic growth. Finally, there are those who for personal reasons disbelieve the scientific consensus, perhaps from a psychological need to be contrarian.

Key players in the fossil fuel industry publicly promote and financially support individuals with real or pretend expertise in climate science who claim that the scientific consensus is wrong. They help these so-called experts present inconsequential uncertainties as somehow devastating to the fundamental scientific consensus. Strategies include trying to undermine the reputation of leading climate scientists and key institutions like the IPCC.

Naomi Oreskes and Erik Conway explained in *Merchants of Doubt* how the same so-called scientists masqueraded through the years as experts innocently denying the risks, and thereby helping to delay policies, on acid rain, second-hand smoke, the hole in the ozone layer, and climate change.[14] A report of the Union of Concerned Scientists stated that ExxonMobil funneled $16 million between 1998 and 2005 to think tanks and individuals seeking to undermine climate science in the eyes of the public.[15] In *Private Empire*, his book on ExxonMobil, Steve Coll concluded that effective actions on the climate risk "will come later than they might have due to the resistance campaigns funded by oil and coal corporations – particularly ExxonMobil's uniquely aggressive influence campaign to undermine legitimate climate science."[16]

In *Climate Cover-Up*, James Hoggan and Richard Littlemore detailed the tactics of entities like the Heartland Institute, funded by the Koch brothers.[17] The starting argument is that evidence of a rising CO_2 concentration is incorrect. If that doesn't work, then the evidence of global warming is incorrect. If that doesn't work, then the warming detected by scientists is attributed to the oscillations of the earth's temperatures through the millennia. Finally, if this too fails, then we must recognize that fossil fuel use is inevitable, and we can adapt to a cozier, more productive planet.

When he was the CEO of ExxonMobil, former US Secretary of State Rex Tillerson acknowledged in a public speech in 2012 that burning fossil fuels is warming the planet, but assured the audience that "we'll adapt."[18] He conveniently failed to elaborate on those future conditions to which humans could adapt, since scientists claim we have enough burnable fossil fuels to raise oceans almost 35 meters (100 feet) and temperatures to scorching levels approaching those of the planet Venus. Which is why scientists respond to the "we can adapt" argument with catchphrases like "come hell and high water," and "first Venice, then Venus."

Another strategy is to undermine the credibility of leading climate scientists and the IPCC. One sophisticated operation produced 'climate-gate,' when a hacker penetrated a server at the Climate Research Unit in the UK, and released e-mail excerpts just before the 2009 climate nego-tiations at Copenhagen. Removed from their context, with no explana-tion of scientists' slang expressions, these excerpts were cleverly selected by conservative media outlets like Fox News to imply that global warming was a fraud perpetrated by a conspiracy of climate scientists. Climate-skeptical politicians, like former Republican Senator James Inhofe, refer-enced climate-gate in support of his claim that "global warming is the greatest hoax ever perpetrated on the American people."[19]

Ultimately, eight separate entities, including the UK House of Commons and the US Environmental Protection Agency, conducted independent inquiries into the climate-gate allegations.[20] All found no evidence of scientific misconduct. Not surprisingly, the conservative media ignored or downplayed these findings. For the hackers and their backers, it was mission accomplished, as polls showed an increase in public skepticism of climate science.

Michael Mann, a leading climate scientist, described climate-gate and similar efforts to vilify climate scientists in *The Hockey Stick and the Climate Wars*.[21] As an expert in long-term temperature trends, he was an origina-tor of the 'hockey stick' graph of the global average temperature since 1000, estimated from tree rings, corals, ice cores, and historical human records. The graph shows the temperature almost flat and then rising after 1900 (the stick blade). While climate scientists accept the shape of the stick, this didn't deter fossil fuel-funded experts from repeatedly claiming to refute it, which conservative elements of the US media slav-ishly reported.

Figure 3.1 on US climate science beliefs parallels Figure 2.1, which showed public views about smoking and lung cancer. As with smoking, the US public's willingness to accept the findings of science depends on self-interest and convenience, namely if one lives in a region that

| Year | Believe humans cause global warming (%) | | |
	Fossil-fuel focused regions	Other regions	All (average of both)
1990	25	35	30
1997	40	60	50
2001	45	65	55
2007	50	70	60
2012	35	55	45
2018	55	70	65

Figure 3.1 Climate science beliefs

produces oil, coal, or natural gas (such as Texas, Wyoming, and West Virginia) or that heavily depends on coal for electricity generation (such as the US southeast and midwest). The greater the self-interest benefit from rejecting a scientific fact, the greater the likelihood of that rejection. Hence the different polling responses between people living in "fossil fuel-focused regions" and those living outside these regions.

The table differs from the smoking surveys in showing a period in which public acceptance of climate science actually declined, from 2007 to 2012, before returning to its upward trend in recent years. One explanation for this reversal in the US is that climate science got caught in partisan battles between Democrats and Republicans. Polls show that while the percentage of Democrats believing climate science is high and steadily rising, the percentage fell among Republicans, especially in the period 2005 to 2015. For one thing, campaigners against climate policy threatened Republican politicians with losing fossil fuel industry political contributions and with internal challenges during Republican nomination campaigns if they failed to back the anti-climate science position. When almost all Republican political leaders are singing from the same song sheet about climate, it increases the chance that Republican voters will believe their party's leaders when they discredit the evidence from climate scientists.

Another explanation is that it might be easier to undermine climate science than smoking science. With smoking, the process is fairly simple.

We gradually notice that the people who get lung cancer are often smokers, sometimes family and friends. Once we open our eyes, the causal link gets increasingly obvious. In contrast, we may notice some changes in the weather, but it's always variable, and as long as those changes are not yet hurting us, we can sustain our delusion.

Unfortunately, the honesty of scientists about the complexity of the earth's climate helps the deniers. Many phenomena are inter-connected and complex. Higher temperatures cause more droughts. Droughts cause more forest fires. More forest fires increase CO_2 in the atmosphere, which increases temperatures. But more forest fires also increase soot in the atmosphere, which can decrease tempera-tures temporarily. Imagine trying to build a high precision model with all these confounding effects. The honesty of scientists about this complexity is used by the denier industry to distract the public from the fundamental scientific consensus.

So while scientists are certain that we are warming the planet, which will melt ice, raise sea levels, and cause major impacts, they will remain uncertain about the timing and location of specific repercussions, right up to when they actually happen. The planet will warm. Climate will change. Weather will change. Ecosystems will change. Oceans will change. How much, when, and where? Scientists cannot be certain.

* * *

In a 2012 episode of his *Colbert Report* TV show, comedian Stephen Colbert commented on the real-life response of North Carolina politi-cians to a state agency's prediction that sea levels will rise 39 inches by 2100 because of global warming.[22]

"North Carolina Republicans have written a new bill that would immediately address the crisis predicted by these climate models – by *outlawing* the climate models!"

"The law makes it illegal for North Carolina to consider scenarios of accelerated sea-level rise due to global warming. To fix that problem, GOP lawmakers want scientists to take the sea-level rise over the last 100 years and use that to predict what will happen in the future. That changes a scary 39-inch rise into a much more pleasant 8-inch rise."

Figure 3.2 Cartoon by Jacob Fox

"I think this is a brilliant solution. If your science gives you a result that you don't like, pass a law saying that the result is illegal. Problem solved."

"I think that we should start applying this method to even more things that we don't want to happen. For example, I don't want to die. But the actuaries at my insurance company are convinced that it will happen, sometime in the next 50 years. However, if we consider only *historical* data, I've been alive my entire life. Therefore, I always will be! So I say bravo North Carolina. By making this bold action on climate change today, you're ensuring that when it actually comes, you'll have plenty of options – or at least two: sink or swim."

With the support of influential media personalities like Stephen Colbert, scientists are fighting back, in a multiplicity of ways. One obvious strategy is for climate scientists and science writers to appeal directly to the public with accessible books.

Bill McKibben's *The End of Nature* in 1989 was the first climate book to reach a wide audience.[23] In the 1990s, international efforts to address the threat seemed likely to succeed, and so less was written. But this hope faded in the early 2000s with the election of President George W. Bush, the failure of the Kyoto Protocol, and the shift in global focus to wars in the Middle East after the 2001 terrorist attacks on the US. Hence the appearance of many more books after 2004. I have already mentioned Al Gore's movie and book, *An Inconvenient Truth,* Jim Hansen's *Storms of My*

Grandchildren, and Michael Mann's *The Hockey Stick and the Climate Wars.* Tim Flannery's *The Weather Makers* was not just a best seller, several influential political leaders claimed it played a role in motivating their climate policy efforts.[24] And Jared Diamond applied his skill at depicting how geo-ecological factors affect human survival in *Collapse: How Societies Choose to Fail or Succeed.*[25] While many of these books, as best sellers, were translated into other languages, an impressive list of similarly themed books were published first in languages other than English.

These talented writers provided clear and effective descriptions of climate science for non-experts. Yet many climate scientists are, like other types of scientists, poor communicators when it comes to the public. In the daily cut-and-thrust of conventional and social media, this leaves them seriously outmatched against the sophisticated and well-funded climate science denial campaign when required to explain the causes of extreme events, like floods and wildfires, and climate science uncertainties.

To help correct this imbalance, Randy Olson abandoned a professorship at the University of New Hampshire and moved to Hollywood to study film production and apply its techniques to the public communication of scientific controversy. In his book, *Don't Be Such a Scientist,* he suggested techniques to help scientists become better communicators.[26] His provocative chapter titles include: "Don't be so cerebral," "Don't be so literal minded," "Don't be such a poor storyteller," and "Don't be so unlikeable." Olson has produced documentaries on evolution and global warming as demonstrations of the approach he espouses. Nancy Baron provides additional tips for scientists in the use of stories and metaphors and in their public engagements, be it in writing or on camera, in her book, *Escape from the Ivory Tower.*[27]

The ongoing failure with the climate threat has motivated some of these writers to return to the issue, this time focused less on climate science and more on technological solutions, civil and political efforts to raise public concern and activism, and strategies for survival under climate change. Three prominent examples are Bill McKibben's *Eaarth,*[28] Tim Flannery's *Atmosphere of Hope,*[29] and Michael Mann and Tom Toles' *The Madhouse Effect.*[30]

No matter how good scientists and science communicators are at explaining the climate threat, they won't achieve complete success if too many people decide about climate science based mostly on the opinions of people they trust.[31] Which takes us full circle to the interplay of myths, evidence, and social cognition that I explored in Chapters 1 and 2. Frustration with the inability to convince everyone about the climate threat has focused the minds of social scientists and climate activists, leading to a host of books on the interplay of human cognition and scientific evidence, such as Mike Hulme's *Why We Disagree on Climate*,[32] George Marshall's *Don't Even Think About It*,[33] and Andrew Hoffman's *How Culture Shapes the Climate Change Debate*.[34]

Strategies for applying this knowledge cover a wide range. James Hoggan interviews psychologists and political scientists for suggestions to improve public discourse between interests in *I'm Right and You're an Idiot*.[35] A 2019 article in *Nature Climate Change* organizes the methods for combating scientific misinformation into four categories: public inoculation, legal strategies, political mechanisms, and financial transparency.[36] Inoculation involves better informing the public, as with the books I have listed above. The shortcoming of this approach on its own explains the necessity of combining it with the other more aggressive strategies.

Another strategy is ridicule, perhaps even more aggressively than that of Stephen Colbert. The TV personality, Bill Nye the science guy, has long been willing to debate climate science in unfriendly venues, such as on the Fox News Channel. But he turned it up a notch in 2019 on the TV show, *Last Week Tonight with John Oliver*. In a skit in which he lit a globe on fire, he angrily expressed his exasperation with climate science deniers, culminating in "the planet is on f***ing fire and we need to grow the f*** up."[37] This tactic might not sway hard-core climate science deniers, but it may boost the morale of climate-concerned scientists and citizens who are often told that their poor communication skills, rather than the stubborn motivated reasoning of climate science deniers, is why some people still don't get it.

If we are honest, climate science denial is not the fault of scientists or science communicators. If they want to be, most humans are pretty good at understanding probabilistic causality. When scientists say that smoking killed about 400,000 people in the US in 2015, surveys show that most people understand that not every lifelong smoker will get lung cancer, and not every incidence of lung cancer is caused by smoking. They understand that the causal relationship is probabilistic, even though they may use a common poker-playing term like 'the odds' when explaining these probabilities.

Will we get to this same understanding with GHG emissions and climate change? We seem to be getting closer. Perhaps it helps, sadly, that climate change impacts are increasingly experienced, with more and more people willing to attribute these impacts to climate change. Perhaps school science teachers are having an impact. As the years pass, an increasing percentage of the adult population has learned basic climate science in school. And unlike the challenge of teaching evolution to people belonging to fundamentalist religions, the teaching of climate science poses less of a direct challenge to most religious beliefs.

Most importantly, experts in communications are adamant that stories and anecdotes can help us grasp new information and reappraise our assumptions. I have followed this advice in writing this book. While I try to be faithful to the leading research on how citizens can contribute to climate-energy success, I sometimes present this information by recounting historical events and the experiences of individuals. Some of these latter stories present specific people I know (albeit with some of their names changed), while some are fictitious characters who represent an amalgamation of two or more people. From my decades of discussing these issues with concerned citizens, I am confident that the stories of both my fictive characters and real acquaintances will remind many readers of their own experiences in navigating the issues of the climate-energy challenge.

CHAPTER 4

All Countries Will Agree on Climate Fairness

We associate truth with convenience, with what most closely accords with self-interest and personal well-being or promises best to avoid awkward effort or unwelcome dislocation of life.

John Kenneth Galbraith

O N JANUARY 30, 1933, PRESIDENT PAUL VON HINDENBURG appointed Adolf Hitler Chancellor of Germany. Hitler's Nazi party had won only 33% of the vote, but he pledged to govern in a coalition with other right-wing parties. Instead, over the next two months he issued executive decrees that overruled existing laws and consolidated his power. Soon, political opposition in Germany was illegal, and newly constructed concentration camps held the leaders of all parties except those closest to the Nazis.

During Hitler's 12-year reign of terror and war, over 60 million people died. With hindsight, we can say that German citizens should have stopped him before he consolidated his fascist dictatorship. But is it fair to judge people who lived at that time? Is it fair to say they should have anticipated the horrific global outcome and acted in time to prevent it?

There were in fact people inside and outside Germany who tried early to convince others of the urgency of preventative action. Hitler had stated his intentions in his book, *Mein Kampf*, which he wrote while serving a short prison term after his failed *coup d'état* of 1923.[1] In this personal manifesto, Hitler claimed it was the destiny of the German people, as the superior Aryan race, to struggle for world domination, and his personal duty to lead them.

Once Hitler had eliminated the option of defeating him in democratic elections, some Germans organized themselves into clandestine resistance groups. These activists included communists, socialists, liberals, conservatives, Christians, and members of the military. Some tried in vain to convince their political and social contacts in neighboring countries of the need for military intervention from outside Germany. From within, some conspired to kill or capture Hitler in hopes that the police and army would transition the country back to democracy. But Hitler had merged his Nazi paramilitary forces with the police, and compelled army officers to swear personal allegiance to him.

Adam von Trott zu Solz was an early participant in the German resistance. Educated at Oxford as a Rhodes scholar, he was training as a lawyer in Germany when Hitler attained power. During the next 11 years, he conspired with other German resistors, but several efforts to overthrow or assassinate Hitler failed. After the failed attempt in July 1944, von Trott was arrested by the Gestapo. He was executed on August 26, 1944, at the age of 35.

In a post-war interview in the movie *Restless Conscience*, his wife recalled von Trott trying to rally others to resist right from the day Hitler was appointed Chancellor. She recounted his agitated response to friends suggesting he was overreacting, "How can you not see it? Hitler says *exactly* what he will do in his book. We must stop him now, before it's too late."[2]

In spite of far-seeing, courageous people like von Trott, the opposition within Germany failed to stop Hitler. Not enough people were willing to act. And while the threat from Germany grew with each year of Hitler's reign, the rest of the world did little.

Winston Churchill is famous for his resolute leadership in World War II, especially during the perilous year when Britain stood alone against Germany, between the fall of France in June 1940 and Hitler's surprise invasion of the Soviet Union in June 1941. He is less well known for his efforts in the 1930s to convince people in Britain, Europe, and America of the urgency of opposing Hitler sooner rather than later. Although not alone in this, Churchill was the most emphatic and eloquent political leader to recognize the global threat and urge pre-emptive action to avert a horrendous outcome. In hindsight, his efforts in the 1930s to prevent a global war were even more impressive and prescient than his war leadership in the 1940s.

Churchill's response to Hitler's 1936 occupation of the Rhineland is noteworthy. The Treaty of Versailles, signed in 1919 at the end of World War I, prohibited Germany from maintaining a large army and stationing troops in the Rhineland along its border with France. But soon after attaining power, Hitler started to remilitarize and in 1936 brazenly marched German troops into the Rhineland. The other treaty signatories, including the US, should have immediately required Hitler to withdraw his forces or face military intervention. Success against Germany at this stage was certain since his army was still small and ill equipped. Also, as it turns out, a group of German army officers were ready to overthrow Hitler the moment foreign powers sent in troops to repel the German soldiers from the Rhineland.

An opposition politician at the time, Churchill pleaded in the British Parliament for immediate intervention against German remilitarization.

> The turning-point has been reached and new steps must be taken ... Germany is arming – she is rapidly arming – and no one will stop her ... I marvel at the complacency of ministers in the face of the frightful experiences through which we have all so newly passed ... A terrible process is astir. Germany is arming.[3]

But England and other countries did nothing to oppose Hitler's abrogation of the treaty, and the movement within Germany to oust Hitler lost its chance. Hitler's successful defiance of foreign powers and re-acquisition of the Rhineland bolstered his popularity, reducing support among conservatives and the military for removing him by *coup d'état*. The opportunity was missed.

Churchill was increasingly bitter at the inability of others to recognize an obvious threat and act pre-emptively. In the following years, as Hitler occupied Austria, then part of Czechoslovakia, then the rest of Czechoslovakia, the major powers of the world did nothing, leading to Churchill's rueful comment in early 1939.

> If you will not fight for right when you can easily win without blood-shed; if you will not fight when your victory is sure and not too costly; you may

come to the moment when you will have to fight with all the odds against you and only a precarious chance of survival.[4]

As an avid 20th-century history reader, I see parallels in how individuals and countries responded to the global threat posed by Hitler's Germany and the global threat posed by climate change. These are different threats. Still, I note similarities in how people justify ignoring the threat and dismissing the compelling arguments of compatriots on the urgent need for pre-emptive action.

Von Trott and other brave people tried to rally resistors, but not enough Germans recognized their personal responsibility to take risks to prevent a disaster. Citizens of other countries had their own excuses for complacency. Many Americans believed that US participation in World War I had been a mistake and now favored an 'isolationist' foreign policy, free from the frequent conflicts in Europe and Asia. They refused to acknowledge the clearly global nature of the threat.

As Hitler's Germany intensified its aggressiveness, humanity's inability to coordinate a global response became increasingly apparent. The League of Nations, which had been created after World War I to reduce the risk of another major conflict, lacked the military force necessary to discipline rogue states. The only hope was if major powers coordinated economic sanctions and, if necessary, military intervention. But their national interests differed. Britain and France were concerned, but wishful thinking bias led most of their political leaders to downplay the threat. Neither country wanted the inconvenience of re-militarizing to confront Germany so soon after World War I. The Soviet Union felt threatened, given Hitler's anti-communist rants and prophesies of Germany's eastward expansion, but mutual distrust prevented it and capitalist countries from cooperating.

These countries eventually fought together in World War II as 'the Allies,' but the powerful coalition of the US, the USSR, and the British Empire that defeated Germany was created by Hitler, not by the coalition members. Britain and France were committed by treaty to protect Poland. Hitler attacked Poland in 1939 anyway, which compelled Britain and France to declare war. After France was defeated by Germany in 1940, Hitler tried to convince Churchill to make peace, but he refused. Hitler's invasion of the Soviet Union in June 1941 made it by default an instant ally of the British Empire. A grateful Churchill ruefully commented on his new allegiance with the hated communist Joseph Stalin, "If Hitler invaded hell, I would make at least a favorable reference to the devil in the House of Commons."[5]

After the Japanese attack on Pearl Harbor in December 1941, Hitler made the fateful decision that guaranteed his defeat. Four days after the attack, to the shock and dismay of his military commanders, he declared war on the US, enabling Roosevelt to finally bring the US into the conflict by reciprocating Hitler's declaration. While much was later made of the Allies' united front against a global threat, their coalition was created by Hitler. Only after his blunder in declaring war on the US could Churchill finally note in his diary, "On that night I experienced the sleep of a baby, confident that our cause must surely now prevail."[6]

While some impressive people frantically sought a concerted, preventative response to the global threat of Hitler, there were not enough of them. Not enough people recognized the enormous importance of acting sooner rather than waiting. Not enough were willing to incur a relatively small cost, personally or nationally, to avoid an enormous future cost. Not enough were willing to yield national interests to global collective interests. Even a threat as grave as the aggression of Hitler's Nazi Germany was insufficient to motivate the great powers to form a coalition. It was not by *voluntary* initiative that countries united to address a serious global threat.

* * *

Reducing GHG emissions is a 'global collective action problem' – humanity must act together to solve it. This is because the atmosphere is a 'global common property resource,' something that no one owns and therefore everyone owns. Common property resources are challenging to manage sustainably because of the difficulty of controlling their exploitation, such as their use for dumping harmful emissions or effluents. If a common property resource is located entirely within national boundaries, like an urban airshed or some lakes and rivers, then an individual government can restrict the dumping of pollutants. But the protection of global common property resources, like the atmosphere and oceans, requires global collective action.

Global collective action to reduce GHG emissions is difficult for obvious reasons. Since the problem results from the GHG emissions of all countries, the emissions of one country are just one part of the problem. Actions by one country cannot prevent the harm from occurring. China is the biggest GHG emitter, accounting for 25%. If China reduced its emissions a whopping 40%, that's only a 10% reduction of global emissions. And most countries' emissions are tiny compared to China's.

This small potential contribution of each country to the solution makes it difficult for a national government to convince its citizens to unilaterally reduce emissions. Indeed, if one or even several countries tried to show leadership by reducing emissions, they could not prevent other countries from 'free-riding' on their efforts. If burning low-cost fossil fuels helps enrich an economy, the countries that did nothing to reduce emissions would see an improvement in their industries' competitive position, leading to greater wealth. The incentive is strong to free-ride if there is no penalty for doing so. And the likelihood that some countries will free-ride discourages others from acting.

Note the similarities and differences with a risk like lung cancer from smoking. With both smoking and GHG emissions, scientists and concerned citizens must overcome the concerted efforts of powerful, wealthy interests to mislead the public about the threat. But with smoking, at least the threat can be addressed within a single jurisdiction. Once enough people accept the science and elect governments willing to act, domestic policies can reduce the harms of first- and second-hand smoke. It doesn't matter what other countries do. But with GHG emissions, even when enough people accept the science and elect a climate-sincere government, citizens are aware that their national effort won't avert the threat. In case they might forget, economically powerful private interests and their agents remind them daily in the media of the futility of unilateral action – "There's no point reducing our small share of global emissions as long as there are still coal plants in [name your country]."

If there were a global government, it could require all countries to reduce their GHG emissions and levy penalties to ensure universal compliance. But we don't have a global government. All we have is the United Nations. This institution was established after World War II with a primary goal of reducing the risks of another world war. But like its predecessor, the League of Nations, the UN's authority is restricted. The major powers have been unwilling to yield much of their national sovereignty to a global authority. Thus, the UN is limited to functions agreed upon by all major powers: development assistance, peace-keeping forces, and international coordination.

The UN can also lead negotiations for global agreements, such as an international treaty to reduce GHG emissions. At the Rio de Janeiro Earth Summit in 1992, all countries agreed to establish the Framework Convention on Climate Change, which mandated the UN to negotiate a climate treaty. They also created the Intergovernmental Panel on Climate Change to provide unbiased assessments of the latest climate science research, the climate change impacts on humans and the environments on which we depend, the ways in which these impacts could be mitigated, and the technologies and policies for reducing GHG emissions to prevent the impacts.

Once a year the UN Framework Convention on Climate Change convenes a negotiating meeting with delegates from all countries, called the Conference of the Parties. Success depends on all countries voluntarily agreeing on the fair contribution of each to the global GHG reduction objective, including payments from wealthier countries to help poorer countries with the costs of following a low-emission energy development path. The meetings have occurred annually since 1995 without yet achieving a binding treaty that would cause global GHG emissions to fall.

The meetings in Kyoto in 1997 and Paris in 2015 appeared to make significant progress. But appearances can be deceiving. In the 1997 Kyoto Protocol, industrialized countries agreed to reduce their emissions, in aggregate, to 5% below their 1990 levels by 2010. They agreed on an allocation of that reduction among themselves. They also agreed on mechanisms to help fund emission reductions in "economies-in-transition" (the former East Bloc communist countries) and developing countries. World political leaders and many climate advocates trumpeted the agreement as demonstrating that the United Nations' voluntary consensus approach could work.

Their conclusion was premature. The protocol failed as a global agreement that would eventually reduce emissions. The reasons were predictable, and many people said so at the time, an example being David Victor's book *The Collapse of the Kyoto Protocol and the Struggle to Slow Global Warming.*[7] First, this was not an agreement that restricted global GHG emissions, notwithstanding how political leaders presented it. Poorer countries did not have GHG limits, while richer countries did. Second, it was not a binding agreement, although there was a commitment to develop a mandatory compliance mechanism in future. Without this, wealthier countries knew that failure to achieve their targets had no repercussions. Compensation of some kind was threatened for countries that missed their commitments, but they could avoid this by withdrawing from the treaty.

The next decade witnessed a painful unraveling. Vice-president Al Gore had negotiated the treaty for the US, but he and President Bill Clinton were unable to convince the US Congress to ratify it. Prior to Kyoto, the US Senate had voted 95–0 not to approve any agreement that failed to also impose binding targets on developing countries. But at Kyoto, these countries were unwilling to talk about restricting their own emissions until wealthier countries acted first, and wealthier countries were unwilling to implement a mandatory global mechanism with penalties – presumably tariffs – for non-compliant countries. The absence of such a condition in the Kyoto Protocol made it easy for the next US president, George W. Bush, to refuse to pursue congressional ratification of the treaty that Al Gore had negotiated.

The ensuing years saw rapid emissions growth in China and other developing countries, which overwhelmed the slowing of emissions growth in wealthier countries. The European Union reached an agreement to implement its own cap program for industrial emissions, but the effect was not significant. The efforts of other wealthy countries oscillated depending on the vagaries of public will and electoral shifts. National debates about GHG targets and policy were increasingly disconnected from the Kyoto targets.

Public concern for GHG emissions in the US declined after the 2001 terrorist attack on the World Trade Center and the Pentagon. But by 2005, the combination of Hurricane Katrina and Al Gore's award-winning book and movie, *An Inconvenient Truth*, caused a resurgence in climate interest in the US, with a ripple effect in other countries.[8]

In 2008, the election of President Barack Obama along with a Democratic majority in the US Congress led to renewed hopes for a revision of the Kyoto Protocol or the negotiation of an entirely new treaty. However, at the 2009 Copenhagen meeting of the Framework Convention on Climate Change, Obama's efforts to reach a new global agreement failed. Developing countries, including China, were still unwilling to commit to restraining their growing emissions, and wealthier countries were still unwilling to offer sufficient financial support for these countries to voluntarily forgo the benefits of burning fossil fuels, nor to implement a system of carbon tariffs to incentivize an effort by all countries.

While the Democratic majority in the US House of Representatives was able in 2009 to pass a bill (Waxman-Markey) to establish a GHG cap-and-trade policy, that bill never came to a vote in the US Senate. The Democratic setback in the mid-term elections of 2010 removed the last chance for US GHG legislation during Obama's presidency, making an effective global agreement all the more elusive.

The failure to reach an agreement at Copenhagen in 2009 convinced frustrated negotiators to set a distant future date for the next major effort at a global agreement, that being the 2015 annual meeting slated for Paris. This gave time for strategic discussions in advance of the meeting, with negotiators finally deciding that each country would be allowed to voluntarily set its target prior to the Paris summit – its "nationally determined contribution." Countries announced these commitments in the year prior to the meeting.

International consensus is easy if each country comes to the negotiating table simply to ratify its own target. Thus, the Paris Accord was signed by virtually all countries in June 2015. Soon after, though, scientists confirmed the obvious. Even if all the national commitments were achieved, total emissions would still increase enough to raise average temperatures about 3.5 degrees Celsius by the end of the century.[9] And like previous agreements, the Paris Accord lacks a mandatory compliance mechanism, so there is no incentive for individual countries to achieve their national commitments if they can instead free-ride on the efforts of others, and others can free-ride on their efforts.

Climate negotiators are dedicated people. But, as defined, their mission is impossible. We have tasked them with convincing countries to voluntarily agree on the allocation of the costs of rapidly transforming the global energy system. We forget that even when facing the immediate, existential threat from German militarism in the 1930s, the world's major powers were unable to voluntarily combine forces in time to avert a global catastrophe.

When it comes to the climate-energy threat, countries have widely different interests that frustrate efforts at preventative action. Fossil fuel-rich countries have the most to lose from decarbonization and not surprisingly some of these have resisted efforts to reach a global agreement, especially in the first two decades of negotiations. These included Saudi Arabia, Iran, Iraq, other members of the Organization of Petroleum Exporting Countries (OPEC), and also non-OPEC oil-rich countries like Russia and Mexico. Endowments of coal and natural gas are also important, with, for example, China, eastern Europe, and India relying on exploitation of these indigenous resources. Even wealthy countries, like the US, Canada, and Australia, are challenged by high concentrations of fossil fuel resources in specific regions, which in a federal system of government can cause intra-national political and even constitutional tensions if the national government is seen as too eager in setting and achieving GHG commitments issuing from international processes.

Poorer countries understand the need to reduce emissions, but they note that today's wealthier countries got that way by exploiting the high quality of fossil fuels to industrialize their economies and improve living conditions. To forgo that path, poorer countries expect to get help with the substantial costs of developing carbon-free energy systems. Richer countries agree they need to help the poorer countries. But the support poorer countries request at the annual negotiations far exceeds the amount wealthier countries feel they can provide. These countries have provided some support for adoption of low-emission technologies. But the amount is far below what is needed to divert developing countries from constructing coal and natural gas plants for generating electricity and expanding transportation infrastructure and vehicles dependent on gasoline and diesel, not to mention relying on emissions-intensive steel, cement, and aluminum production processes. Without this effort, as Figure 4.1 shows, the global growth in GHG emissions will be increasingly driven by growing fossil fuel consumption in developing countries, a point I return to in the final chapter.

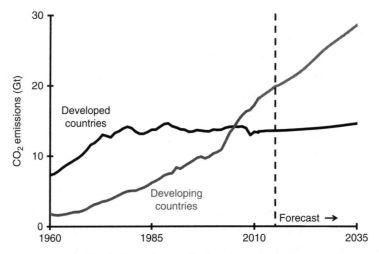

Figure 4.1 Global CO_2 emissions: developed and developing countries

Thus, just as national self-interest biased the views of countries on how to bear the burden of pre-emptively stopping Hitler and Nazi Germany, national self-interest looms large in global GHG negotiations. There is no universally agreed criterion for allocating the cost of global GHG reduction among countries. Poorer countries often argue that the cost should be allocated according to "ability to pay" and "historical responsibility." This means that wealthier countries, which have been emitting GHGs since the start of the industrial revolution in the 18th century, should bear much of the cost. Countries with low per capita emissions, which are usually but not always poorer, argue that each human should have the same allocation of atmospheric rights for GHGs. This would mean that countries with higher per capita emissions should quickly reduce their emissions and make polluter pay transfers to other countries during that transformation.

At one time, this implied that wealthier countries should pay more as the greater polluters. However, China is now in an interesting situation. While three decades ago it squarely fit the description of a poorer, low-emission country, its dramatic economic expansion between 1985 and 2015 led to an equally dramatic increase in its GHG emissions. The expansion depended in part on the rapid construction of coal-fired electricity plants and emission-intensive steel and cement plants such that today China's CO_2 emissions exceed those of the US and EU combined.

* * *

In 1992, I was appointed to the *China Council for International Cooperation on Environment and Development* as one of six foreign experts on its energy sub-group. The council's mission is to foster long-term collaboration between foreign experts and senior Chinese officials and academics in advising the Chinese government on improving environmental performance and living standards. Over the years I served on the council, I participated in various energy-related assignments. My last assignment was as co-chair in 2009 of a task-force on sustainable use of coal. We delivered our final recommendations to Premier Wen Jiabao in November 2009, just before he left to participate in the failed Copenhagen climate conference.[10]

My two decades of engagement with Chinese researchers, bureaucrats, politicians, and, increasingly, non-government organizations have been fascinating. I experienced the changing views of Chinese people as their country rapidly evolved from a poor, technologically backward and internationally insecure nation to an increasingly modern, wealthy, and self-assured world player. This has also been reflected in their changing views of energy, trade, global responsibility, and climate. While the Chinese may still refer to themselves as a poor nation that must prioritize economic growth to better people's lives, that message is combined with recognition of the country's status as a major power with global responsibilities.

My first assignment in 1992 for the council was focused on coal. Back then, our team of six Chinese and six foreign experts recommended to the Chinese government that it eliminate its large coal subsidies, which would raise the price of coal for electricity plants, industry, and even households (much coal was burned in homes for heating and cooking). This would reduce coal consumption, favoring cleaner but more expensive fuels. The government graciously thanked us, and did nothing. We also designed environmental taxes that the government should apply to fuels, including coal, to reflect their environmental damages. The government graciously thanked us, and did nothing. And we designed a renewable electricity mandate, a policy that would require state-run electricity firms throughout the country to attain a minimum level of renewable electricity generation, an amount that would rise over time to slow and even reduce coal use. Again, the government graciously thanked us, and did nothing.

The years went by and we earnestly forged on. Then, in 1997, the Kyoto Protocol happened, and the Chinese government flipped. In rapid succession, it implemented all three of our recommended policies: it cut coal subsidies; introduced modest, but rising, environmental charges on some energy-related pollutants; and implemented a renewable electricity mandate. (For this work, I still have my thank-you letter from the Chinese president.) The government even gave us new marching orders, asking for advice on developing carbon capture and storage so that coal could be used with minimal carbon pollution.

I was dumbfounded by the swift reaction to Kyoto. I didn't see why the government would respond this way when the protocol required nothing of China. Five years of collaboration had brought us quite close to our Chinese counterparts, so we asked them to candidly explain their government's actions.

"It's obvious. We don't trust the rich countries."

"What do you mean? They've required nothing of you. Kyoto is a free-ride for developing countries."

"But rich countries cannot be trusted. They seem to be getting serious about climate change. They will come after us with tariffs and trade sanctions. We need to be one step ahead."

This created a sense of optimism. Even if Kyoto was deeply flawed, it might nonetheless set the stage for something better. It clearly had symbolic value for the Chinese. They were already anticipating the kind of trade pressures that would follow as countries like the US imposed costs on its own industry and moved to protect that industry from its competitors in countries with less stringent GHG policies.

But for reasons I have already explained, Kyoto fizzled out after the election of President George W. Bush and the 2001 terrorist attacks. The prospect for global collective action diminished. The Chinese grasped this new reality and we returned to the old pattern on the China Council. Our next policy proposals were again graciously accepted and ignored. With the Chinese economy steaming along, coal power plant construction reached record levels, as did the growth of carbon pollution. A golden opportunity for preventative action was missed.

The effect elsewhere in the world was predictable. In developed countries like mine, one increasingly heard that tiresome refrain: "Why should we do anything when the Chinese are completing at least one coal-fired power plant per week?" It was tiresome, but it had a ring of truth. To be effective, preventative action on GHG emissions has to be global. But countries of the world could not voluntarily agree on climate fairness.

I have not been involved directly in China for the last decade. But from a distance, the change during this period has been remarkable. The expansion of coal-fired power has finally abated. The government now aggressively develops wind, solar, hydropower, biofuels, other renewables, and nuclear power. It is using more natural gas, which at least has less emissions than coal. China is a major exporter of wind turbines and photovoltaic cells, and the world's largest producer and consumer of electric cars.

Without a global GHG treaty, China became in just 20 years the single biggest cause of rapidly rising global emissions. Now, still without a treaty, China is becoming the most important developer and adopter of the technologies that are essential for reversing the path of those emissions. Looking back, I can't help wondering about China's development path had we been able to preventatively address this global collective action problem two decades ago.

* * *

I believe today, as I did two decades ago, that a *voluntary* international agreement to deeply de-carbonize the global energy system in a few decades is extremely unlikely. While I appreciate the efforts of the negotiators, I believe that the threat of trade barriers and carbon tariffs is essential for achieving a significant global effort within the next decade. Otherwise, like people, countries have a strong self-interest bias which prevents them from voluntarily accepting what other countries argue is their fair allocation of the burden of transforming the global energy system.

If we cannot hope for this, what can we realistically hope for? First, we can no longer talk about pre-emptive action. Unfortunately, just as the global community failed in the 1930s to pre-emptively avoid major harm from Hitler, we failed in the 1990s and 2000s to act in time to avoid all the harms from our GHG emissions. Today's higher atmospheric CO_2 concentration, plus the effect of emissions in the coming years from recently built fossil fuel infrastructure, is causing damages that will intensify over the next few decades, even if all GHG emissions stopped today.

If we continue for another decade on our current GHG trajectory, the parallels with Hitler are even stronger. At some point, the negative impacts will be so great that citizens in many countries will compel their governments to unilaterally close coal plants and ban sales of gasoline cars, even without a global treaty. Perhaps we are on the cusp of this stage of the struggle, given the increasingly aggressive unilateral decarbonization efforts of some countries.

If we abandon the myth that humans can reduce GHGs in a way that seems fair to everyone, those countries making a significant effort to reduce emissions would now levy tariffs on imports from countries that are not, regardless of whether these latter are rich or poor. In his book, *Global Warming Gridlock*, David Victor explains how climate-leading jurisdictions could join forces in applying carbon tariffs to imports from climate-laggard countries whose economies have high emissions.[11] As the trading power of these 'climate clubs' increases, the incentives for laggard countries to join their GHG-reducing efforts also increases, as Bill Nordhaus explains in a recent article titled, "Climate Clubs: Overcoming Free-riding in International Climate Policy."[12]

Had China faced carbon tariffs from importing countries 20 years ago, its energy development path would have differed significantly. Today, it is rapidly developing zero-emissions electricity sources. But had there been carbon tariffs imposed by Europe and the US, which almost happened in the mid-2000s, China would have started much earlier, and built far fewer coal plants. Its economy may have grown more slowly, and the Chinese government would have complained bitterly and justifiably about unfair treatment by wealthy countries. But the Chinese would also have accelerated low-carbon technological development and adoption just as they are doing now, with much fewer of the GHG emissions that today impose costs on everyone, including themselves.

Who will take the lead in creating climate clubs? Perhaps the US will start its own climate club. In that regard, I note that every US climate bill proposal, including the Waxman-Markey bill, contained tariff-like mechanisms imposed on imports from countries that insufficiently regulated or priced their own emissions. Some say the wording in these bills was directed at China, with its rapidly growing emissions at the time. During the presidency of Barack Obama, it looked like the US and China might start their own club. While they did not advance to discussions of carbon tariffs, they signed an agreement in 2014 to limit their GHG emissions, which helped form the basis for the wider Paris agreement in 2015. Needless to say, President Trump stopped further progress.

Perhaps the first climate club with carbon tariffs will be Europe. Perhaps it will be an eclectic mix of middle-sized countries like France, the UK, Scandinavia, and Canada. Perhaps it will be China in concert with these other countries. While the game-changing development of a climate club does not seem likely in the near term, its chances for generating an effective collective effort by some countries seems substantially better than the global voluntary consensus approach of the annual UN-led negotiations.

Will climate clubs with carbon tariffs be fair to developing countries? This is unlikely, given that the citizens of wealthier countries are only willing to transfer a small percentage of their GDP to help people in developing countries. There will be modest support. But not nearly the amount that developing countries would find fair. Thus, global progress on decarbonization, when it finally happens, will likely involve a combination of carrots and sticks, namely a combination of modest financial support with substantial carbon tariffs.

Figure 4.2 Cartoon by Kallaugher, K. 2009. Climate Change Summit 2040. *The Economist* (November 19)

Will developing countries be better off with this approach relative to a continuation of ineffective international negotiations? Yes, definitely. First, the costs of forgoing the use of coal and oil are falling thanks to the efforts of wealthier countries and now China to cut their emissions. This means that zero-emission energy will be less costly for a developing country than it would have been for China to have pursued two decades ago. Second, the impacts of climate change are becoming increasingly severe, so the prevention of GHG emissions has greater value. Developing countries are less well equipped to handle the impacts of droughts, heat waves, wildfires, hurricanes, floods, and disease. If we prevent the worst effects of climate change, even though not achieved in a perfectly equitable way, developing countries will be far better off.

From a global equity perspective, the scenario I propose is not ideal. But since that ideal scenario is extremely unlikely, we cannot hold the urgent need to act hostage to our wishes for global fairness. People in poorer countries will be better off if key powers take the lead on the GHG threat and don't allow anyone to free-ride. For it is the poorest people in the poorest countries who will experience most brutally the impacts from our reckless emissions of GHGs and our multi-decade inability to take globally effective preventative action, just as it was often the poorest and most helpless people who suffered the consequences of our global failure to prevent the rise of Nazi Germany and the disaster of World War II.

Demanding that the global climate agreement only happen if it is seen as equitable by every country on the planet is to ensure that it won't happen. Those who demand this need to look in the mirror when it comes to allocating blame for a continued global failure that is now especially harming the poorest people on the planet. And this failure to make unpopular decisions two decades ago has had another unfortunate repercussion. It has bought time for those who profit from rising GHG emissions to convince political leaders and the public in fossil fuel-rich jurisdictions and fossil fuel-dependent regions to accept actions that keep us on this disastrous path, as we'll see in the next chapter.

CHAPTER 5

This Fossil Fuel Project Is Essential

It is difficult to get a man to understand something, when his salary depends upon his *not* understanding it.

Upton Sinclair

INDIVIDUAL COUNTRIES HAVE STRONG INCENTIVES TO DELAY GHG-reducing actions that might disadvantage their economy relative to laggards, and this is especially so if they are fossil fuel-rich. The default path in such cases involves government talking about a national energy transition – especially when under the media spotlight at international climate negotiations – but doing little domestically to cause that transition. This optimal strategy from a national perspective causes humanity to fail with the global collective action challenge of climate change.

Although the incentives are against it, political leaders occasionally emerge who want to act decisively at a national or sub-national level. Perhaps the politician is concerned and sincere, recognizing the need for political leadership and accepting the duty to act despite domestic political risks and the lack of an effective global effort. Perhaps the jurisdiction lacks its own fossil fuels or is less dependent on them because of the dominance of an alternative like hydropower or nuclear, making it easier for citizens and corporations to envision a non-fossil fuel energy system. Perhaps there is greater public support for action due to a combination of higher education, wealth, global awareness, and trust in government and public institutions.

For corporations and individuals whose real or perceived self-interest is linked to the fossil fuel path, various strategies are available to delay or undermine climate-energy policy efforts in such jurisdictions. In a previous chapter, I explained how some have followed the strategy of the tobacco industry by misleading us about the science. In this chapter, I explain the one-at-a-time technique of convincing people who want action on the climate threat to nonetheless accept that this proposed coal mine, coal-fired power plant, oil pipeline, oil extraction project, natural gas development should proceed because it is somehow clean or valuable or a tiny GHG contributor or ethical.

To succeed in the art of illusion, magicians use a technique called 'sleight-of-hand.' They divert your attention elsewhere so that you fail to see what they're actually doing. With fossil fuels, tragically, the goal of the magic act is to acquire wealth without anyone realizing you are hastening climate change with its catastrophic impacts. The sleight-of-hand succeeds if people continue to support, or at least allow, investments and activities that extract and emit carbon, even though these same people don't want climate change. The magic act diverts their attention by incessantly harping on the jobs and other benefits from fossil fuel development, while avoiding any mention of the inevitable disaster. If the jobs and wealth message is repeated enough, the effect is hypnotic.

The fossil fuel industry has deep pockets to fund professionals whose job is to convince us that a particular fossil fuel extraction, transport, or burning activity is somehow good. These people are usually well paid thanks to the money we provide when buying gasoline from an oil company and electricity from a coal-burning utility. In the cruelest of ironies, we who are still somehow dependent on fossil fuels are bankrolling the people who work to keep us on a destructive path.

An American friend of mine, Steve, who once worked in marketing, recounted to me a day in which he felt particularly inundated with fossil fuel industry messaging. In the online version of his paper he read about the jobs and tax revenue a proposed oil pipeline would generate. In that one morning, he read this same message in an op-ed, the main editorial, a news article, and an info-ad designed to resemble a legitimate news article. Later that day, driving home from work he passed a bus emblazoned with the message "powered by natural gas: the green energy future." On the same trip, a radio ad informed him that the gasoline he buys is "good for his engine and the environment." And that evening, a TV ad by his electric utility trumpeted its "clean coal powerplants that help sustain local coal mining jobs."

Because of his marketing background, Steve is attuned to the techniques of his former profession. Had he not deliberately reflected on the coordinated biases in these messages, he too would have assumed these activities were good for both the environment and the economy. He reminded me of the strategy behind the Marlboro Man and other techniques to sell harmful products. Never mention lung cancer. Never mention climate change. Inundate the viewer with images of a thriving economy, along with tax revenues supporting local schools and hospitals.

If you read the promotional material of fossil fuel corporations in support of any coal mine, oil or gas well, oil pipeline, oil refinery, coal port, or coal-fired power plant, you will never see an explanation of how this project is consistent with limiting global warming to 2 degrees Celsius. Instead, you'll find vague claims that this project is the cleanest of its kind in the world. You'll hear about its economic and social benefits. You'll even hear that this corporation cares about climate change and is doing its part by improving plant efficiency or planting trees or something equally innocuous. But you'll never find an explanation of how this project is consistent with preventing climate change.

There are various techniques for deluding us that a project is clean when, if examined from the deep decarbonization imperative, it is clearly not. One technique involves finding a 'worse-than' comparative. In the case of coal, this is not easy because it is the most carbon-intensive of the three fossil fuels. But marketers for even the dirtiest coal plant in America can ostensibly find a still dirtier plant in some corner of the world for comparison. "Our coal plant is far better than those dirty plants in China."

The worse-than comparisons are ubiquitous. Since newer coal plants are more efficient, which means they burn less coal and produce less emissions, marketers morph this simple fact into the deceptive term 'clean coal.' Branding campaigns portray new coal-fired technology with slick info-ads explaining that continued development of coal plants is good for America and the planet. In *Big Coal*, Jeff Goodell recounted the efforts of the coal industry to rebrand itself as clean in the eyes of Americans.[1] In a *Rolling Stone* article in 2010, he described the American

Coalition for Clean Coal Electricity, with its $18 million advertising campaign, as "a front group for coal companies and utilities."[2]

For those skeptical about the coal industry, it has developed a second line-of-defense. There are a few plants in the world that generate electricity from coal while capturing most of the carbon and storing it permanently deep underground in porous layers of sedimentary rock. Few companies have this. But the mere possibility enables coal promoters to present new plants as 'capture-ready,' which is nothing more than conventional coal plants with adjacent parking lots where they might one day build a CO_2 capture facility.

In contrast to coal, the natural gas industry requires less trickery for its worse-than-me claim because its power plants produce only half the carbon emissions of coal plants. And with the low prices of natural gas over the last decade, which should continue for years, the industry can further claim that switching from coal to gas does not increase electricity prices.

The natural gas industry is, nonetheless, regularly confronted by environmentalists and independent researchers who note that natural gas combustion also heats the planet. One industry response is to present its product as the 'bridging fuel' on the road to lower emissions. This is used for electricity generation but also transportation, since switching cars, trucks, and buses from gasoline and diesel to natural gas would slightly reduce emissions.

Oil's traditional dominance of the transportation sector has so far obviated the need for a worse-than comparative. Until recently, it was difficult for most people to visualize switching to cars powered by electricity, biofuels, or hydrogen. Now, however, electricity is becoming a real threat to gasoline, with the emergence of many commercial models of plug-in hybrid and battery-electric vehicles. Hydrogen might also do well in fuel cell vehicles, while cleaner forms of biofuels, especially renewable diesel, are a threat for trucks and long-distance transport by train and ship. Thus, the challenge is growing for marketers of gasoline and diesel.

In Canada, where I live, one oil industry strategy is to change our vocabulary, just like Big Brother in George Orwell's *1984*.[3] When I was training at an energy institute in the 1980s, all of our energy dictionaries and encyclopedias used the term "Athabasca tar sands" or "Athabasca bitumen" to refer to the tar sands of Alberta. Those were the only names I knew. Then one day in the late 1990s, while speaking at a conference in Canada, one of the other panelists, from the oil industry, kept correcting me when I said tar sands. "It's oil sands." Having decided this term sounded more benign, the industry was determined to change our vocabularies. I and others stubbornly stuck with tar sands, but eventually gave in if only to be understood when speaking to the public and media. The industry had the marketing power to impose its will on our language itself. More recently, I have noticed in the media that the Canadian oil industry has replaced "developing our oil sands" with "developing our energy resources" and "developing our natural resources." Even the word oil is falling out of favor. One wonders what Orwellian euphemism is next – the "green sands"?

My discussion of these issues with my friend Steve was illuminating, as he helped me understand the various techniques of marketers. But he wanted something in return. He wanted to know how energy system researchers like me could tell if a particular project, like the Keystone XL oil pipeline from the Alberta "oil sands" to the Gulf, was consistent or not with the 2 degrees Celsius (4 degrees Fahrenheit) limit. Having often heard the industry refrain, "we can't stop using oil tomorrow," Steve wanted to know what investments today and tomorrow are consistent with preventing temperatures from rising more than the 2 degrees Celsius limit, or an even tighter limit such as 1.5 degrees. He wanted to know what he should oppose and what he could allow. He wanted to know whose evidence he could trust.

* * *

John Weyant and Hill Huntingdon have directed the Energy Modeling Forum at Stanford University for over three decades. Almost no one in their field is better known than these two professors, who built the forum into the world's premier institution for coordinating studies of national and international energy markets. Their studies involve the world's leading energy-economy modeling institutes, each with its own particular model that simulates how our energy producing and using technologies are likely to evolve, given key assumptions about population and

economic growth, technological innovation, costs, consumer preferences, and public policies.

Each year since its inception, the forum launches a new project in
which academic, industry and government experts study scenarios of
interest. These are numbered EMF 1, EMF 2, EMF 3, etc. Often, the
EMF studies focus on climate-energy policies at the US or global level.
The same modelers who coordinate their work for the Energy Modeling
Forum also do this for the global assessments of the Intergovernmental
Panel on Climate Change.

I told Steve to visit the Energy Modeling Forum website and skim some
of the key articles pertaining to EMF 27, a 2010 study that explored
pathways for keeping the temperature increase below 2 degrees
Celsius.[4] In studies like EMF 27, the models run identical climate-
energy policy scenarios designed to achieve the same outcome for the
global temperature in 2100. Differences in the model results indicate the
extent to which differences in model algorithms and assumptions are
a source of uncertainty.[5]

A key takeaway from EMF 27 and similar studies is that we can only
burn a small percentage of the remaining fossil fuels in the earth's crust if
we are to keep the temperature increase below 2 degrees Celsius.[6] Since
the carbon of burned fossil fuels goes into the atmosphere as CO_2, we can
work backward from the maximum possible atmospheric GHG concentration to define the 'carbon budget,' the amount of remaining coal, oil,
and natural gas we can burn.

Prior to the industrial revolution, when humans started increasing the
combustion of coal, followed by oil and then natural gas, the atmospheric
concentration of CO_2 was 280 parts per million. Since 1750, it has
increased exponentially to pass 415 parts per million in 2019.
According to climate scientists, we should have started two decades ago
to hold it to 350 parts per million to have a decent chance of preventing
the temperature increase from exceeding 2°C in 2100. Today, after two
decades of procrastination and rising cumulative emissions, this means
reducing emissions rapidly.

Our carbon budget is the rectangle in the middle of Figure 5.1. To the
left is the carbon we released from 1850 to 2000 (1,020 gigatons) and
from 2000 to 2015 (380 gigatons). On the right of the figure, the carbon

in unexploited fossil fuels is divided into the current reserve estimates of coal, oil, and natural gas companies (745 gigatons) and additional amounts that some experts conservatively estimate still reside in the earth's crust (2,050 gigatons). The actual amount is much greater, as I explain in Chapter 7.

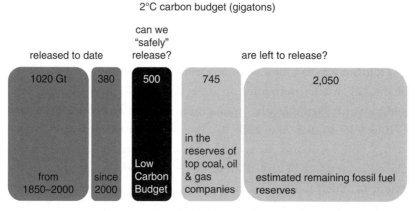

Figure 5.1 Carbon budget

This figure lumps all three forms of fossil fuels into one carbon source in order to compare them as a whole with the carbon budget. But studies like EMF 27 indicate the implications of the carbon budget for individual forms of energy. These studies show the effect of that budget on the global consumption of coal, oil, and natural gas over the next decades if we are to act effectively on the climate threat.

The general finding is unsurprising. Since our global energy system is more than 80% dominated by the burning of coal, oil, and natural gas, we need to stop building coal plants, and phase out existing ones over the next few decades (or retrofit these with carbon capture and storage). We need to rapidly phase out gasoline and diesel in transportation, meaning that global oil demand would soon start to fall. And while natural gas might still rise, as we use it to help phase out coal in electricity generation, within a couple of decades its demand too should be falling.

On my suggestion, Steve visited the Stanford website and read some EMF 27 articles. (I didn't see the point of sending him to the 2018 IPCC report on attaining the even-more-difficult target of 1.5°C.[7] Although the report is an excellent resource, the 1.5°C target is almost impossible to achieve without a sustained global economic collapse or a magical low-cost means of extracting CO_2 or deflecting solar radiation.) Steve noted the evidence for immediate action to meet emission targets for 2050, especially if we expect rich countries to bear more of the initial costs of energy system transformation. But he wondered how he could explain to his neighbors that even though we won't stop using oil right now, we should be acting now to reduce its consumption. I suggested he estimate the time required for significant emissions reductions from all vehicles in his neighborhood, especially since we know we must have a carbon-free transportation system.

Steve is a keener. Over the next two weeks, he interviewed almost everyone on his block. After completing his survey, he sent me his calculation for the amount of time needed for carbon-free vehicles to conquer his neighborhood, and the challenges he faced with neighbors who were initially unwilling to purchase zero-emission vehicles. Steve had learned that the market penetration of a new technology takes time, first for a few adventuresome people to try it, then for the bulk of the population to accept it after witnessing that experience, and then for the transformation of the entire vehicle stock as the oldest models are retired.

Since the average vehicle lasts 15 years, virtually all cars, vans, and pick-up trucks purchased after 2040 had to be zero-emission to achieve a 75% market share by mid-century. This left only one decade to transition from a few early adopters to wider consumer acceptance. For profound technological change, this is a tight timeframe. Consider that the hybrid cars, Toyota Prius and Honda Insight, were introduced in the US in 2000, and took a decade to reach 3% of new car sales, in spite of government subsidies and high oil prices.

Figure 5.2 summarizes the results from Steve's survey and forecast. He figured that the zero-emission vehicles must attain 30% of sales within 10 years, which translates into only 10% of the total vehicle stock, and 100% within 20 years to achieve 75% of total vehicles in 2050.

As Steve's exercise shows, what must happen is straightforward. To reduce GHG emissions, we must switch to alternative technologies. These are available today, but their rate of adoption is constrained by the rate of transformation of our existing energy-using factories, buildings,

Market share of zero-emission personal vehicles	2030	2040	2050
Share of *new* cars purchased	30%	100%	100%
Share of *all* cars on the road	10%	25%	75%

Figure 5.2 Market share of zero-emission vehicles

equipment, vehicles, and infrastructure. Even if government implemented aggressive policies today that mandated a rapidly growing investment in zero-emission technologies for all of these activities, it would take decades to transform the energy system, especially since long-lived investments like buildings, industrial plant, and infrastructure require much more time for renewal than vehicles.

Through this exercise Steve also realized that emission reductions must happen everywhere at the same time. It does little good for vehicles to switch from gasoline to electricity if that electricity is generated in coal-fired power plants. The falling emissions from vehicles would be offset by rising emissions from the power plants. Thus, the electricity system needs to rapidly decarbonize at the same time. And since only a small percentage of electricity plants are retired in a given decade, it is imperative that all new electricity investments are zero-emission and that coal plants are phased out. As an example, my colleague, Jonn Axsen (and former student George Kamiya) simulated the combined effect of energy transformation in the electricity and transportation sectors in different Canadian provinces.[8] Their study shows that electric cars already reduce emissions, even in jurisdictions with coal-fired power. Since the complete phase-out of coal may take one to two decades in some wealthy countries, pushing hard now for electric vehicles synchronizes the energy transformation in these two key sectors.

The technological path for an 80% reduction of global emissions by 2050 entails greater electricity use in industry, buildings, and transportation because electricity causes no emissions at the point of consumption. On the flip side, this path has a falling demand for oil, which is obvious from the table prepared by Steve, in which gasoline vehicles fall to only 25% of the total stock by mid-century, and continue their decline thereafter.

The computer models used in the studies of the Energy Modeling Forum keep track of the stock of houses and cars on Steve's block, and virtually everything else associated with GHG emissions. They keep track of the rates at which infrastructure, buildings, industrial plants, and equipment are retired and replaced. They map how this system-wide inertia determines what things we need to do today, tomorrow, and the next day in order to achieve a 2050 emissions target. And by keeping track of all these components and how they must change over time, the models provide a reality check on the "we-are-clean" claims of industry and the "we-are-acting-in-time-to-hit-our-target" claims of politicians.

The university research team I lead has an energy-economy model of the US and another of Canada, and we participate in some of the studies of the Energy Modeling Forum. Like others, we produce a dizzying array of results; there are many scenarios with differing assumptions about technologies, global energy markets, and policies. But some common lessons emerge from all the models. First, as I have said, we need to be making zero-emission technology and fuel investments today, even to meet an emissions target that seems safely distant. Second, if we pace our reductions to the rate at which technologies are naturally renewed, even the cost of deep decarbonization is modest. In 2015, for example, we estimated that the cost of achieving an 80% reduction in US emissions by 2050 would be equivalent to a year and a half of lost economic growth. One of my graduate students, Sally Rudd, decided to compare these costs to other items Americans spend money on. She found that this dramatic reduction of emissions would annually cost Americans slightly more than they spend on cosmetic surgery, less than on gambling, and far less than on going out for lunch. Her punch line? "There may be no free lunch, but reducing carbon pollution costs less than lunch."[9]

Steve's case study of his neighborhood gave him insights into the challenges of the deep decarbonization transition. We have the needed zero-emission and low-emission technologies. But it takes years, even decades to replace all equipment, buildings, factories, and vehicles. Then there is the human side. Some people readily adopt new technologies. But it takes time to convince the majority of consumers to switch, even when government policies make these technologies an affordable option. Then there is the political side. Some politicians are keen to enact policies that support zero-emission technologies and penalize polluting technologies. But the fossil fuel industry and other vested interests work hard to confuse the public about the need for and benefits from these policies. And without a clear and certain global effort it is easy for naysayers to discourage unilateral efforts by individual jurisdictions.

Steve was now eager to hear more about case studies from my research team's modeling of climate and energy policy in Canada and the US. I thought he would be interested in one story in particular, since it has dominated Canadian news for almost a decade.

* * *

As one of the world's wealthiest countries, Canada is expected to be a global leader when it comes to reducing GHG emissions. However, Canada is also plentifully endowed with all three fossil fuels. The distribution of these resources is regionally diverse, and in Canada's federal system, resource ownership resides with provincial governments. This creates a tension between those provincial governments that want to develop their fossil fuel resources, and are therefore usually biased against deep decarbonization policy, and other provincial governments that place greater priority on emission-reducing policies.

In 2015–19, the Liberal government of Prime Minister Justin Trudeau pursued GHG reductions, promising that Canada would achieve its Paris commitment of a 30% reduction by 2030. But the oil sands of Alberta make a significant contribution to the Canadian economy and the Alberta government wants production to expand over the coming decades. For this to occur, new oil pipelines are needed to transport that additional output to market. From 2012 to 2015, opposition to the proposed Keystone XL pipeline from the Alberta oil sands to the Gulf of Mexico became a *cause célèbre* for environmental activists who wanted a serious deep decarbonization effort. To improve the chances of approval, the project's proponents claimed that increasing oil pipeline capacity would not cause increased oil sands output and emissions.

I was called to testify in Washington in 2013 before the US Congressional Subcommittee on Energy and Power. I explained the linkage between oil pipelines and oil output, and how approval of a pipeline like this would facilitate oil sands expansion and higher

GHG emissions from Canada. While the experience of testifying was intriguing, I noticed that the Republican congressional committee members were not listening to my responses to their questions, which were really just lengthy statements anyway. It seemed like their focus was not me, but somewhere else, perhaps the voters in their home districts or the fossil fuel companies that might contribute campaign funding.

After years of deliberation, President Obama rejected the Keystone XL application in 2015. He accepted the argument that more oil pipelines lead to more oil sands production. Not surprisingly, his decision was overturned two years later by President Trump.

Another pipeline proposal that received less attention in the US, but has been a major issue in Canada, is the TransMountain Pipeline expansion. For decades the original pipeline transported crude oil and refinery products like gasoline and diesel from Edmonton to Vancouver. In 2004, the pipeline was purchased by Houston-based Kinder-Morgan, which applied in 2013 to triple the pipeline's capacity so that diluted bitumen from the oil sands could be transported to the west coast for shipment to overseas markets. The tripling of capacity helps the ongoing oil sands expansion, although again proponents and politicians avoided all discussion of the consistency of oil sands expansion with global carbon budgets.

To shed light on the debate, my research group used results from the EMF 27 study to assess whether oil sands expansion, and thus more oil pipelines, is indeed compatible with the global carbon budget. We took the global oil demand from the EMF 27 model results where humanity keeps the temperature increase at 2°C, estimated the effect on the oil price over the next few decades, and compared this to the likely production cost of oil sands over this time. If the cost of producing oil from the oil sands, including the costs of almost completely eliminating GHG emissions in its production process, exceeded the market price of oil, oil sands expansion would be uneconomic, as would new oil pipelines.

The price of oil depends in part, however, on the production decisions of the Organization of Petroleum Exporting Countries (OPEC), a price-influencing cartel of major oil producers. If OPEC tried to sustain its current production level, while the global demand for oil fell, the price of oil would fall below $30 per barrel for decades. With its low production costs, OPEC would outcompete other producers. If, however,

OPEC reduced its output in line with the declining demand for oil, to sustain a constant 40–45% market share of oil production (as it has been for 25 years) then the price of oil would settle at higher levels, probably in the $45 range.

Research by ourselves and others showed, however, that even if OPEC followed this latter strategy, ensuring a higher oil price, oil sands expansion would still be uneconomic. The reason, as we showed in a paper entitled "Global carbon budgets and the viability of new fossil fuel projects," is that deep decarbonization policies would increase the oil sands cost of production.[10] Since this source of oil produces more GHG emissions during production than most sources, what is already a high cost source of oil would see its production cost rise above $50 per barrel, either because of paying a carbon tax on production emissions or paying to eliminate these.

* * *

Governments and fossil fuel corporations avoid the cognitive dissonance caused by simultaneously discussing their fossil fuel expansion and GHG reduction commitments. This is why more citizens need to 'connect the dots' between the two, as I next explained to Steve.

An effort to stop the expansion of fossil fuel infrastructure, such as an oil pipeline, is referred to as a supply-side action. While stopping a pipeline ultimately requires a government decision, citizen efforts to influence that decision range from campaigns to disinvest from fossil fuel companies to acts of peaceful civil disobedience that hinder the construction of fossil fuel projects. In the case of Steve and his neighbors, their potential role as decarbonizing consumers is a demand-side action. Such actions may happen without any policy effort by government. But as the last 30 years have shown, humanity is not going to spontaneously walk away from fossil fuels in time to avert dramatic climate impacts. Government policy is required.

Figure 5.3 depicts government policy options to motivate GHG-reducing actions by individuals and firms. At the top tier, government can choose between non-compulsory and compulsory policies. With non-compulsory policies, it tries to convince people to voluntarily change their technology choices and behavior for reasons of altruism or financial self-interest. Labels on appliances and vehicles inform buyers of the benefits of a more efficient model. Subsidies to products like efficient fridges also focus on self-interest. Governments and advocacy groups also apply moral suasion to encourage individuals and businesses to voluntarily reduce their emissions, efforts known as 'corporate social responsibility' and 'green consumerism.' Finally, because government owns buildings, vehicles, transit systems, and more, it can reduce its emissions via internal investment and management practices.

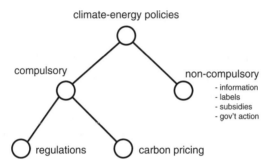

Figure 5.3 Climate-energy policy

All of these non-compulsory policies are attractive to politicians because they don't have to compel anyone to do anything. But if emissions reductions are costly or inconvenient, these policies have negligible effect. Non-compulsory policies played a role in reducing smoking because the harm is 'internalized' – we do it to ourselves. With second-hand smoke and GHGs, where our emissions harm others, we need compulsory policies.

Most governments have tried to look sincere by applying non-compulsory policies for much of the last three decades, extolling the virtues of low-emission lifestyles and technology choices, and doling out subsidies to lure some people to more energy-efficient devices. But if we look at what happened to emissions while governments were doing this, we know that compulsory policies are necessary for the energy transition.

The diagram shows compulsory policies divided into two major categories: regulations and carbon pricing (also called standards and emissions pricing). Our economy is rife with regulations that govern everything from the efficiency of your fridge to the emissions from your vehicle. We can rely exclusively on regulations to reduce GHG emissions if we want. This is a scary thought to people who prefer less government. They fear a swarm of bureaucrats scrutinizing and controlling everything they purchase or do.

But it doesn't have to be this way. We can design regulations that oblige industry to reduce its emissions or shift to a broad category of technologies (like zero-emission electricity generation) and then let businesses decide how to achieve it, perhaps with those who find reductions more expensive paying those who find it cheaper to do more. In the next chapter, I explain and provide real-world examples of this more flexible regulatory approach.

Since economists focus on economic efficiency, they prefer policies that achieve our environmental objectives as cheaply as possible, leaving us with more money for education, healthcare, social services, cosmetic surgery, monster homes, expensive watches, luxury cars, whatever we prefer. Lots of evidence shows that if forced to pay for our pollution, we'll pollute less. With carbon pricing, we can decide for ourselves how and by how much we'll reduce our emissions. You see the price of gasoline gradually rising while the price of ethanol or renewable electricity remains stable. You decide your next car will run on ethanol or electricity instead of gasoline. Your neighbor decides to stick with gasoline, paying more because of the added emissions charge. The net effect is that emissions fall as desired. Government stays in the background, allowing each person to decide their response to the emissions charge based on their preferences.

This free choice for businesses and individuals is good not just because of our beliefs in individual freedom and responsibility. It's also good because each of us may have different costs of reducing emissions: old factory versus new factory, suburban commuter versus inner-city dweller, inhabitants of cold climates versus hot climates. Emissions pricing allows everyone to decide on their technologies, fuels, investment, and lifestyle based on their unique costs and preferences. As a result, we reduce emissions at the lowest possible cost and least possible inconvenience.

When it comes to carbon pricing, there are two main options: carbon tax and cap-and-trade. A carbon tax is the easiest to explain. Since government already taxes energy, it simply adjusts its tax rates to match the carbon content of each fossil fuel: high for coal, low for natural gas, medium for oil products like gasoline. A second option for emissions pricing is to set an emissions cap and distribute tradable permits that in total sum to the cap. By allocating tradable permits (sometimes called allowances) government replicates the individual freedom of the carbon tax. Those who find it relatively cheap to reduce emissions might do additional reductions, leaving them with surplus permits they can sell to those who find reductions relatively costly. The permit trading price gives the same emissions pricing signal to everyone, just like the carbon tax. Government stays out of the decision. I elaborate on the pros and cons of these policy options in the next chapter.

* * *

Had the international community achieved global agreement on national commitments to stay within 2°C, and had that agreement included an effective compliance mechanism, then each country would domestically apply one or a combination of carbon pricing and regulations to meet its commitment and avoid non-compliance penalties (probably international carbon tariffs). If this occurred, the demand for coal, oil, and eventually natural gas would decline, just as shown in studies reported by the IPCC and the Energy Modeling Forum.

In this world, there would be no need for citizens like Steve to worry about climate-energy policy or the proposed projects of the fossil fuel industry. Only economically viable projects in a decarbonizing economy would proceed. Of course, such projects may have local impacts and risks that citizens may be concerned about. Environmental assessment processes would still be required. But the contribution of such projects to GHG emissions would be of no concern, since citizens would already know that humanity has implemented deep decarbonization policies.

Unfortunately, that is not the world in which Steve and the rest of us find ourselves. So we need to be vigilant, as Steve now is. His investigation of the small picture, the cars on his block, and the big picture, global studies by Stanford's Energy Modeling Forum, has given him a level of awareness that won't help him sleep at night. Yet, he says he feels empowered. Although not an expert, he is now better equipped to deal with fossil fuel advocates and politicians trying to convince him to accept the continued extraction and burning of fossil fuels in a world that is not yet on a path to climate success, not by a long shot.

Steve now understands that "fossil fuels are clean" is a marketing ploy. He knows that we already have commercially available technologies and energy forms to shift our energy system on to the deep decarbonization path. He knows what must be happening today in his country and his region as part of the global effort to avert a climate disaster. We cannot be allowing new projects that 'lock-in' the extraction and burning of fossil fuels.[11] Our new electricity plants, new factories, new buildings, and new vehicles must be zero-emission or close to it. And this energy transition won't happen without compulsory climate-energy policies.

Steve can now 'connect the dots' for himself and friends to help counter the effect of those who are preventing us from addressing this threat. As Figure 5.4 shows, he knows that to keep the temperature increase to no more than 2 degrees Celsius, we need to return atmospheric concentrations of CO_2 to 350 parts per million. Steve also knows that for this to happen, CO_2 emissions must fall 50% globally by 2050 and 80% in richer countries. He knows that this can only happen if every major investment today is on the path to CO_2-free technologies and fuels.

Steve can now see through the misinformation campaigns. He is now able to respond to the numerous rationalizations for why *this* fossil fuel project is essential.

connect-the-dots

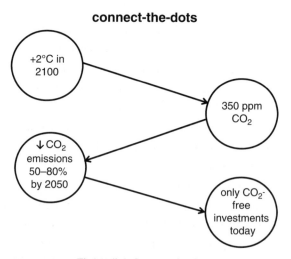

Figure 5.4 Connect the dots

When they say, "We're not going to stop using oil tomorrow, so this project should proceed," Steve sees that if this project proceeds, we certainly won't stop using oil in time to avert a catastrophe. If, instead, we enacted compulsory transportation policies of rising stringency, and work to spread these to developing countries, using globalization campaigns that likely require carbon tariffs, oil sales would decline as plug-in hybrids, battery-electric, biofuel, and other clean vehicles captured market share. We won't stop using all oil tomorrow. But we must try to stop most new investments to extract carbon from the earth's crust.

When they say, "We need the jobs and tax revenue from this fossil fuel project," Steve now knows that if we capped or priced carbon pollution, we would use more electricity, biofuels, and hydrogen in our vehicles, and these would be produced using solar, wind, wood, grains, hydro, perhaps nuclear power, and perhaps some fossil fuels with carbon capture and storage. And, of course, all of these alternatives would also produce jobs and tax revenues.

When they say, "Electric, ethanol, biodiesel, and hydrogen cars and trucks are expensive, unreliable, and inconvenient," Steve now knows that these options may appear relatively expensive today, but that is only because fossil fuels have a huge subsidy by using the atmosphere as a free dump. The economics change once we correct this terrible oversight with carbon pricing or regulations. Then we'll see these alternatives become cheaper and more reliable as they compete with each other in the rapidly growing market for low- and zero-emission vehicles.

When they say, "There is no point reducing our emissions until the Chinese, Indians, and other developing countries act," Steve now sees that there is no point in developing countries reducing emissions until the richer countries take serious action. As this happens, the leaders of developing countries know that voters in these well-off countries will require that their efforts not be nullified by rising emissions in other countries. Carbon tariffs will likely follow, and we need to be open about this now. If we allow the fossil fuel industry to paint our domestic efforts as globally futile, these efforts will be thwarted.

When they say, "Our oil, coal, or gas is ethical because when you buy from us your money doesn't go to terrorists," Steve now wonders, "How ethical is it to harm current and future generations with climate change simply to enrich yourself?"

These are just some of the justifications for continuing on our high-risk path. The false logic and biased evidence are easily refuted, but informing the public is not easy. This is why people who understand the need to act quickly on the climate threat must lobby for and support compulsory policies, domestically and globally, and actively help their neighbors, friends, and family achieve this same understanding.

And whether we refer to the challenge as a climate emergency or a deep decarbonization urgency or an energy transformation necessity, we must understand that success requires a policy transition as well. Climate-concerned jurisdictions, followed quickly by all jurisdictions, must shift from the all-too-common milquetoast policy stringencies that tinker at the edges of our fossil fuel-dominated economies toward policies that cause the rapid GHG reduction that is essential. A slight reduction in coal burning, a bit more biofuels in gasoline, improved energy efficiency of fossil fuel-burning devices will not do the job. We need now to enact and sustain transformative policies that phase out coal in electricity generation, gasoline in transportation, natural gas and heating oil in buildings, and a host of other wholesale transitions.

Implementing and sustaining such policies in the realm of real-world politics will not be easy. Which is why we must be willing to compromise on our preferred compulsory policy, where this accommodation might increase our chance of political success. In the world of climate-energy policy, we must heed Shakespeare's warning that, "Striving to better, oft we mar what's well."[12]

CHAPTER 6

We Must Price Carbon Emissions

When the facts change, I change my mind. What do you do sir?

John Maynard Keynes

Ⅰ N ITS BUDGET SPEECH OF FEBRUARY 19, 2008, THE GOVERNMENT OF the Canadian province of British Columbia announced its imple-mentation of a 'revenue-neutral' carbon tax.[1] The tax started at $10 per metric ton of CO_2 on July 1, 2008 and would follow a scheduled increase of $5 per year to reach $30 in 2012. Because I had been advising the government on climate policy, including design of the carbon tax, the premier of the province invited me to the budget speech along with environmentalists and business leaders. The idea was to show broad support in a high-profile event that included the official speech in the legislature, a gala reception, and media interviews. I declined to attend.

My reason was not that I opposed the tax. Rather, I was anticipating the political battle ahead, and wanted to maintain my position as a non-partisan academic expert who avoided hobnobbing with politicians at public events.

I have always been non-partisan in my climate policy advisory work, helping politicians across the political spectrum if they seemed sincere about climate action. But I knew that those opposed to the tax would try to paint my support as biased, motivated by a partisan preference for the governing, right-of-center party. They would try this even though I had been appointed a decade earlier by the left-of-center party to a five-year term as chair of the British Columbia Utilities Commission, had been an advisor to Canada's Conservative minister of environment, and before that Canada's Liberal government as it assessed options for achieving the country's GHG reduction target under the Kyoto Protocol.

I correctly anticipated that there would be a vicious fight over the carbon tax in the year between its announcement and the provincial election. I also anticipated that this fight would be far from the evidence-based battles in which we academics engage. But even with my long experience in the cut-and-thrust of political policy debates, I did not anticipate how blatantly the tax's opponents would lie about its effects. A new tax, even one that does not cause a net tax increase, is an enticing target for political shenanigans.

Why then did the BC government pursue such a politically risky policy? It's important to understand the context, both globally and in this particular jurisdiction.

Globally, the period 2005 to 2008 was a 'policy window' for political action on GHG emissions. While ongoing conflicts in the Middle East were still dominating public attention, a shift began as Hurricane Katrina in 2005 set the stage for Al Gore's 2006 movie, *An Inconvenient Truth*,[2] and Nicholas Stern's comprehensive report for Tony Blair's UK government on the economic benefits of acting now to reduce GHG emissions.[3] In 2005, the European Union implemented a cap on industrial emissions.[4] In the US, Republican and Democrat senators and representatives were negotiating various bi-partisan bills to cap US GHG emissions, and international discussions intensified to bring the US back into either the Kyoto Protocol or, more likely, a new international agreement that would set emission limits for *all* countries, not just the wealthier ones. And Republican governors, like Mitt Romney in Massachusetts and Arnold Schwarzenegger in California, were pushing aggressive state-level climate policies to counter the reluctance of Republican President George W. Bush.

Although the Canadian Conservative government of Stephen Harper was also reluctant to act, as a minority government it needed to give lip-service support for Canada's Kyoto target. In reality, it did as little as possible.

However, British Columbia's premier, Gordon Campbell, was a policy wonk who was willing to show policy leadership even when that entailed political risk. In 2006, he got religious on the climate threat, and decided he should push to make British Columbia a model for climate policy. His new climate deputy minister, Graham Whitmarsh, contacted me and we began discussing policy options.

Campbell soon expressed interest in a revenue-neutral carbon tax because, as a right-of-center politician, he preferred its minimalist approach to government: giving a simple price signal that left businesses and households to decide for themselves if and by how much they would respond to the rising cost of fossil fuels. To be revenue neutral, government would lower personal and corporate income taxes to ensure that in each year these reductions in government revenues would equal its carbon tax revenues. To those low-income individuals who didn't pay taxes, and thus would not benefit from a tax cut, the government would send lump-sum payments three times a year. The policy design team used the energy-economy model I had developed over the previous decade to estimate how carbon tax revenues would change as people changed technologies and perhaps behavior in response to the rising after-tax price of gasoline, diesel, heating oil, and natural gas. The price of electricity would change little because there are few electricity-derived GHG emissions in our hydropower-dominated jurisdiction.

Instead of the carbon tax, I had suggested that Campbell start with less politically risky policies, such as the flexible regulations I describe later in this chapter, while waiting to see if British Columbia could eventually join the emissions cap-and-trade policy that California was trying to convince western US states and some Canadian provinces to implement together. Campbell agreed, but also wanted the carbon tax. Ultimately, his was a shot-gun approach, adopting multiple pricing and regulatory policies, some of which overlapped significantly. After years of unsuccessfully trying to convince politicians to implement pricing or regulatory policies, I now found myself arguing for parsimony: reducing such policies to minimize regulatory complexity and implementation cost.

The 'carbon tax war' started on February 19, 2008. I experienced first-hand why politicians associated with carbon pricing have a high casualty rate.

During his previous seven years as premier, Campbell easily outpolled the opposition. With over a year until the next election, he held a 20-point lead. This is enormous in Canada's first-past-the-post electoral system, where three and sometimes four parties split the vote, such that capturing only 40% of the total votes can deliver a landslide victory.

Recognizing the political gift, and desperate for any chance to improve its prospects, the left-of-center opposition party immediately launched an "ax-the-tax" campaign. No matter that this party's own policy program promised a carbon tax. No one read these things anyway. And this sudden reversal enabled it to position itself at the head of mass opposition to the carbon tax which came from all directions – climate change deniers, fossil fuel interests, representatives of northern, suburban, and rural voters who claimed the tax was not revenue neutral for them, anti-tax advocates, truckers, talk show hosts, columnists, editorial boards. The major newspapers published a steady stream of anti-carbon tax op-eds, full of untruths.

My innocent and dumbfounded graduate students kept asking me why anyone would lie about the carbon tax. Why would opponents say it was a tax grab when it was revenue neutral? Why would they say it especially hurt the poor, when ours and the government's widely publicized analysis showed the opposite, thanks to the direct payments to low-income people? Why did opponents say it would destroy the economy when the evidence showed it wouldn't? Why did truckers say it hurt them when their costs could be passed on to customers? Why did northerners say it was unfair to them because of colder temperatures when data showed they had better insulated homes and so consumed the same amount of natural gas as southern British Columbians, and many also used untaxed wood for space heating? This is a sample of the relentless misinformation which my research group tried to correct by producing carefully researched reports and evidence-based op-eds in the weeks and months before and after the tax's implementation.

My students also learned that political battles involve character assassination, with anyone as a potential target. We found out my house was under surveillance when reading in the newspaper about my hypocrisy as a carbon tax advocate who left his home fully lit during Earth Hour. As it turns out, on that fateful evening I was visiting friends in Toronto, where we dutifully extinguished all lights in a politically correct, candle-lit vigil. Meanwhile, back in Vancouver, my teenage kids were hosting a raucous Saturday night party, oblivious to the fact it was Earth Hour. Later, they were confused when, instead of lambasting them for an unsanctioned party, I groused about their choice of lighting. "Why couldn't you have used candles?" "But you always said candles were a bad idea at teenage parties?"

Surveys by political scientists and professional pollsters confirmed that the ax-the-tax campaign was a huge success. Although publicized analysis by the government and my research team showed that 30% of British Columbians would be net financial losers under the revenue-neutral carbon tax (years later confirmed with hindsight analysis by my former student Nic Rivers and colleagues[5]), polls showed that the public believed the opposite, with 70% assuming they were net losers. People notice the posted price of gasoline far more easily than a change in the percentage of their income tax rate. Who other than accountants and economists knows their income tax rates?

Since many British Columbians hold strongly pro-environment views, there was substantial support for the carbon tax. But what matters for any political leader's survival is to find enough support in key swing electoral districts (ridings) to win a general election. For Campbell, that likelihood was diminishing fast. In just six months, his 20-point lead evaporated, and the trend indicated he would lose the May 2009 election because he would be defeated in key swing districts. A sudden collapse of this magnitude only happens after a sex or corruption scandal.

However, Campbell got lucky in the fall of 2008. As the world spiraled into a financial crisis, British Columbians suddenly had bigger economic concerns, and Campbell had always polled best on managing the economy. Moreover, the global recession that followed the financial crisis caused the price of oil to drop from its high level of the previous four years. In the six months preceding the election, anti-tax campaigners had difficulty sustaining anger among the electorate since the carbon tax came into effect just as gasoline prices were plummeting. The first year of the carbon tax would have increased gas prices by only two cents per liter, but thanks to the oil price collapse, they actually fell by 15 cents.

As the graph of political support over time in Figure 6.1 shows, the ax-the-tax campaign helped the left-of-center party, the NDP, overcome in just six months the 20-point lead of Campbell's Liberal Party. But the economic crisis in late 2008 reversed the trend, and he held his support to win the election, just barely. The BC carbon tax survived its first electoral test. But, as the Duke of Wellington purportedly said after defeating Napoleon at Waterloo, "It was a near run thing."

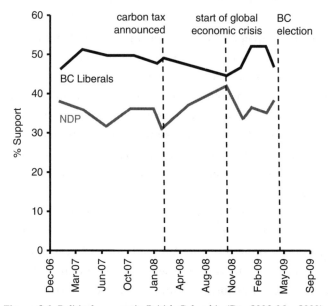

Figure 6.1 Political support in British Columbia (Dec 2006–May 2009)

Campbell stepped down in 2011 and his replacement froze the carbon tax, meaning that its effect declined with each year of inflation. For a while it looked like she might rescind it. But politicians in British Columbia are expected to annually balance the budget, so she would have needed to raise income taxes to offset the lost revenue from a canceled carbon tax. Those of us who had argued for revenue neutrality when designing the tax felt vindicated. This design gives the best chance for sustaining the tax. If it is linked to spending on energy efficiency, electric cars, or other GHG-related actions, the next government can cancel these while it eliminates the carbon tax to demonstrate its solidarity with "downtrodden motorists." Implementing and then sustaining climate-energy policies of rising stringency is not politically easy.

* * *

I explained in Chapter 4 that GHG reduction is a global collective action problem – all countries, or at least all major GHG emitters, need to act in concert for global success. This requires a global enforcement mechanism, without which each country's efforts are likely inconsequential, making it difficult for sincere politicians to push for domestic energy transformation.

But even if GHG emissions were only a domestic rather than a global environmental challenge – meaning that each country could prevent climate change within its borders by reducing its own emissions – public acceptance of transformative climate-energy policies would still be elusive. Deep decarbonization imposes near-term real and perceived costs, some of them seemingly concentrated in fossil fuel-endowed regions, to produce society-wide long-term benefits. This timing disconnect of costs and benefits is always politically difficult, and the geographical imbalance of real and perceived costs makes it even more so. Regions, corporations, and consumers with a vested interest in fossil fuels will impede energy transformation policies, with some propagating misinformation about climate science and the cost of deep decarbonization.

In the face of this opposition, politicians must recognize the low odds of achieving a climate-energy consensus. They must show leadership by enacting effective policies while knowing that fossil fuel interests will use aggressive tactics to prevent or delay these. Under this relentless pressure, few politicians stay the course, even those who are concerned and sincere.

Moreover, the divergence between the four-year electoral timeframe of most democratic systems and the multi-decade timeframe of deep decarbonization facilitates the deception strategies of insincere politicians, who promise to lower gasoline and electricity prices today *and* to dramatically reduce GHG emissions within 15 years. These faking-it politicians know they will have retired by the time their false GHG promise is exposed. And the challenges from these insincere politicians often compel the sincere politicians to retreat toward safely distant GHG targets and largely ineffective climate-energy policies.

Political scientists who research policy-making in democracies note that the challenges facing climate-energy policy are not unique. In his 1960s book, *The Logic of Collective Action*, Mancur Olson explained why policies that might broadly benefit society have a higher likelihood of failure if their costs (real or perceived) are concentrated among a smaller group that is highly motivated to campaign aggressively to prevent them.[6] Some countries, and some regions within countries, certainly fit the bill for an agenda determined by their fossil fuel endowment.

Success in the face of powerful interests might be helped by broad-based efforts to educate and build consensus on the need for transformative climate-energy policies. But to rely on this alone is naïve. Indeed, politicians and climate action advocates who base their strategy on rationally convincing most people in fossil fuel-endowed regions of the necessity and fairness of energy-system transformation share responsibility for our ongoing failure. Instead, they must recognize the real-world constraints on rational policy-making, as explained by political scientists, sociologists, and social psychologists, and from this recognition develop strategies less dependent on a policy consensus for success.

In their book, *Democracy for Realists: Why Elections Do Not Produce Responsive Government*, Christopher Achen and Larry Bartels explain, "Group and partisan loyalties, not policy preferences or ideologies, are fundamental in democratic politics ... For most people, partisanship is not a carrier of ideology, but a reflection of judgments about where 'people like me' belong."[7] Daniel Kahneman in his book, *Thinking Fast and Slow*, refers to our various group thinking cognitive biases, such as the 'halo effect' in which we give the benefit of doubt to someone from our group, even though their position may now be at odds with our initial position.[8] And political scientists have long referred to the 'Nixon goes to China' phenomenon, whereby a political leader with unassailable credentials in the eyes of a particular group is allowed to effect change they would strongly oppose if pursued by a political leader external to their group. (Known as a hardline anti-communist, Republican President Richard Nixon visited China in 1972 to re-establish diplomatic relations, a more difficult gesture for left-of-center Democrat presidents, lest they be seen as soft on communism.)

As the popular leader of a right-of-center political party, Gordon Campbell was able to garner support from the political party most likely to oppose compulsory GHG policy, because *he* was a highly trusted leader of the tribe. If he thought they should act on climate, maybe they should. Thus, after years of ignoring the climate threat, members of this party were suddenly interested. It was particularly entertaining to watch previously skeptical cabinet ministers, whose narrative had been "there's no sense acting until everyone acts," suddenly arguing that "the time for action is now." I was reminded of this reversal a decade later when observing US Republican politicians, who had earlier slammed Donald Trump as outrageous and despicable, changed their tune once he became president and leader of their party.

In its 2005–2009 term in office, the popular Campbell government was into its second mandate after a successful first four years. This aura of political success accorded Campbell almost dictatorial powers in pursuing his new passion for GHG policies – including a carbon tax. In fact, in just two years he legislated virtually *all* of the compulsory policies for reducing emissions.

Figure 6.2 is a more detailed version of Figure 5.3 in Chapter 5. The initial version stopped at the level of regulations and carbon pricing, the two generic alternatives for compulsory policies. This abridged version of the figure enables me to focus on the distinction between non-compulsory policies, that on their own cannot cause a major energy system transformation, and the compulsory regulations or carbon pricing that can. The extended version in Figure 6.2 includes a bottom row showing multiple regulatory and carbon pricing options. While I have already explained the distinction between carbon pricing and cap-and-trade, the diversity of regulatory options, as depicted in the two

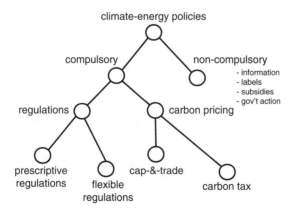

Figure 6.2 Climate-energy policy: details on regulations and pricing

categories on the bottom left, is often ignored in discussions of our climate-energy policies.

The carbon tax is well understood, or at least by the tiny percentage of the public that is interested. To apply the tax, the government changes the tax rates it charges consumers of coal, natural gas, gasoline, diesel, heating fuel, jet fuel, and so on to reflect their carbon content, the assumption being that all of the carbon will eventually end up as atmospheric CO_2. If, however, a coal plant is capturing and safely storing some of its emissions, the quantity of captured carbon is subtracted from the quantity of carbon in the consumed coal, so that the tax only applies to emissions that reach the atmosphere. The $30 carbon tax in British Columbia increased the price of gasoline by 7 cents per liter or 28 cents per gallon. The tax per liter of diesel is slightly different because this fuel has a different carbon content per liter.

Some industries, such as cement and aluminum, and some sectors of the economy, such as agriculture and forestry, emit CO_2 and other GHGs that are not the result of burning fossil fuels. Government can require producers of these emissions to report them so that it can charge the appropriate tax. But this gets complicated with the more difficult-to-measure emissions, such as methane released from a pile of cow manure. The government exempted these emissions to minimize the administrative challenges of implementation, not to mention the political costs of aggravating farmers with a new tax.

Government can use the carbon tax revenues in various ways. Some people argue it should subsidize emission reductions, with grants for home insulation, electric cars, transit expansion, and wind turbines. The counter argument is that the tax already incentivizes these actions, so revenues should be allocated where they best benefit society. According to economists, societal benefits are maximized by cutting taxes that hinder economic growth, which explains the Campbell government's decision to cut corporate and personal income taxes.

People concerned with political acceptability, however, focus on more visible ways of returning the tax revenue. An 'atmospheric dividend' is one of many marketing terms suggested for periodic lump-sum payments that would return all carbon tax revenue directly to households. I confess to some skepticism with the argument that carbon taxes will be politically popular once we label and use them a certain way. For decades, I've heard arguments that carbon taxes would be accepted *if only* government used a clever label. "Don't call it a tax, call it a carbon levy." "No, call it a pollution charge." "No, call it an atmospheric user fee." "No, call it a (fill in the blank)." I've also heard for decades that *if only* the carbon tax revenue were used in such and such a way, then it would be politically acceptable. "Don't keep the money in general revenue, cut income taxes." "Don't cut income taxes, give subsidies for voters to insulate their homes and buy low-emission vehicles." "No, give money to those most impacted by the tax." "No, give equal 'dividend' payments to each individual or household since they are all potential voters." "No, give the money back as (fill in the blank)."

My review of the evidence and my anecdotal experience suggests that no matter what euphemism proponents offer, it takes no time at all for carbon tax opponents to convince an electorally significant share of voters (which only need be a few percent if this becomes *the* single issue that determines these people's votes) that the tax is harming them financially, while government wastes millions in postage and advertisements to buy their vote with their own money. Barry Rabe explores this issue of how to 'frame' the carbon tax in his book, *Can We Price Carbon?*, and indeed finds that some strategies are less objectionable than others.[9] But my point is that the framing of carbon tax implementers must overcome the well-financed 'reframing' campaign of carbon tax opponents, complete with well-funded and therefore widely circulated lies that confuse the public about the benefits and costs of the tax and the various ways of using its revenues. Research on the challenges of framing and reframing strategies for garnering public support of climate policies seems generally consistent with my skepticism.[10]

We learned from our experience in British Columbia that many people could not grasp how a revenue-neutral carbon tax would lower emissions. I was a regular on radio talk shows, which, to the chagrin of the government, intensified their focus on the carbon tax around July 1 each year, the date of its annual scheduled increase. The media loved this boost in ratings, as angry callers defiantly argued "I'll use the carbon tax rebate to buy the same amount of gasoline when I fill up my pick-up truck, so this stupid policy changes nothing."

I am never satisfied with my attempts to clarify in one-minute radio-clips why a revenue-neutral carbon tax would optimally reduce emissions, hence my sympathy for the poor politician trying to explain this in a candidates' debate. Given more time to explain this in my undergraduate sustainable energy course, I've had some success. Still, an amazing number of students perform poorly with this on exam questions. They keep forgetting that each person or household or taxpayer receives an identical rebate, regardless of how much carbon tax they paid. One person might pay $120 in carbon taxes and another $80, yet both receive a rebate of $100. Both have an incentive to reduce their carbon emissions, and thus their carbon tax payments, since that reduction will not affect the size of their rebate. If the person originally paying $80 finds a way next year to pay only $60, they still get the $100 rebate. Because the carbon tax increases the relative prices of fossil fuel products, some people will consume less than previously, perhaps by changing behavior, perhaps by changing technology. The pick-up truck driver might not reduce his consumption in response to the carbon tax. It's his prerogative to do nothing and call the tax stupid. But smart people will explore their options.

Thus, another challenge is to respond to comments like, "It's unfair because I can't change my behavior. I still need to get the kids to (name your activity) and there are no alternatives to the car where we live." Again, it is easier explaining to my captive students that a carbon tax is not focused on changing behavior. It lets each person decide if they will change technology, change behavior, or do nothing and pay the full tax. They, rather than government, decide what is best for them, depending on their preferences and costs. Some people, like the pick-up driver, may use the same technology in the same way. But some will choose a more efficient gasoline option or a plug-in or biofuel option for their next vehicle purchase, without changing behavior. Some will carpool more frequently for kids' events or commuting. Some will move to higher density suburbs or the inner city where destinations are closer, so that they drive less, and where vehicle alternatives like transit, walking, and cycling are more accessible. The net effect of these diverse individual responses to a rising carbon tax is a reduction in GHG emissions, without mandating that anyone behave in a particular way or purchase a particular technology. But good luck trying to get all voters to grasp this argument, especially that small percentage of suburban voters who have a disproportionate influence on the outcome of close elections.

I could go on about the travails of defending a carbon tax. This activity has been a big part of my life for over a decade. The experience helps explain my jaded response to those economists who refer to "the ease of explaining why the carbon tax is the best policy." It didn't help my attitude that throughout the past decade economists from around the world made pilgrimages to British Columbia to study our 'ideal' carbon tax, yet showed little interest in the real-world evidence I and others provided on how easy it is for opponents to mislead a modest, but electorally significant, share of voters with blatant lies.[11]

Because the other carbon pricing policy in Figure 6.2, cap-and-trade, avoids the word tax, there is hope that it may be more politically acceptable. As I described in Chapter 5, government sets a cap on emissions for all or some sectors of the economy, and auctions or freely allocates (called 'grandfathering') tradable emission permits (also called 'allowances') that sum to the total emissions cap. In future years, the cap declines according to a schedule, meaning that the number of permits issued by government each year also declines.

As with a carbon tax, this policy does not require a specific change in technology or behavior. If the policy is applied to industry, a given firm may reduce enough emissions that it has a surplus of tradable permits to sell to other firms. Or, it could do less reductions and be a permit buyer. The trading price of permits acts the same as a carbon tax, putting a price on emissions but letting individuals decide how to respond, depending on their costs and preferences. Because of this common feature, economists estimate that the carbon tax and cap-and-trade cost the economy about the same for a given reduction of GHG emissions.

The implementation of cap-and-trade does not require that individual households become active in the permit trading market. Instead, their electric utility, natural gas utility, and gasoline company buy and sell permits on their behalf, based on the carbon content of each form of energy they use, from production through to the final product, and this cost gets passed on to consumers in their electricity and natural gas rates, and in the price of gasoline. They react to this price increase just as they do to energy price increases caused by a carbon tax. This is why both the carbon tax and cap-and-trade are called carbon (or emissions) pricing policies.

They differ, however, in that cap-and-trade requires the establishment of a government institution to allocate permits and regulate their trading. In contrast, the carbon tax incurs no extra administrative costs. Government simply changes the rates of the taxes it already imposes on energy products. The emissions cap also differs in providing greater confidence that a given GHG target will be achieved – if the cap is binding and the allocated permits equal the cap. In contrast, people's response to the carbon tax is less easy to predict, so we are uncertain of the GHG reductions that will result from a given carbon tax. The tax does, however, provide price certainty if government announces its level (whether constant or rising) for the next several years. This was something I lobbied strongly for as we designed the BC carbon tax, as this helps people trying to guess the future price of energy when buying their next long-lived technology like a furnace or car. We legislated its rising value from 2008 to 2012. In contrast, the price of GHG emissions (and therefore of energy) is uncertain under cap-and-trade, since it depends on the uncertain market for emission allowances.

Because of this uncertainty, real-world applications of cap-and-trade may include a modification which makes the two policies even more similar. The government sets a floor and a ceiling price for permits in the permit trading market, by promising to adjust the available permits each year to keep the price within these upper and lower bounds. This reduces price uncertainty, but on the flip side it increases uncertainty about the emission reductions. Finally, the two policies can be even more similar if government auctions some or all of the emission permits instead of freely allocating them. The auction revenues are similar to carbon tax revenues, presenting the same dilemma for government in terms of how best to use them from an economic and political perspective.

The most notable examples of GHG cap-and-trade policy are the European Union system applied to industry since 2005 and the California system applied to economy-wide emissions since 2013. The Canadian province of Quebec joined the California program in 2014, followed by the province of Ontario in 2017. In 2018, however, a newly elected Ontario Conservative government canceled the province's cap-and-trade policy, having promised during the election campaign that, as a friend of struggling motorists, its first act would be to eliminate it. To gain votes, it incessantly referred to the cap-and-trade policy as "a carbon tax by another name." It won in a landslide – having also promised cheaper beer.

* * *

Economists generally don't like regulations. They argue that regulations (also called standards in the US) are not as economically efficient as carbon pricing because they constrain the choices of consumers and firms, with government regulators determining the technology that each should adopt. In contrast, by allowing each individual or firm to determine their preferred (presumably cheapest) response to rising fossil fuel prices, carbon pricing ensures that GHG emissions decline at the lowest possible cost – notwithstanding the claims of dishonest politicians that it's an "economically disastrous" way of reducing emissions.

When regulations are particularly inflexible, we refer to them as 'prescriptive' or 'command-and-control,' terms that have been around since the late 1960s, when a surge in environmental concerns in wealthier countries triggered a wave of environmental regulations. Hindsight studies by economists showed that many of these prescriptive regulations had high costs relative to a pricing approach, for the same environmental benefit. And this is why economists keep proposing carbon taxes as the right response to the climate-energy challenge.[12]

However, not all regulations are created equally. Under pressure from industry and economists, regulators have increasingly opted for what are called 'market-oriented regulations' or 'tradable performance obligations' or 'tradable standards' or 'flexible regulations.' I call them 'flex-regs,' which non-experts tell me they find easiest to remember. Flex-regs have features that mimic the flexibility of carbon pricing.

While I distinguish only two categories of regulations in Figure 6.2 – flexible and prescriptive – we should place regulatory options along a continuum. At one end, extremely prescriptive regulations tell industry or consumers exactly how much to emit or which specific technology to adopt. At the other end, flex-regs focus on a market-wide outcome without dictating the specific behavioral or technological choices of individuals and firms. Flex-regs allow those under regulation to trade among themselves, with some overperforming and some underperforming, as long as the net effect is to achieve the aggregate market requirement.

In 2007–2008, I helped the British Columbia government implement two flex-regs – the clean electricity standard and the low carbon fuel standard. And in 2018 it launched the zero-emission vehicle standard. These flex-regs are similar to US policies of recent decades.

Almost 30 US states have a 'renewable portfolio standard,' a flex-reg mandating that a minimum percentage of electricity is generated from renewables each year.[13] Because this is a requirement for the entire market, individual electricity providers are not required to achieve the minimum percentage, as long as they pay other providers to exceed the minimum. They make this payment by buying surplus renewable electricity credits from those electricity suppliers that exceed the market obligation. Its adoption by so many US states suggests that this flex-reg is less politically challenging than carbon pricing. Its adoption by Texas in 1999 is notable for contributing to a rapid deployment of windpower, which in turn helped lower the cost of this electricity source.[14]

Since the 1990s, I had been lobbying for a renewable portfolio standard in British Columbia, but with a twist. As an economist, I argued that the policy would be more economically efficient if it was not restricted to renewables, but instead open to any low-emission electricity source. In 2007, I found a receptive ear in the Campbell government and helped design a 90% 'clean electricity standard,' meaning that the mix of new electricity-generation investments must match the current generation mix, that being 90% clean (near-zero-emissions) in our hydropower-dominated jurisdiction. The remaining 10% could be natural gas turbines for regional backup, diesel generators in remote off-grid communities, or industrial cogeneration facilities using natural gas.

This was a big deal. Large hydropower is politically difficult in British Columbia. The first project in 40 years is under construction, but it will be the last. Called "Site C," this project was reviewed and then shelved because of environmental opposition in the 1970s. The province also has vast deposits of low-cost, high-quality coal and natural gas. Thus, when we implemented the clean electricity standard in 2007, the main electric utility, BC Hydro, had already signed agreements for two private coal-fired power plants and was planning to construct its own 600-megawatt natural gas plant. The policy forced it to abandon these fossil fuel projects.

This type of policy in a jurisdiction with existing coal plants, such as the province of Alberta next door, would be less efficient than carbon pricing – which incentivizes the operators of existing coal plants to find a cost-minimizing balance of reduced operation of some plants and the shut-down of others. But in British Columbia, with its hydropower dominance, our analysis indicated that the flexibility of our clean electricity standard would result in similar total costs as a carbon tax for a given GHG reduction. And because the BC carbon tax of $10 rising to $30 by 2012 was not high enough to deter construction of new coal and natural gas plants, the clean electricity standard presented a less controversial way of preventing these investments. For the same environmental outcome, the carbon tax would have had to rise much faster.

The second key flex-reg we implemented in British Columbia in 2007 was the 'low carbon fuel standard,' a policy similar to the one California innovated a year earlier. The low carbon fuel standard requires that the average carbon intensity of energy sold for use in transportation decline over time. Although it is called a fuel standard, it is really an energy in transportation standard because it includes electricity, hydrogen, and any other form of energy used in transportation (even though these are not traditionally called fuels). The required reduction in carbon intensity applies to each form of energy's 'full-cycle emissions' – the emissions when gasoline is burned, but also the 'upstream emissions' that occur when extracting oil, processing it, and then refining it into gasoline. This inclusion of upstream emissions applies equally to the production of diesel, biofuels, electricity, hydrogen, and any other form of energy used in transportation.

Policy commentators sometimes suggest that while flex-regs like the renewable portfolio standard and the low carbon fuel standard can contribute to GHG emission targets, they must be applied alongside carbon pricing policies for deep decarbonization. This is incorrect. With, for example, a target date of 2050, governments can set a clean electricity standard that achieves an extremely low electricity-carbon intensity and a low carbon fuel standard in which aggregate full-cycle emissions achieve near-zero for the slate of energy forms used in transportation. In 2017, my former student, Tiffany Vass, played the lead role in modeling a low carbon fuel standard for Canadian transportation that achieved an 80% reduction by 2050, including the cost-effective reductions in the upstream production of each form of energy.[15]

Like the renewable portfolio standard, the low carbon fuel standard is flexible in that individual transportation energy suppliers don't need to achieve the required carbon intensity in a given year, as long as they buy credits from suppliers that surpass this requirement. A supplier of electricity, biofuels, or hydrogen for vehicles is given credits for selling these forms of low-emission energy for transportation. When gasoline sellers purchase some of these credits, so that their sales portfolio satisfies the carbon intensity requirement of the low carbon fuel standard, the ultimate effect is to lower the price of electricity and biofuels while raising the price of gasoline. But the policy is flexible because it doesn't force consumers to buy electric or biofuel or hydrogen vehicles. It lets them decide how they will respond to the combination of a rising price for gasoline and a falling price for the electricity, biofuels, and hydrogen used in vehicles. They might get a more energy-efficient gasoline car, drive less, or switch to a low-emission vehicle.

Some economists argue that in spite of their flexibility, the low carbon fuel standard and renewable portfolio standard can be fairly expensive ways of reducing GHG emissions relative to the carbon tax and have not yet had a big impact.[16] But many of these studies focus on near-term, modest targets for these flex-regs rather than on their likely performance if applied as lead policy for deep decarbonization. In this latter application, we and others have found that rising gasoline prices under both carbon pricing and this flexible regulation would become similar as the carbon intensity in transportation energy fell to very low levels. At that point, the economic efficiency difference between the flex-reg and carbon pricing is modest.[17]

A third important flex-reg, also in the transportation sector, is the vehicle emission standard. While the US has had vehicle 'energy efficiency' standards since the oil crisis of the 1970s, California has long focused its vehicle regulations on emissions that affect local air quality. However, since 1990, it has increasingly incorporated GHG emission limits into its vehicle regulations. Plug-in electric and hydrogen cars can have zero GHG emissions at the point of consumption, which California refers to as ZEVs – zero-emission vehicles.

California's ZEV mandate gets the most attention. By notifying vehicle manufacturers years in advance that they must achieve minimum percentage targets for ZEV sales, and imposing penalties for non-compliance, the ZEV mandate incentivized the development and commercialization of plug-in electric and hydrogen fuel cell vehicles. The former are now developing quickly, in part thanks to Elon Musk's brainwave of targeting wealthier buyers with a high-performance status car. Since Tesla obviously exceeds its annual ZEV percentage sales requirement, each year it has surplus credits to sell to other manufacturers, and the revenue from these sales helps it lower the price on its electric vehicles.

To pay for these credits, or to sell more of their own ZEVs in an effort to meet the mandate, sellers of gasoline vehicles must increase the price of these, in effect creating a cross-subsidy from gasoline vehicle purchasers to ZEV purchasers. Buyers of gas-guzzling pick-up trucks and luxury cars may pay $1,000 to $2,000 more for these planet-harming acquisitions, but with the typical extra costs of vehicle features, they're unlikely to notice they are subsidizing ZEV purchasers.

From a cost perspective, the ZEV is more expensive than a carbon tax because it doesn't price gasoline. The carbon tax gives consumers more flexibility, as some may opt to drive a gasoline car less as the carbon tax rises. But the ZEV has flexibility attributes that help reduce compliance costs. As noted, its credit trading feature allows manufacturers to decide who among them will produce more electric and hydrogen cars, presumably those for whom this activity will be most lucrative. Also important, it does not favor specific technologies, allowing vehicle sellers and buyers to determine through their choices the ultimate mix of electric, hydrogen, and perhaps plug-in hybrid vehicles that fulfill the ZEV mandate in a given year. And the policy drives competition that continuously lowers the costs of deep decarbonization of personal vehicles. A similar policy can be applied to commercial trucks of various sizes, perhaps including biofuels as a near-ZEV (ultra-low-emission) option.

In sum, flexible regulations, like the renewable portfolio standard, the low carbon fuel standard and the vehicle emission standard, are not as cost-effective as carbon pricing for a given GHG reduction. But, if designed to maximize the flexibility for firms and households as they respond to these flex-regs, the cost-effectiveness difference may be reasonable, especially for the full energy system transformation required by deep decarbonization. This is something that more researchers are exploring, especially since the two policy approaches appear to perform so differently in terms of political acceptability and their likelihood of implementation.[18] My research team is contributing to this work.[19]

* * *

After the 2009 failure in the US of the cap-and-trade bill (the Waxman-Markey bill),[20] President Obama spent the remaining seven years of his presidency pursuing sector-specific regulatory alternatives to economy-wide carbon pricing. He focused his efforts on the electricity and vehicle sectors, where US executive powers are well established through the regulatory mandate of the Environmental Protection Agency.[21]

In the vehicles sector, he tightened energy efficiency standards (called "Corporate Average Fuel Economy" or "CAFE") and incorporated stricter emission performance criteria. However, the challenge, from a deep decarbonization perspective, is that energy efficiency has diminishing returns: better fuel economy means that driving costs less, which motivates more vehicle use. Because of this 'rebound effect,' which I return to in Chapter 10, the increased use of a more energy-efficient device negates some of the reduction of energy and emissions it was intended to cause.

In the electricity sector, Obama implemented the "Clean Power Plan," a regulation under the Environmental Protection Agency that required declining emissions from coal-fired power plants.[22] In order to make the regulation less costly, it included multiple flexibility provisions. Emission reductions could be measured by intensity or absolute amounts. While each state was given a target based on past emissions, states could trade among themselves to lower costs.

These efforts by President Obama to use his executive powers were laudable. But, given the limited terms of US presidents, this is a tenuous approach to deep decarbonization, as the next occupant of the White House can reverse executive orders. Donald Trump wasted little time in halting Obama's tightening of vehicle regulations and his clean power plan.

These reversals raise an issue that is debated by climate policy advocates and experts. Is it easier for future governments to reverse regulations or carbon pricing? Some people have strong views on this. But it seems to me that no climate policy can be inoculated against the will of future governments to eliminate it. The best chance is if the stringency of the policy rises fast enough to cause much of the desired energy transition *before* a future government can reverse it. If many coal plants are closed before a climate skeptic like Donald Trump attains power, he will have greater difficulty resurrecting them.

The elimination of coal-fired power plants in the Canadian province of Ontario is one such example. From 2004 to 2014, one political party held office long enough to implement an ambitious policy of closing all coal plants, which had previously provided 25% of the province's electricity. The government rushed to finish the transition within a decade, aware that no future government could resuscitate the decommissioned plants. It succeeded.

In contrast, carbon pricing is problematic if intended to play the lead role in energy system transformation. Implementing governments need to retain power long enough for it to have a significant effect, such as forcing the closure of coal plants. But this requires rapidly increasing the tax, which increases the likelihood that the implementing government will lose the next election – Catch 22. This is why in British Columbia we implemented the clean electricity standard, even though we were also implementing a carbon tax. By our calculations, the latter, at its initial level and rising schedule chosen by government, would not have prevented construction of the planned coal and natural gas plants.

Advocates of carbon pricing frequently point to all the jurisdictions that have a price on carbon, be it a carbon tax or cap-and-trade. What they fail to mention is the stringency. I have not seen evidence of a rising carbon price that alone would sufficiently increase coal and gasoline prices to lead a major energy system transformation. The UK has used a combination of carbon pricing and regulation to phase out its coal plants. The carbon price is no doubt contributing, but so are the regulations and other government policies.[23]

Scandinavian countries have had high carbon taxes for over two decades. But the initial implementation of carbon pricing involved modest adjustments to already-high gasoline and diesel taxes that had been raised in the 1970s to reduce dependency on oil imports. Increases in the price of gasoline between 1990 and 2010 were mostly caused by rising world oil prices. In recent years, however, the carbon price in Sweden has been rising, and certainly has had an important effect, especially in the choice of energy for heating buildings – both individual and in district heat systems. Unfortunately, other countries lack the public trust in government that is needed to follow the carbon pricing of Scandinavian countries.[24] And even there, it is not easy to distinguish the carbon price effect from the other subsidy and regulatory policies that reduce energy use and GHG emissions in electricity generation, buildings, industry, and transportation.[25]

Since the failure of cap-and-trade in 2009, the application of carbon pricing in the US seems inconceivable. But that is not the case for the 40 million Americans living in California. That state's cap-and-trade system charges about $20 per metric ton of CO_2, which equates to 16 cents per gallon of gasoline. Thus, Californians have carbon pricing. But how important is this policy to the state's ambitious GHG reduction efforts?

The pie chart in Figure 6.3, made from data of the California Air Resources Board, shows the relative contribution of different policies to that state's projected GHG reductions. Note that carbon pricing (light gray) contributes only 16%, while regulations of various types contribute most of the rest (dark gray). Of these, flex-regs are dominant, including the renewable portfolio standard in electricity and the low carbon fuel standard and vehicle emission standards (and ZEV mandate) in transportation. Economists might wish it were otherwise, but in the most climate-sincere state in the US, this is the climate-energy policy reality.

Many economists talk as if carbon pricing is the *only* legitimate option for driving the energy transition. But the politicians and regulators who are actually having an impact in leading jurisdictions like California view the world differently. While they may pay lip service to carbon pricing,

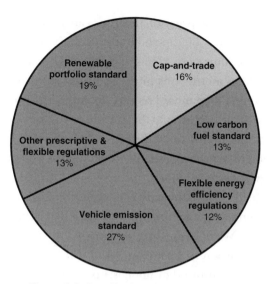

Figure 6.3 Contribution of California policies

the lead policy to drive energy system transformation thus far has been prescriptive regulations and flex-regs. Our experience with the carbon tax in British Columbia has helped me understand why.

* * *

There is a long-standing joke that we economists are a breed of social scientists who try to figure out if what works in our theories could possibly work in the real world. My decades of climate-energy policy experiences keep reminding me of that joke. Politicians who show leadership in the difficult task of energy system transformation are telling us something by their actions. But are we researchers willing to learn from these, and use that knowledge to help them do better?

Because they involve the trading of credits, flex-regs change the prices that influence the decisions of producers and consumers of energy. In fact, the credit or permit trading prices can be used to estimate the 'implicit carbon price' of a flex-reg like the renewable portfolio standard. Taking the difference in energy costs between renewables and emitting generators (coal and natural gas) and dividing this by the difference in the emissions of the two groups, gives a ratio of cost (or implicit carbon price) per unit of CO_2 reduced.

This implicit carbon price of flex-regs can be compared with the 'explicit carbon price' of cap-and-trade or carbon taxes to estimate their relative economic costs. Thus, if a $20/tCO_2$ carbon tax reduces emissions 1 million metric tons in the transport sector while a flex-reg like the low carbon fuel standard requires an implicit carbon price of $40 to achieve the same reduction, the carbon tax is more economically efficient by $20 per metric ton reduced.

This is useful information. But sincere politicians who want to lead on climate-energy policy need more.

First, they need to know the most economically efficient design for the flex-reg in a given sector and how they can mesh that policy with flex-regs in other sectors. What is the best design of the renewable portfolio standard or low carbon fuel standard? And what stringency of flex-reg for each sector will ensure that the costs per ton of GHG reduced are similar across the economy?

Second, sincere politicians need to know the relative political acceptability of each climate policy. For a given level of GHG emissions reduction in a given sector, how much more difficult is one policy than another? We shouldn't tell climate-sincere politicians to stick an electoral bullseye on their backs without first informing them of the political and economic benefits and costs of the policy alternatives. As the failures of the last three decades suggest, this type of analysis is important if we are to accelerate progress on the climate-energy challenge.

I'll bet French President Emmanuel Macron wishes his advisors had done more polling on the relative political acceptability of different climate policies before he announced in 2018 a small carbon tax increase to raise the price of gasoline by 3 cents per liter and diesel by 5. This might have spared him four months of protests by the *gilets jaunes* (yellow vests) – suburban and rural people for whom the tax increase symbolized the disregard for their cost of living concerns by the urban educated elites who dominate French society.[26] Macron was forced to reverse the tax increase, but the severe drop in his popularity seemed irreversible.

Given the simultaneous implementation of multiple climate policies in British Columbia, my jurisdiction provided an excellent test case for comparing the economic costs and political acceptability of a carbon tax and the two flex-regs we implemented – the low carbon fuel standard and the clean electricity standard. (The government also tightened energy efficiency regulations and implemented a carbon offsets system for government agencies, but these are less effective policies, as I explain in later chapters on energy efficiency and offsets.)

In 2012, my former student, Katya Rhodes, led our team in surveying 400 British Columbians to assess their climate-energy policy knowledge and preferences.[27] Our initial questions probed citizen knowledge of climate policy. Even though our jurisdiction had just experienced a high-profile political campaign, in which carbon pricing and other climate policies were center stage, we found that few people knew about these policies. Like researchers and interest group advocates, we climate policy experts tend to mistakenly believe that many non-experts share our interests, a common misconception known as "the curse of knowledge."

Having long been aware of the curse of knowledge, I often caution my research team not to over-estimate public awareness of the climate-energy policies with which we are obsessed. (That's why I encourage them to door-knock in suburban areas to discuss climate-energy policy during election campaigns – the ideal myth-busting exercise for young and old policy analysts.) Our survey results did not disappoint. If given no prior information, only 25% of respondents knew about the carbon tax, and less than 2% knew about any of the other climate policies. When we made it easier, by describing and embedding the five legitimate policies within a list of 15 policies of which 10 were fictional, still only 60% guessed the carbon tax, and none of the other four true policies were identified by more than 15% of respondents. While politicians, interest groups, experts, and media pundits had loudly and continuously debated climate policies for two straight years, most of the public had tuned out. As one grad student later told me, "When would someone on Facebook and Instagram hear about this?"

Our questions also probed the degree of 'strong opposition' to each of the key policies. We believed that strong opposition would be greatest for the carbon tax. Over the years, I had noticed how those opposed to climate policy could more easily incite public anger at the carbon tax, with less success when criticizing flex-regs like the renewable portfolio standard and vehicle emission standards, even when experts explained in the media that these latter were costlier.

During my previous decades of interaction with policy advisors viewing public surveys, I noticed how often they focused on the size of strong opposition rather than on total support versus total opposition. Strong opposition is key because a significant number of people are 'single-issue voters': a politician's view on one key issue, like abortion or gun control or taxes, can be decisive in determining how these people vote. And people often vote against rather than for something. In the US 2016 presidential election, many survey respondents admitted, "While I didn't like Donald Trump, I *really* didn't like Hillary Clinton. So I voted for Trump."

If a policy like the carbon tax provokes enough strong opposition, this offers a 'wedge issue' for opposition politicians trying to gain traction with voters, especially where the issue might tip the balance in critical 'swing' districts. Elections are often won or lost by the voters in swing districts, which in Canada and the US are usually suburban areas. Inner cities and rural constituencies tend to be more stable in their voting preferences.

Considerable evidence supports my anecdotal observations. In his book, *The Myth of the Rational Voter: Why Democracies Choose Bad Policies*, Bryan Caplan reviews a large US opinion survey which finds that many Americans don't agree with economists about the benefits of certain types of policies, notably the economic efficiency gains from using tax changes for societal ends – except in the case of clear and unequivocal tax cuts.[28] This is consistent with surveys in British Columbia, which I noted above, in which most people believed they were net losers under the revenue-neutral carbon tax, even though evidence provided by government and independent academics like me showed the opposite. Like the survey respondents described by Caplan, many people suspected it was a veiled tax grab.

Suburbanites drive a lot. Even though many want action on GHG emissions, some can be persuaded that a carbon tax is so unfair it should determine their vote. And it only takes a shift of 2–5% of voters in swing districts for success in the first-past-the-post electoral systems of the US, the UK, and Canada. Thus, opposing a carbon tax is an enticing strategy for a politician presenting herself as a populist champion of the middle class. And, as we witnessed in British Columbia, this strategy can be compelling even for left-of-center politicians with environmentalist credentials, as they promise to eliminate the carbon tax and reduce emissions thanks to magical policies they were only willing to fully reveal *after* the election.

In the final part of the survey, we thus probed strong opposition as an indicator of 'political acceptability' or 'likelihood of implementation.'[29] Figure 6.4 from the survey results confirms our hypothesis that the carbon tax had by far the largest percentage of strong opposition, a result that did not change even after we provided a neutral description of each of the policies in terms of its cost-effectiveness – which favored the carbon tax. It is noteworthy that all policies had more supporters than opponents – consistent with the strong environmental values of British Columbians. Even the carbon tax had majority support of 56%, a finding that environmental advocates got from their surveys too, which, in their eyes, justified their media mantra that "the public wants politicians to tax carbon." But strong opposition to the carbon tax was ten times its level for the low carbon fuel standard (21:2) and seven times its level for the clean

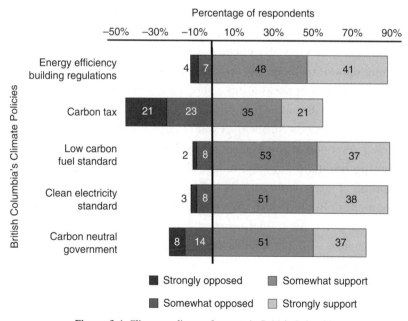

Figure 6.4 Climate policy preferences in British Columbia

electricity standard (21:3). To veteran policy advisors, this would be the critical finding from our survey.

These policy preferences might be understandable if the carbon tax was doing the heavy lifting as the lead policy for causing GHG reductions. But my research team had been commissioned by the government in 2006–2008 to model the combined effects of the policies, and we later simulated the individual effect of each policy if applied on its own.[30] We estimated that expected emissions in 2020 would be reduced 15 metric tons by the clean electricity standard and 3 metric tons by the low carbon fuel standard.[31] In contrast, if used alone, the carbon tax would reduce annual emissions by only about 3 metric tons in transportation and 3 metric tons in electricity from what they otherwise would have reached by 2020.

Our survey findings from British Columbia's policy experiment are consistent with US public opinion surveys. I earlier mentioned Barry Rabe's book, *Can We Price Carbon?*, which is full of valuable insights from survey research on US public opinion with respect to climate science and climate policies.[32] He and collaborators maintain a website which they update with the latest surveys to show how opinions shift over time and with different policy designs. The results tend to support our finding for British Columbia, namely that while total public support for carbon pricing in the US can equal or even exceed total opposition, the 'strong opposition' response consistently receives 30% and higher.[33] In contrast, 'strong opposition' to a flex-reg like the renewable portfolio standard is usually below 10%.

Rabe's surveys also probe the extent to which different uses of carbon pricing revenues in the US, such as subsidizing renewable energy or ensuring revenue neutrality, reduce the size of the strong opposition response. I note, however, that these survey responses tend to be hypothetical. In our British Columbia experiment we learned first-hand that while government might earnestly try to communicate the benefits to individuals and households from its particular use of carbon tax revenues (in our case giving *all* the money back as tax cuts), many people accepted the untrue claims that government was absconding with the revenues. The easy success of this lie illustrates the difficulty of predicting from surveys how competing narratives (one of them false) play out in the real world – with its cognitive biases, competing information, and imbalance of access to communications media.

Real-world climate-energy policy adoption also supports our survey implication that flex-regs would have a higher probability of implementation. Almost 30 US states are using the renewable portfolio standard to transition toward wind, solar, and other renewable electricity technologies. While some industries and politicians have vigorously opposed this policy, blaming it for increased electricity prices and reduced reliability, their admitted successes in slowing the adoption and rising stringency of renewable portfolio standards pales in comparison to their complete success in preventing all state and national efforts to implement carbon taxes and almost all efforts to implement economy-wide cap-and-trade, with the exception of California.

I reiterate that even when we explained that the two flex-regs were costlier than the carbon tax, for a given amount of GHG reduction, the relative ratios of strong opposition between the carbon tax and the flex-regs remained the same. People's policy preferences were more influenced by the word tax than by our statements of relative cost-effectiveness.

* * *

I see our survey as an early contribution to what I hope becomes a growing body of interdisciplinary research that combines the methods of economists in assessing the economic efficiency of different climate-energy policies with the methods of other social scientists in assessing the likelihood of their implementation. We need these disciplines working together because even a slightly better chance for deep decarbonization policy can be critical.

We must keep reminding ourselves that *all* effective climate-energy policies are politically difficult. Even flex-regs, while outperforming carbon pricing, are difficult to implement at stringency levels that would transform the energy system. Success requires a government that is firmly committed to market transformation and unwilling to yield to industry arguments that it cannot produce enough renewable electricity or electric vehicles or biofuels. With flex-regs, government must impose on a few key industries strong penalties for non-compliance, thus incentivizing these players to subsidize between consumer groups to achieve the mandated sales targets. If, instead, government will only implement flex-regs at a stringency acceptable to vehicle manufacturers or electric utilities or fossil fuel distribution companies, the requirements will be unambitious, further delaying the deep decarbonization transition.

At least flex-regs *only* require that sincere politicians prevail in a political struggle with the electric or fuel or vehicle industry, facilitating a divide-and-conquer policy strategy. Carbon pricing, in contrast, requires sincere politicians to overcome widespread misinformation campaigns by a coalition of insincere politicians, fossil fuel companies, and wealthy and powerful anti-climate action advocates. Of course, climate policy opponents will try to distort any effective policy in order to defeat it – branding flex-regs like the low carbon fuel standard as hidden taxes and government overreach. But, if the comparative policy surveys are indicative, the task for these opponents are more difficult with flex-regs than with carbon pricing.

In Figure 6.5, I present my summary assessment of the case study and survey evidence on the relative political acceptability of the four main policy categories, in the case where each is implemented as the lead policy for deep decarbonization. Note that the figure shows *all* climate-energy policies as politically difficult when set at stringencies that would decarbonize the energy system over just a few decades. Thus, the vertical

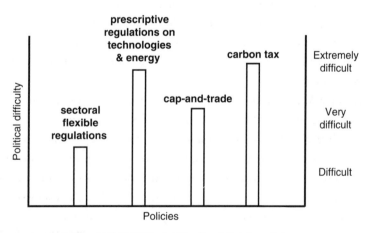

Figure 6.5 Political difficulty of climate policies

axis ranges from extremely difficult at the top to difficult at the bottom. Nothing is easy.

Obviously, I rate carbon tax as extremely difficult. Cap-and-trade scores as less politically difficult for several reasons, most important being absence of the word tax. Prescriptive regulations on individual technologies and energy are almost as politically difficult as the carbon tax because relying primarily on these for deep decarbonization would be very costly, inciting a public backlash against the rapidly rising costs of energy services. Economically inefficient policies can lead to GHG reduction costs that are 10 times higher than they would be under efficiently designed carbon pricing. In contrast, sectoral flex-regs, such as the renewable portfolio standard and the low carbon fuel standard, have proven to be politically easier than explicit carbon pricing. Hence their ranking between very difficult and difficult.

Perhaps we should expect no policy to play a leadership role. In assessing the Swedish carbon tax, I noted how that country also relies significantly on subsidies, regulations, and direct government actions in electricity, district heating, public transport, etc. The use of multiple, overlapping policies to address the same GHG reduction objective might strike many economists as economically inefficient, even dumb. But given the urgency of deep decarbonization, this approach might be acceptable, especially if it has better prospects for transforming the energy system in just a few decades because of political acceptability.

One variant of this would be a policy sequencing approach. Instead of spinning our wheels for another two decades by harping on politically unacceptable levels of carbon pricing, we economists could urge governments to emphasize flex-regs in the early stages of the transition, shifting to carbon pricing later. A renewable portfolio standard, not a carbon tax, has been key in helping solar and wind penetrate the US electricity market and achieve falling costs. The California ZEV mandate, not a carbon tax, has been key in helping electric vehicles develop and capture niche markets, with wider dissemination now imminent. Regulations, not a carbon tax, has helped in the development of biofuels, some of which have low emissions in production. During the early phases of market penetration with flex-regs, it is the producers of coal-fired power who subsidize renewables

(renewable portfolio standard) and the purchasers of gasoline vehicles who subsidize electric vehicles (zero-emission vehicle standard)
and the purchasers of gasoline who subsidize biofuels, electricity, and
hydrogen in transportation (low carbon fuel standard). But in the
consolidating phase, carbon pricing could take over. It will be less
politically difficult to raise gasoline prices with a carbon tax when
40% of cars are electric and 40% of trucks are electric or biodiesel.
Imagine carbon tax opponents trying to incite outrage from die-hard
gasoline users when so many of their friends, family, and competitors
are no longer sympathetic to the complaints of those unwilling to
acquire low-emission options that are readily available and widely
accepted. Carbon pricing as consolidator, flex-regs as catalyst.

One could argue, moreover, that while carbon pricing is the cheapest
policy to reduce GHGs in a mythical world in which politics does not
affect policy choices, it might not be the cheapest option in the real world
in which it does. This would be the case if its dogged pursuit tragically
sustains our multi-decade failure, keeping us on a GHG trajectory whose
devastation dwarfs the economic inefficiency losses from instead pursuing flex-regs.

In my talks, I sometimes use cost estimates from Nicholas Stern's 2006
report, *The Economics of Climate Change*.[34] He estimated that failure to
reduce emissions would devastate global GDP by 20% while a global
carbon tax to prevent that devastation would cost 5% of global GDP in
GHG reduction costs. What if sectoral flex-regs applied to the entire
economy to prevent the 20% loss were likely to cost 7% of GDP, because
they are less economically efficient? And, what if the likelihood of implementation of the flex-regs was 50%, but for the global carbon tax only
20%, because of political acceptability differences? Integrating this information into an 'expected benefit-cost' calculation ('expected' because it
includes probabilities) suggests that insistence on carbon taxes would be
economically inefficient. Multiplying the costs by their likelihoods shows
that the expected GDP effect of carbon tax insistence causes a 17% loss of
global GDP (.2x5% +.8x20%) while the flex-reg strategy causes only
a 13.5% loss of global GDP (.5x7%+.5x20%). (Note that either way the
likely outcome is not good because I assume a high likelihood of continued failure in both cases.)

The key takeaway? Insisting that we price carbon in hopes of a modest cost saving over flex-regs could be, as my mother used to say, "penny wise, but pound foolish."

But in closing this chapter, I should not be too hard on economists. Our training has shaped our policy preferences, making us acutely aware that through economically efficient policies humanity can achieve more good things with the same resource endowment. We certainly cannot afford to waste scarce human and natural resources as we try to simultaneously reduce GHG emissions *and* increase energy supply to the billions of poor people whose lives it would significantly improve. This is why we economists have lots to offer on the climate-energy challenge. We know that, given the attraction and low cost of fossil fuels, humanity *must* either price carbon or regulate technology and energy choices.

Also, we are trained to probe the true effect of these compulsory policies in comparison to the many other "solutions" on offer. This is critical, for as humanity continues to fail with the climate-energy challenge, frustrated, sincere people have earnestly considered a range of actions and approaches. As Mike Hulme noted in his book, *Why We Disagree About Climate Change*, the climate-energy challenge has over time become like a "Christmas tree on which we each hang our own baubles," using it to advance agendas that are tangential to rather than essential for deep decarbonization.[35] Problems arise when these agendas distract us from the few things that absolutely must happen, namely the compulsory policies that cause the rapid phase-out of coal in electricity and gasoline in transportation.

In the following chapters, I describe how some of these agendas, even though based on valid perspectives and aspirations, can deflect us from the simple, basic task of energy system transformation and the necessity of compulsory regulations or carbon pricing to cause that transition. And I suggest how these agendas can be modified slightly so that they don't inadvertently deflect us from that essential task.

CHAPTER 7

Peak Oil Will Get Us First Anyway

The worst of all deceptions is self-deception.

Plato

A FORMER COLLEAGUE OF MINE HAS A COUSIN NAMED DIEGO who lives in the mountains of New Mexico, about 10 miles from the nearest town. He supports his wife and three kids as a jack-of-all-trades who can fix anything: machinery, vehicles, electrical, foundations, plumbing, carpentry, you name it. He does great work and charges little. Because of his multiple talents, Diego is the first person people call no matter how complicated the problem. But he doesn't need much money, so he only accepts jobs when funds are low.

His family doesn't travel. The kids are home-schooled. They grow their food, make and repair their clothes, and have minimal needs. The family doesn't interact much with others: the kids don't partake of sports or other youth activities, and the parents avoid clubs and socializing. They occasionally come to town for supplies and once a month for church. Otherwise, they stick to themselves.

I asked why the family was so self-reliant and isolated.

"Diego is a 'survivalist.'"

"A what?"

"You haven't heard of survivalists? 'Doomsday preppers'? 'Peak oil catastrophists'?"

"I've heard of peak oil catastrophists. They believe we'll soon run out of oil. When that happens, many horrors follow, from food shortages to suburban wastelands to mass migrations – a game of Survivor in which self-reliant people will fare better. Isn't that it?"

"That's it. Armageddon is nigh, and these people are ready."

"But wait a minute. Living on a mountain seems vulnerable."

"Diego has that covered."

He described Diego's hill-top bastion. Being off-grid, he generates his electricity from solar panels, a small wind turbine, and a micro-hydro generator in the stream 300 yards down the hill. Power from these sources is stored in a bank of batteries under the barn, next to an underground bunker. This has emergency living quarters for the family and is fully stocked with preserved food and other critical supplies like first-aid and extra clothing. He has a wood-burning air-tight stove in the main house and another in the bunker if needed. A rooftop solar hot-water system provides domestic hot water, augmented by heat from the wood stove.

Diego runs his truck on gasoline. But in his barn he has an oversized golf cart, with extra seating and a large cargo bed. It can run on an electric motor powered by a rechargeable battery. It also has an internal combustion engine, for which Diego can make ethanol from a wood-burning still that converts grains and vegetable waste into ethyl-alcohol. He rarely runs the still, but he could gear-up if necessary. As backup, he has six horses and two fields of hay to fuel them.

I refer to Diego's place as a bastion for good reason. It makes no sense to prepare for the Dark Ages if you're unable to fend off marauders scavenging for food and fuel. He has an intruder-detection system that covers a half-mile perimeter, and hidden surveillance cameras scan the only access road, which he has mined with remote-controlled IEDs. It was strongly hinted that Diego also has a serious arsenal in the bunker. As for handling horses, his whole family is well trained. For families like Diego's, home schooling encompasses a lot.

As an energy analyst, I occasionally read about people like Diego, who act on their conviction that we should prepare for the day when civilization collapses, perhaps because the oil runs out.[1] These people are rare. But not so rare are those who believe that an energy day of reckoning is imminent and that we should worry about our rapid oil depletion. For many older Americans, this concern dates back to the 1970s, especially the 'oil crisis' of 1973.

In October 1973, the United States provided military supplies to Israel during its month-long Yom Kippur war with Egypt and Syria. In a show of solidarity, Arab oil-exporting states embargoed supplies to the US and some European countries, causing gasoline shortages unseen since World War II. President Nixon appointed an energy czar, William Simon, to control prices. He prohibited gasoline sales on Sundays, and rationed sales on alternating days between even- and odd-numbered license plates. The situation remained tense for months. Truckers went on strike to protest the size of their fuel allocations, leading to violence between strikers and strike-breakers. Queues snaked out from gas stations, sometimes up to 100 cars long. Nixon urged drivers not to exceed 80 kilometers per hour (55 mph) and households to limit thermostat settings to 20 degrees Celsius (68 degrees F).

Some states contributed with their own energy-saving ordinances, with Oregon gaining notoriety for its Grinch-like ban on Christmas lights. Newspapers reported fistfights in gas station queues. Almost overnight, the price of crude oil had jumped from $3 per barrel to $12. While $12 might seem paltry today, it's $75 when adjusted for 45 years of inflation. Thanks to gasoline price controls in the US, the domestic price only doubled, but this was still a huge shock for a gas-guzzling, auto-dependent nation. And because oil generated a fifth of US electricity back then, electricity prices also jumped.

The year 1973 was full of dramatic news. There was the Arab-Israeli war. The US was in the final stages of its painful withdrawal from Vietnam. The Chilean military overthrew the government of Salvador Allende. And the Watergate scandal mesmerized Americans, culminating in the resignation of President Richard Nixon. While the 1973 oil crisis was just one of many dramatic events, for some it symbolized the beginning of the end for humanity's resource profligacy, exposing the impossibility of exponential growth on a finite planet.

* * *

Google the term 'peak oil' and get ready for a tsunami of the frightening scenarios envisioned by Diego and fellow preppers – deserted suburbs, empty skyscrapers, armed battles over food, water, and other resources, mass migrations in a chaotic world. Websites offer instructions on gardening and food preservation, living off-grid on solar, wind, and wood, and defending yourself and family from desperate intruders.

It is misleading, however, to conclude that all the people concerned with peak oil are dystopians awaiting global chaos. From time to time the peak oil concern is widely shared by people whose views are otherwise far from those of people like Diego. This mainstream interest goes in cycles. After a peak in interest during the oil shocks of the 1970s, the concern diminished in the late 1980s and early 1990s, as development of new oil sources kept oil prices low. But the high oil prices from 2004 to 2014 sparked a new wave of peak oil concern. The recent flourishing in the US of plentiful light tight oil (also called shale oil) has reduced media interest in peak oil since 2010. But the concern has not disappeared.

The premise of peak oil is simple. Oil is the critical energy input of the global economy. The annual global consumption of oil is massive, while its quantity is essentially finite. (Although oil is continuously being produced by the decomposition of tiny dead animals and plants, this annual rate of production is minute compared to our annual consumption.) As oil scarcity becomes acute, its price will rise to high levels, creating a crisis for our oil-dependent economies and lifestyles.

To assess the peak oil claim, it seems obvious to ask people who know something about the earth's crust. Colin Campbell, a British geologist who helped found the *Association for the Study of Peak Oil*, offers the following, "It's quite a simple theory, and one that any beer-drinker understands. The glass starts full and ends empty, and the faster you drink it, the quicker it's gone."[2] Campbell and other geologists have studied the oil-endowed regions of the planet to produce an estimate of what's left. They expect a peak in the rate of discovery, followed by the inevitable decline as humans scour the earth's crust for remaining oil deposits in increasingly dispersed and difficult locations.

The global oil assessment by these modern researchers is based on the pioneering analysis in the 1950s of an American geoscientist, Marion King Hubbert. Originally from Texas, Hubbert earned a PhD from the University of Chicago in 1937 and then worked as a petroleum geologist for Shell Oil from 1943 to 1964. At a 1956 meeting of the *American*

Petroleum Institute, he presented his theory that discoveries of oil in a given oil-bearing region would trace a bell-shaped curve over time, with initially a rising rate of discovery, then eventually a declining rate.[3] The peak would be reached when half of the total reserves had been discovered, hence the symmetrical shape. Oil production would have the same bell-shaped curve, but it would lag the discovery curve depending on the time required to bring new reserves into production.

The bell-shape of peak oil is depicted in Figure 7.1. At that 1956 meeting, Hubbert predicted that annual additions in the lower-48 US states would peak about 1970, with production peaking soon after. His prediction went counter to prevailing industry wisdom and was disregarded.

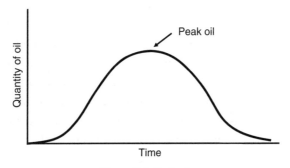

Figure 7.1 Peak oil

But 15 years later, right on cue, US oil supply additions peaked in the continental US (excluding Alaska), which prompted oil analysts to revisit Hubbert's views. His stature within the industry started to climb. Then, the oil crisis of 1973 spread his reputation to the general public, as suddenly everyone was concerned with oil scarcity, especially given the growing US oil dependence and the impacts of the surprise Arab oil embargo.

The media enjoyed the story about this maverick geoscientist who 15 years earlier had predicted the US peak with amazing accuracy. In 1975, the National Academy of Sciences accepted Hubbert's US analysis and publicly acknowledged its earlier mistakes in critiquing it. Today, the Association for the Study of Peak Oil annually bestows the King Hubbert Award on leading contributors, and the terms peak oil and 'Hubbert's peak' are synonymous.

The study of peak oil increasingly shifted from the US to global estimates of oil supply and production, with peak oil alarmists suggesting that that the global peak will be globally catastrophic. Robert Hirsch, who produced a report on peak oil for the US government, said in 2005, "Previous energy transitions were gradual and evolutionary; oil peaking will be abrupt and revolutionary."[4]

Alarm about peak oil was expressed by high-profile personalities with no particular expertise in global energy. In 2006, Kurt Vonnegut said, "What's going to happen is, very soon, we're going to run out of petroleum, and everything depends on petroleum. And there go the school buses. There go the fire engines. The food trucks will come to a halt. This is the end of the world."[5] Visit peak oil websites and you will find similar warnings about the downward slope of Hubbert's curve.

As someone whose career has been devoted to resource and environment sustainability, I sympathize with this view. The modern economy gobbles up the planet's resources at a tremendous rate and spews a massive flow of wastes into the environment. Figure 7.2 visualizes this conundrum: the human economy is like a machine that extracts resources from the environment and converts these into goods and services, expelling a polluting stream of wastes. The two prime threats to sustainability are exhaustion of critical resource inputs and pollution that disrupts the environment's ability to provide clean water, fertile soil, breathable air, and a stable climate. As the economy grows, it swallows more resources and spews more waste. Even if it doesn't grow, current flows are unsustainable, certainly when it comes to GHG emissions.

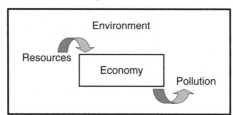

Figure 7.2 Sustainability challenge of resources and wastes

This situation provides lots to worry about. On the resource side, we can fret about exhausting non-renewable resources, like fossil fuels, zinc, copper, and phosphorus. Even if a resource is potentially renewable, we might harvest a fish species to extinction, grow crops in ways that deplete soil fertility, or drain an aquifer faster than natural percolation replenishes it.

On the waste side, the by-products of human settlements and industrial activities have pollution impacts that range from local to global. Over the past half-century, wealthier societies have reduced some local impacts, like effluents despoiling rivers and emissions causing smog, in part thanks to the power of NIMBY – 'not-in-my-back-yard.' Global threats are more challenging. Still, there have been some successes, such as the quick international agreement in 1989 to phase out chlorofluorocarbon gases that were creating a hole in the ozone layer.

It is perhaps no coincidence that the oil scarcity fears of the 1970s coincided with a rising general alarm over the twin threats of resource scarcity and environmental degradation. In 1972, a think tank called The Club of Rome published *The Limits to Growth*, a book which illustrated how exponential growth of resource use and pollution on a finite planet could not endure.[6] The book triggered a vigorous debate. On one side are people concerned with impending resource scarcity. On the other are optimists who believe that human ingenuity, in concert with market forces of supply and demand, will respond to these sustainability challenges by switching away from scarce resources and controlling pollution before it reaches truly harmful levels.

Who is right? Difficult to say. Bjorn Lomborg argued in *The Skeptical Environmentalist* that environmental conditions are not as dire as claimed by environmentalists, and Matt Ridley argued in *The Rational Optimist* that the exponential growth of human ingenuity will keep us dodging the twin swords of resource depletion and environmental destruction.[7] Less optimistic books are Clive Hamilton's *Requiem for a Species*, David Wallace-Wells' *The Uninhabitable Earth*, and Nathaniel Rich's *Losing Earth*, who lament our environmental predicament, especially the role of powerful corporations and individuals in preventing humanity from acting on the threat of climate change.[8]

As these books attest, assessing if and how humans will overcome a wide array of threats to sustainability is a difficult endeavor. While I agree that we often underestimate human ingenuity, I also agree that humans are ill equipped to deal with a threat like climate change, which requires a coordinated, global effort to address the pollution output side of Figure 7.2. Over two decades of failure suggest the odds are not in our favor.

The concern for peak oil, however, is not about the wastes we produce, like GHGs, but rather about the threat of exhausting key resources, the left input side of Figure 7.2. But how urgent is this threat compared to climate change? And since oil is involved in both cases, are these two sustainability concerns – resource depletion and pollution accumulation – connected in some way?

* * *

The bell-curve of Hubbert and his followers depicts the annual supply additions of a specific resource – oil. This sounds simple, but it's not. The definition of oil has changed continuously in the past, and will continue to change in future. And each time it changes, the estimated oil supply increases, and Hubbert's bell-curve gets tossed aside and replaced by a taller and wider version. Yet this seems to go unnoticed by those concerned with peak oil.

When Hubbert's career started, the definition of oil did not include oil under the deep ocean, as in the North Sea and off the coast of Brazil. Nor did it include the additional oil that could be extracted by injecting gas or water into depleted oil reservoirs to force more oil from wells that would otherwise stop producing – called 'enhanced oil recovery.' Nor did it include oil-impregnated sand, as in western Canada's oil sands. Nor did it include molasses-like heavy oil, as in Venezuela. Nor did it include oil trapped in shale rock, as in North Dakota. Technologies to exploit these substances either did not exist or were too costly, so these 'unconventional oil resources' were excluded from oil supply estimates even though geologists knew about them.

The petroleum industry progresses in fits and starts from the easier to the more difficult, incorporating these unconventional resources along the way. Yes, we are *always* running out of the easier stuff, such as conventional oil which flows freely from a well under its own pressure. But as this happens, we develop technologies that reduce the cost of exploiting the more difficult stuff, such as the various forms of unconventional oil. This transition forces industry to broaden its definition of oil to progressively incorporate more of these unconventional supplies, especially as their costs of production fall with technological innovation.

Every year British Petroleum issues a highly regarded energy statistical update that includes estimates of global oil supplies.[9] Just 20 years ago, Canadian oil sands were not considered economic and so were excluded from the BP global estimate. But cost-reducing technological innovations and rising oil prices led BP to change its oil supply estimate for Canada from 40 billion barrels in 1990 to 180 billion in 2000, on par with the oil supplies of Saudi Arabia. This process was repeated for the heavy oil of Venezuela. In 2000, BP's oil supply estimate for Venezuela was 75 billion barrels, but by 2010 it had ballooned to 300 billion barrels.

Since 2010, BP has also been revising upward its estimates of light tight oil, as found in North Dakota, Texas, and elsewhere. The earth's sedimentary rocks are full of carbon from the remains of dead animals and plants accumulated over billions of years. We find conventional supplies of oil and gas because some of these carbon-rich remains, after high pressure transformed them into liquids, migrated through porous rock until they accumulated under an impervious layer, such as limestone. But much of the earth's carbon was unable to migrate and accumulate, remaining trapped in layers of mud and clay that eventually compressed into shale rock.

Thanks to recent technological innovations, we now combine the fracturing of carbon-rich shale rock, a process called 'fracking,' with horizontal drilling that can find small, isolated oil deposits in shale and associated rocks. This technology also enables the extraction of a lot more natural gas. Thus, the development of fracking and horizontal drilling has dramatically increased the estimated supplies of oil and natural gas in North America, and a similar development is gradually occurring on other continents. This unconventional source of oil and gas is enormous.

If, instead of living in the mountains of New Mexico, Diego was tucked away in the backcountry of North Dakota, he would probably know about shale oil. In 1953, just as Hubbert was developing his peak oil theory, geologists identified a major subsurface shale deposit on the land of Henry Bakken, a farmer near Williston, North Dakota. Eventually, they determined that the Bakken formation underlies 200,000 square miles of North Dakota and Montana. This is a huge source of oil. Yet, for the next 50 years the petroleum industry ignored it. There was no incentive to exploit the more difficult oil sources while the easier stuff was plentiful, and lower cost to produce.

But once oil prices started climbing in 2003, some oil companies scaled up their fracking efforts and cost-reducing innovations soon followed. Oil output at Bakken, which was close to zero in 2003, grew exponentially to 200,000 barrels per day in 2009, 600,000 in 2012, and over 1 million in 2015. With the development of light tight oil in North Dakota, Texas, and other states, total US oil production increased from 5 million barrels per day in 2008 to 10 million in 2018. The US is now virtually self-sufficient – producing as much oil as it consumes.

In trying to make sense of this rising output from a resource that is supposed to be in decline, Diego might take a break from peak oil websites and briefly turn to an independent assessment by some of the world's leading energy experts called the *Global Energy Assessment*.[10] Released in 2012, after five years of collaborative research, this report presents multiple dimensions of the global energy system. It shows that humans have consumed about one trillion barrels of conventional oil, but the earth's crust still has over two trillion barrels. Enhanced oil recovery adds another trillion, oil sands and heavy oil another trillion, and light tight oil yet another trillion. This makes five trillion barrels available. In other words, we have only burned about one sixth of the oil and oil-like substances that we currently know are available.

Peak oil analysts claim that the peak occurs when about half of the resource is consumed. They further claim that peak oil is imminent. But, if we have consumed only one sixth of the resource, then a peak oil crisis is hardly imminent. And the amount of oil remaining might not matter anyway once we acknowledge the fact that oil is but one fossil fuel option for making products like gasoline and diesel. Germany produced synthetic transport fuel from coal during World War II when British ships and Soviet armies blocked its access to oil supplies. Today, South Africa produces much of its gasoline and diesel from coal, having adopted the same German technology in the 1970s to circumvent the oil embargo imposed to discourage its racist apartheid system. Meanwhile Qatar exports diesel that it produces from its plentiful natural gas supplies and there are similar facilities elsewhere in the world.

These 'coal-to-liquids' and 'gas-to-liquids' processes can expand dramatically if oil scarcity provided a market opportunity. In such a scenario, the authors of the *Global Energy Assessment* estimate that natural gas supply could equal six trillion barrels of oil and coal 10 trillion. This means that we have used but 1/20th of the fossil fuels available to economically produce gasoline and diesel, a devastating ratio for the peak oil paradigm. There are now analysts arguing that the oil price will stay low for a long time.[11]

How can the peak oil analysis be this wrong? One problem for people concerned about oil scarcity is the tendency to overlook the response to higher oil prices, as Daniel Yergin explained in his book *The Quest.*[12] Economic history abounds with instances when the rising price of a scarce commodity triggered exploration and innovation in the development of alternatives. Some of the best evidence comes, ironically, from the very 1970s oil crisis that is so symbolic for peak oil catastrophists.

The 1973 oil price increase was followed by a second jump to $40 per barrel during the Iranian revolution in 1979. The price stayed at that level for six years. But, in 1986 it collapsed to below $20 and, except for a brief spike during the 1991 first Iraq war to expel Saddam Hussain's army from Kuwait, it remained low for the next 15 years.

Why didn't oil prices keep rising through the 1980s and 90s as many had expected? The answer is the predictable supply-demand response to the 1970s price increases. On the demand side, industrialized countries stopped generating electricity from oil by switching to coal, natural gas, nuclear, and renewables. Oil use in industrial boilers and residential furnaces plummeted, mostly replaced by natural gas, while vehicle efficiency regulations reduced consumption of gasoline and diesel.

On the supply side, increased exploration led to supplies from new conventional sources, such as the north slope of Alaska. Technological improvement increased the take from enhanced oil recovery and enabled offshore development, as in the North Sea. With government help, investment also flowed to unconventional sources like oil sands, shale oil, light tight oil, and coal-to-liquids. But most of these develop-ments stagnated once the oil price collapsed in 1986, when what was an oil seller's market became a buyer's market.

This rapid response explains why historical graphs of global and US oil production show a different pattern from the singular pinnacle predicted by Hubbert and his followers. Figure 7.3, constructed from data of the US Energy Information Administration, shows the 1970 production peak, as predicted by Hubbert. But since 2003, US production is rising again.

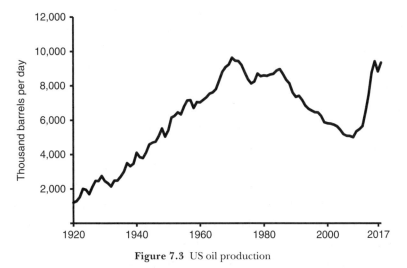

Figure 7.3 US oil production

This development undermines the beer-drinker metaphor for oil depletion. A more accurate version has an industrious bartender who responds to depleting stocks of ale by rummaging through the inner recesses of his pub's cellar to find more kegs. Yes, supplies are finite. But the huge cellar has many uncharted nooks and crannies. Although some of the pub's stored ale is more difficult to retrieve, it far exceeds the amount in the kegs currently on tap. It is incorrect to assume the pub's beer will be exhausted when these are drained.

* * *

Many people misinterpreted the oil crisis of the 1970s as signaling the end of oil. In fact, the price rose because a geopolitical crisis caused a temporary shortage. When the crisis abated, supply increases from market competition caused the price to fall in 1986 back down to oil's cost of production. It stayed there until 2003, when growing demand, especially in China and India, outstripped the discovery rate for new supplies, and speculators in a tight market drove the price higher. But this higher price triggered a market response that increased supply and moderated demand, so prices settled far from the lofty heights predicted by peak oil catastrophists.

When asked why prices are today not at $200, some peak oil believers credit oil supply shortages with causing the economic recession of 2008–2010. They claim that high oil prices in 2008 caused the economic crisis, which in turn reduced oil demand, causing its price to fall. It doesn't matter that leading authorities on the economic crisis, such as Paul Krugman in *The Return of Depression Economics and the Crisis of 2008*[13] and Joseph Stiglitz in *Freefall*,[14] do not finger oil prices as causing the crisis. Instead, they explain how a lethal combination of lax financial regulation and simple greed wreaked economic havoc.

The price of oil, like that of any commodity, rises and falls in response to short-term market changes, which can be triggered by war, geopolitical tension, facility failures, major new discoveries, and rapid demand increases and decreases. Those who believe that peak oil is imminent tend to interpret each significant price increase as the start of a unidirectional ascent brought on by the peaking of oil supply. This leads to claims that oil prices will reach $200 or $300 per barrel and stay there. The likely market response to such high prices is ignored.

When pressed with all of this contrary evidence showing a huge supply of alternatives to conventional oil, some peak oilers offer one last argument – the declining rate of 'energy-return-on-energy-invested' (referred to as 'EROEI'). They claim that although there is a huge supply potential from the alternatives to conventional oil, the conversion of these into gasoline and diesel requires a lot of energy, forcing the economy to "run faster just to stand still." They note that in the 1930s the US oil industry consumed one barrel of oil for every 100 barrels it produced, while today that ratio is down to one to 15, and even lower in the case of shale oil and oil sands. This declining rate of EROEI will cause, so they say, rising energy prices and a peak oil crisis. In other words, the peak in the discovery and production of conventional oil is still critical, despite a plethora of high-cost unconventional alternatives, because exploitation of the latter requires too much energy.

But while this ratio indicates a greater input of energy to produce each unit of oil used in the economy, it is not true that a rising EROEI automatically leads to rising oil prices. Before such a conclusion, we must first determine the effect of ongoing innovations that improve the productivity of the industrial plant, equipment, buildings, infrastructure (called 'physical capital') used to produce the oil. If the cost of these investments per unit of oil declines fast enough, this offsets rising costs due to consuming more energy inputs per barrel produced, especially when those energy inputs are cheap.

As an example, assume that it costs $100 to produce a barrel of oil, and that this is comprised of $10 for energy inputs, $75 for physical capital, and $15 for all non-energy operating costs, including labor. (The relative costs in this example are close to reality, and I picked an oil cost of $100 for simplicity.) Now, assume that a declining EROEI over the next two decades necessitates a three-fold increase in energy input for each barrel of oil. If nothing else changes, this increases the production cost to $120 per barrel, with total energy inputs now costing $30 instead of $10.

This suggests a rising cost of oil, and therefore higher energy prices because of a declining EROEI. But before concluding this we need to know what happens over this period to the cost of the physical capital per barrel, especially since we know that innovations are continuously improving the productivity of plant and equipment in any industry. What if this rate of improvement was a conservative 1% per year over the next 20 years? If so, the cost of physical capital per barrel would fall from $75 to about $58. The net effect of these two processes – a dramatic decline in EROEI and a gradually falling physical capital cost – would together result in an increase in the production cost of oil by $3 over 20 years. It would rise from $100 to $103 ($30 + $58 + $15). This is hardly the frightening jump in production costs that people fear. Yet it closely reflects what actually happened over the past half-century as we depleted the easy oil.

Returning to the big picture, we've burned one trillion barrels of oil and we still have over five trillion barrels of oil and oil-like substitutes, and over 16 trillion barrels of oil-equivalent coal and natural gas substitutes. That's a lot of fossil fuels, and potentially a lot of carbon pollution. No wonder that we experts who worry about climate change see the world so differently than people worried about peak oil. Our worry is that we *won't* run out of oil fast enough.

Most people concerned with peak oil acknowledge that global warming is also a threat to sustainability. So maybe it's harmless if they continue to worry about peak oil. But maybe it's not harmless, especially when it inadvertently helps the fossil fuel industry convince politicians and the public of the urgency of increasing oil production. Whenever oil prices rise because of some short-term crisis, industry echoes the peak oil argument to convince governments to approve and even assist new fossil fuel projects. Since we already have enormous capital resources and technical know-how in this industry, the quickest response to an apparent energy supply shortage is to stay on the fossil fuel path, which is also the GHG-increasing path.

Thus, focusing on the peak oil concern can have the unintended consequence of helping the fossil fuel industry increase carbon pollution. It also can justify complacency on the climate-energy threat. Why enact policies to phase out gasoline use if we'll soon run out of oil anyway?

But it doesn't have to be this way. By tackling the climate change threat we also address the peak oil threat. Hitting a peak in emissions requires us to shift the transportation system from reliance on oil-derived gasoline and diesel to a rapidly growing use of electricity, ethanol, biodiesel, and hydrogen. As this shift happens, the consumption of gasoline and diesel will peak and then fall. On the surface, the peak in oil consumption would appear to vindicate Hubbert. But in this case, the peak would occur not because of a decline in oil discoveries and reserves, as he predicted, but because of a decline in oil demand, while supplies remained plentiful. Just as the Stone Age did not end for lack of stones, the Oil Age would not end for lack of oil.

I share many of the concerns of peak oilers. Like them, I cannot ignore how the growing global economy gobbles up resources and spits out wastes. For long-run sustainability, humans need to find a way to transform our economies so that they mimic biological systems, recycling wastes and resources in a closed loop. But now we must focus on rapidly cutting GHG emissions. We can't let the myth of peak oil help the fossil fuel industry keep us on this disastrous path.

CHAPTER 8

We Must Change Our Behavior

The truth that survives is simply the lie that is pleasantest to believe.

H.L. Mencken

HOW EMISSIONS-INTENSIVE IS YOUR SEX LIFE? IF YOU CAN'T answer this question, you're probably not alone. But I know someone who can.

It all started when a grad student of mine (who wishes to remain anonymous) discovered a book offering advice on being a green consumer. One of the sections focused on "greening your sex life." It suggested consumer products that reduce the use of energy and non-renewable resources, as well as cutting down on GHG emissions.

My student was intrigued. Being an engineer, and a skeptic by nature, she wanted some hard numbers to assess these claims, and learn more about her own ecological footprint in the pursuit of tantric pleasure. Soon she was riveting my earnest research group with lists of alternative products for every imaginable and unimaginable pleasure. For some of our young researchers, it was an unexpected educational experience.

You can get into the mood with candles made from beeswax, organic wine in a goatskin, and alluring lingerie produced from hemp, bamboo, or seaweed. Edible underwear may be out of style, but if it's organically produced, it shouldn't be taboo. If whipped cream is your thing, never buy an aerosol-spray canister; hand-whip it instead.

Condoms should be latex, possibly from the sap of a rubber tree on a sustainably managed plantation. Sex toys should be PVC-free. Vibrators should use rechargeable batteries or run on solar power. Lubes and massage oils should be made from organically based silicon, not petroleum. Feathers should come from real animals: naturally shed, not plucked. And for those who like it a bit rough, there is hemp rope and handcuffs from recycled metal.

Sure, these sustainable, high-quality products cost a bit more, but acquiring them will make you feel good. The edible massage oil is just $16 a bottle. The deluxe eco-rechargeable vibrator goes for only $139. The list of green sex products and activities is endless.

At first blush, it all seemed reasonable: "We must change our behavior and consumption to reduce our environmental impact." But the hypothesis troubled our Ms. Skeptic. Her suspicions were aroused by the sheer volume of devices and consumable products in the modern sex life, green or not. She wanted to see for herself if our shifting preferences of the past five decades, since the sexual revolution in the 1960s, had caused an increase or decrease in energy use and pollution. She wanted to know if a significant effort to green our consumption, in this case related to sexual activity, would truly cause a decrease in energy use and GHG emissions, both directly in the act itself, say the electricity used in vibrators, and especially in the production and delivery of all the devices and products now involved. She wanted to know if 'green consumerism' was a canard when it came to sex, perhaps when it came to everything.

Some people were shocked by the revealing information about American sexual activities in the earlier surveys of Masters and Johnson, Kinsey and Hite. But the shocker for my student was that these earlier authors never collected data on the energy and emissions associated with sexual paraphernalia. To her, this was sacrilege.

As one of our most tenacious researchers, she soon developed her own methodology that combined spot surveys of sexual activities over the years with data on sales of sexual products. She then generated estimates of energy consumption from use rates and of material waste from discard and replacement rates. With these data assembled, she started number crunching.

She estimated that in the wild and natural 1960s, people's sex-related energy and material consumption actually declined. The widespread adoption of the pill undermined sales of condoms, diaphragms, and IUDs. Use of lubes and massage oils was rare compared to today.

According to the surveys, S&M was less common too, which is borne out by the sales data, if it is to be believed. But after that decade, the energy- and emissions-intensity of sex, on a per-person basis, has maintained a steady increase. The ownership of various sexual props, at one time limited to the promiscuous and kinky, has become almost *de rigueur*. Most people have at least some kind of device or liquid in the bedside drawer. For some, it's a full closet.

In her research, my grad student focused on what is involved in making an object and getting it to the consumer – the energy and materials used in production, transport, and delivery. In production, one can calculate the materials and energy required in manufacture. In transport and delivery, energy use depends on weight and size, so again it's possible to find data from comparable products.

She found that energy use for production and delivery of sexual props has grown much faster than the US population; an average American today has many more sexual products and devices than four decades ago. For example, Kinsey found that less than 1% of women in 1953 had a vibrator and Hite put the figure at less than 5% in 1976.[1] Contemporary surveys put the number at 40–55%, with many women having several.

Each of these products and devices takes energy to produce and deliver. The material itself is often produced from petroleum or natural gas, but this 'feedstock' use of energy is tiny compared to the energy consumed for production and transport. The energy required for pro-duction of a sexual product is usually a combination of electricity and a fossil fuel like natural gas. The transport of sexual products produces more carbon pollution due to the burning of gasoline and diesel by trains, semis, and local delivery trucks, or ships and planes if imported from overseas.

Does switching to 'green' products change any of this? Not much. With a few devices and liquids as indicators, our intrepid investigator estimated the reduction in energy use and carbon pollution from a widespread shift to greener sexual products and activities. Her results presented a diverse range, depending on the product and activity. But once she had mapped these onto the sales data, the takeaway was unequi-vocal: the trend to consume more overwhelms even a complete switch to greener consumption. Per person, we consume a lot more for sex than we did 50 years ago. The energy and emissions impact of almost everyone greening their consumption might offset 5% of this effect.

To her credit, our Ms. Skeptic did distract me from my climate worries. I started worrying about how granting agencies would view our research group if she published her findings.

Greening the consumption side of our sex lives might make us feel good about ourselves. But it's not the path to climate bliss. In fact, across-the-board research on human consumption shows that this truth holds for more than just sex. As we get richer, we consume more. If the economy is dependent on burning of fossil fuels, that greater consumption translates into more GHGs. In this context, changing our consumer choices and behavior can only make a small contribution to the 50–80% emissions reduction scientists say we must achieve by 2050. As I once heard at a conference, "we're not going to buy our way out of this one."

* * *

If you ask a person on the street if behavioral change is necessary to prevent climate change, surveys show that most agree. People can't tell you what behavioral change means. But they agree it must happen, whatever it is.

We hear this refrain from environmentalists, of course, but also from politicians, corporate leaders, celebrities, and the media. In 2006, John Hofmeister, the former President of Shell Oil, said, "We need to change the hearts, minds, values and behaviors of Americans toward a culture of conservation."[2] In 2010, the Natural Resources Defense Council said, "Behavioral change and personal action are critical to any successful effort to curb greenhouse gas pollution and avoid the worst impacts of climate change."[3] And in 2012, Dr. Karen Ehrhardt-Martinez of the Garrison Institute's Climate, Mind and Behavior Program said, "Behavioral approaches offer the promise of large, rapid and relatively inexpensive means of reducing carbon emissions ... We don't need to change beliefs, we need to change behavior."[4]

When people are pressed to explain what behavioral change might entail, the response is a patchwork. Some talk about being a greener or more ethical consumer. Some talk about changing their lifestyle. Others talk about consuming less altogether. And some argue that the only way to really consume less is to earn less. Vancouver, where I live, is the birthplace of the Work Less Party, inspired by Conrad Schmidt's book, *Workers of the World Relax.*[5]

Either way, the concept of behavioral change is frustratingly vague. Is it a behavioral change to buy green devices and liquids for sex? Or do we need to buy fewer things for sex? Or stop having sex? (What is the sexual carbon footprint of a monk or a nun?) Or should we make sure that our sex lives don't produce new lives, since the total human population drives our environmental impact? Or, instead of shopping, should we spend more of our time having sex, but without devices except contraceptives? People having sex are not in a shopping mall, at least not usually.

We energy analysts spend a lot of time thinking about this – behavioral change, not sex. We define behavioral change as consciously acting differently and doing so on a regular basis that requires mindfulness, at least initially. Sorting one's garbage for recycling eventually becomes unthinking, automatic. But initially it requires a conscious, daily effort. Busing or biking instead of using the car is a behavioral change since it requires continually acting differently.

Think of the needs and wants that underlie human behavior. We need food, clothing, and shelter. We want security, comfort, and convenience. Many of us want power and status. We seek entertainment and pleasure. We can be quite sedentary, but also quite mobile. Witness the spread of aboriginal peoples throughout America after arriving from Asia 20,000 years ago, and the travel bug of modern people.

Through the millennia, humans have learned how to better exploit the earth's energy and materials to satisfy these needs and wants. And, as we've gotten wealthier, our use of resources has increased dramatically. In the world's poorer countries, people want more electricity and modern fuels because these enable better homes, hospitals, schools, infrastructure, and other key goods and services. But a rising use of energy and materials is still happening in wealthier countries too. Affluence does not appear to satiate all human wants, at least not those of most people. As we get richer, our firms process more energy and materials to provide us with more desirable goods and services. And if firms in other countries can provide these more cheaply, we import them. Thus, we also cause the energy and materials consumption resulting from the production of these goods and services in far-away places.

With rising wealth, people can satisfy more of their wants. One widespread want is bigger houses. In 1970, the average American single-detached house was 1,500 square feet. In 2010 it was 50% larger. Not everyone prefers a bigger house. But monster homes are now a worldwide phenomenon as some of the newly wealthy emulate the opulent lifestyles of the rich.

And as our wealth rises, our mobility demand increases. With air travel, that increase has been rapid. Figure 8.1 shows the growth of commercial airline passenger travel since 1970 compared to the growth of global Gross Domestic Product (GDP). (For comparison, the data sets have been modified so that both start at 100 in 1971.) Air travel's exponential growth shows no sign of abating, especially as a greater share of global GDP growth occurs in developing countries where more people are reaching income levels that enable increased travel.

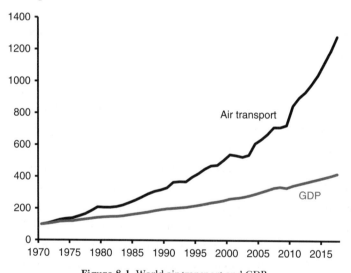

Figure 8.1 World air transport and GDP

In a positive feedback loop, the more we travel, the more our desire and need for travel increases, as we tell friends and neighbors about exotic destinations, meet and marry people from distant places (causing additional travel by family and friends), and develop far-flung business and professional connections. Rather than a behavioral change, we might best characterize this as a behavioral trend, one of many that leads to more energy use and, in a fossil fuel energy system, more GHG emissions.

In *The Economic Naturalist's Field Guide*, Robert Frank describes how our consumption can be motivated by our wealth relative to the other people in our social context.[6] Simply put, we consume in part to keep up with the Joneses. And if our incomes climb and we enter new social contexts, we invariably find new Joneses to keep up with.

This drive for status has obvious implications for material and energy consumption. But even if status comparison were not a factor, humans are drawn to novelty and this has big implications for energy consumption. If a neighbor, friend, or relative acquires a new gadget, we often think it might benefit us too. So even those who are not particularly status-conscious are drawn in, for reasons that might go all the way back to our emergence as a species. As Bill Rees, the academic who invented 'the ecological footprint,' explained in a 2010 article, humans seem coded for acquisition – throughout human history, acquisition success meant evolutionary success.[7]

Empirical evidence of the energy consumption caused by our acquisitiveness was clearly shown by one of my grad students, Steve Groves, in his 2009 thesis entitled "The Desire to Acquire: Forecasting the Evolution of Household Energy Services."[8] He found that in 1970, the average American house had 12 energy-using devices, excluding the light bulbs. These comprised the furnace or air conditioner, other major appliances, and smaller devices like TV, iron, toaster, vacuum cleaner, and a few radios and alarm clocks. Forty years later, in 2010, the much larger average American house had 48 energy-using devices. To the 1970s list, add many of the following: freezer, ice-dispenser, garburator, coffee maker, cordless and mobile phones, several computers, CD players, consoles and hand-held devices for gaming, multiple TVs and DVD players, mp3 players, blender, bread maker, food processor, wine and/ or beer cooler, microwave oven, patio heater, hot tub, leaf blower, high-powered lawn mower, an array of power tools, power washer, and barbecue. Also, dishwashers and air conditioners made the transition from luxury to necessity.

Since the 1970s, regulations and occasional energy price spikes have motivated significant improvements to the energy efficiency of furnaces, air conditioners, and major appliances like fridges, clothes washers, clothes dryers, and stoves. But this reduction has been offset by the growing size of houses packed with these new energy-using devices. As a result, energy use per person has grown significantly among the wealthiest 25% of Americans. This is especially so if one includes all the energy used by firms throughout the world making stuff or providing services for these people, like the aviation fuel for their ski vacation, the energy to produce their ski equipment and clothing, the energy for the hot tub at their ski resort, and, increasingly with climate change, the energy to make snow at their ski resort. And then there's all the stuff we don't see or think about, like internet servers with their skyrocketing energy use.

Layered onto this is a secondary trend: the accelerating rate of turnover of some of these devices. Ten years ago, the average person kept their mobile phone for three years. Today this average is much shorter, as people race to buy the latest upgrade, meaning that energy use in production and transport is rising faster than the number of devices actually in use. Someone once referred to the mounting volume of discarded devices as "the Steve Jobs legacy."

People who call for behavioral change can be vague on what we do that causes GHG emissions, and thus on how behavioral change might reduce these. My research group cannot afford such vagueness, so we keep asking for specifics in order to numerically estimate the effect.

The work of my research group on human mobility illustrates this point. We run computer models that estimate how and at what cost humans can reduce GHG emissions. We frequently hear from environmentalists and public transit advocates that since people use cars to get from point A to point B, public transit in the form of bus, light rail, or rapid transit offers the same mobility service. They note, moreover, that public transit uses less energy and costs less than a car per person-kilometer-traveled (as long as the bus or train has a decent ridership), especially when you consider the cost of a car, its maintenance charges, insurance, and fuel. Once people are educated about this cost advantage, some will shift to transit – or at least that is the assumption.

But this rarely happens. One reason is that person-kilometers-traveled is just one of the values a car provides. Other behavior-determining wants and needs are important, such as comfort, convenience for transporting goods and other people, entertainment, power, and status. We are not effective as researchers, policy advisors, and concerned citizens if we ignore these critical factors when predicting the receptivity of people to the call for behavioral change.

Thus, a key task of my group's research is to undertake surveys asking people under what conditions they would switch from their personal vehicles to public transit. We also compare survey responses to actual behavior to make sure we have designed the questions to prevent respondents giving biased answers because of 'wishful thinking' or 'wanting to please.' From these surveys we've become aware of the extent to which a personal vehicle is much more than a device for delivering person-kilometers-traveled. Other key vehicle attributes include convenience for short trips, privacy for personal conversations, quick flexibility when plans change, ability to move bulky or heavy objects, cost advantage over public transit when transporting several people, avoiding exposure to hot or cold weather when walking to and waiting for the bus, and less direct interactions with people who are rude, ill, or threatening.

At some point, our research findings led me to propose that we no longer refer to a vehicle as a CAR in our computer model. I wanted us to call it a PMD, 'personal mobility device,' to reflect the high value many people place on the convenience of having their own mobility device. I wanted this kept in mind as we assessed policies attempting to lure people on to transit.

As it turns out, my desire to change CAR to PMD opened a can of worms. Our next set of surveys, and those of our colleagues, further assessed human motivations in mobility choices. Before I knew it, one of the researchers in our team altered the PMD acronym to PMSED, a 'personal mobility and status-enhancing device.' I initially protested, but the research showed that car ownership was for many people as much about status as mobility.

It didn't end there. (These are grad students after all.) Soon more surveys led to still more debates about the correct acronym. Quietly, one of our researchers changed it yet again. The rest of us were left to ponder the meaning of the new acronym, PMSESICD.

We should have guessed. This student was surveying the willingness of young males to pay a substantial premium for excess horsepower combined with an appearance of speed, a muscle car, or strength, a large pick-up. When the acronym's meaning was finally revealed, it seemed obvious and appropriate. In the case of many young males, and some older ones, a personal vehicle is more accurately labeled as a 'personal mobility, status-enhancing, and sexual-insecurity-compensatory device.'

If we want people to change their behavior, we better know why they behave a certain way and exactly how we could motivate them to behave differently. We may have success with some behaviors. But new fads, inventions, and processes can continuously swamp these successes.

One example of these unpredictable developments is the emergence of bitcoins. Bitcoin trading is enabled by what are called 'blockchain technologies.'[9] These require huge amounts of electricity to progress through protocols designed to ensure that bitcoin transactions can be trusted, without involving an overseer, like a government regulator. Figure 8.2 shows the incredibly rapid growth in electricity use by the

Figure 8.2 Bitcoin electricity consumption

bitcoin industry in just over one year. Between January 2017 and September 2018, bitcoin electricity consumption reached and then surpassed the entire electricity consumption of one modest-sized country after another.

The bitcoin phenomenon was unforeseen 10 years ago. It is impossible to predict the energy-intensive activities that will emerge over the next 10 years. But we can be sure there will be many. Humans love to innovate, and they love novelty. Often that leads to more energy use. If we have not decarbonized our energy system, GHG emissions will rise.

* * *

The next time someone tells you we must change behavior to reduce GHG emissions, ask them how they changed behavior to reduce emissions that were causing acid rain, smog, dispersion of lead, and destruction of the ozone layer. You will get a blank stare. No one changed behavior. Instead, we changed technologies, with considerable success. We did this with the compulsory policies, especially regulations, I described in Chapter 6.

Acid rain was a major problem in the 1970s and 80s, killing forests and lakes, reducing agricultural production, and damaging buildings and infrastructure. It was caused by sulfur and nitrous oxide emissions from burning fossil fuels in power plants, factories, buildings, and vehicles. We needed to change technologies and fuels throughout the economy. And that's what we did. Governments required refineries to remove sulfur from transport fuels. In fact, it required them to dramatically reduce the sulfur content in all fuels, from home heating oil to bunker fuel for ships. In blissful ignorance, we now emit much less sulfur when driving a gasoline vehicle.

Coal-fired electricity plants were another major source of acid emissions. Governments gradually tightened standards, forcing the development of flue-gas-desulfurization. As this technology became commercially available, the US government enacted in 1990 a sulfur emissions cap-and-trade policy that contributed to sulfur emission reduction from power plants.

While acid rain was once a great concern of environmentalists and scientists, today it's rarely mentioned. We adopted regulations and some emission pricing to drive technological changes that dramatically reduced the environmental harm caused by burning fossil fuels in all sectors of the economy. Behavioral change played virtually no role.

This pattern repeats for urban air quality. Today, our cities are not smog-free, by any stretch. But when compared to 1970, urban air quality has improved significantly in industrialized countries. Again, we did not change behavior for this environmental improvement. We simply regulated the fuels and technologies that caused emissions. New regulations required refineries to reformulate fuels and vehicle manufacturers to install catalytic converters and other emission control devices. By 2000, a typical gasoline-fueled car emitted 96% less smog-creating emissions than its 1970 predecessor. Industrial plants in and near urban areas were also regulated for their emissions, leading to the adoption of selective catalytic reduction to reduce nitrous oxides, and the installation of bag-house filters or electro-static precipitators to capture particulates. In Los Angeles, government instituted a cap-and-trade system for nitrous oxides, which reduced these by 25%. The net consequence of these regulations and some pricing mechanisms is substantially improved air quality in most US cities. Ask a baby boomer what it was like when they were a child, and you'll hear about teary eyes, hazy vision, and labored breathing.

This pattern recurs with other environmental threats. Scientists alert people to the problem. Environmentalists are the first to believe them. Corporations that are implicated as contributing to the problem initially either deny the threat or balk at the cost of addressing it, fearful of government red tape and loss of profits. Eventually, enough public concern prompts politicians to act. They respond with tougher standards, and on rare occasions with policies that change prices. The standards force technological change. The threat is diminished. Afterwards, almost no one can say what technologies and what policies were involved. But if asked, they admit they didn't change their behavior.

Why would anyone think that reducing GHG emissions will be any different? One reason on offer is the magnitude of the problem: "surely a major transformation of the global energy system in just a few decades will require behavioral change." But why assume this? Why not focus on implementing the policies we know are essential, and then see what happens? Getting effective policies adopted is very difficult, but far less difficult than convincing virtually everyone to voluntarily change their behavior. As the compulsory policies are tightened, it may well be that some people will change their behavior. But we should not bank on this. Focus on pricing GHGs or regulating GHG-emitting technologies, and let individuals and industries decide the mix of behavioral and technological change as they respond to these policies.

As public awareness of acid rain and smog grew through the 1970s and 80s, an increasing number of people understood that their vehicles were part of the problem, in some cases a big part. Environmental campaigners talked about the need for people to use their cars less. But few did, as average vehicle use continued to rise. What made the difference was the rising public demands for political action, which eventually forced politicians to enact tighter regulations that forced the necessary technological change. The successful response was political and technological, not personal and behavioral. Of course, there was no explicit decision to forget about behavioral change. But governments quietly acknowledged that to rely on it alone would be insufficient.

With climate change, everyone has had the option over the last three decades of changing their behavior. We know the result. On average, we built larger houses and transported more goods and people – and even produced more emissions for sex. Fortunately, as with the other environmental threats, there are technological options to use less energy, to use zero-emission forms of energy, and to use fossil fuels while capturing the carbon, just as we now capture sulfur and particulates. When we finally do enact policies that compel GHG reduction through regulations or carbon pricing, corporations and individuals will decide on the mix of behavioral and technological change that suits them.

"If only everyone else lived sustainably,
then I could consume whatever I want."

Figure 8.3 Cartoon by Jacob Fox

I have frequently heard people say that we must severely curtail vehicle use to succeed against global warming. But should we bet the future of the planet on this when all we need to do is stop emitting carbon from our mobility devices, be they public transit or PMSESICDs?

As a politician having to deal with all people, not just the environmentally focused, Arnold Schwarzenegger understood this when, as Governor of California, he pushed for GHG reductions. He understood that there was little chance young males would give up their love of powerful vehicles. So he showed car and truck enthusiasts how he'd converted one of his Hummers to biofuel and another to hydrogen. (How many did he have?) When regulations dictate that muscle cars will only run on biofuels and electricity, this is what young males (and some females) will buy. Some might gripe about it. But compare this to the difficulty of convincing all of them to voluntarily sell their vehicles and take the bus.

In the same vein, I once heard a conference speaker confidently say, "Someday, flying will be viewed with the same disgust associated with lighting a cigarette indoors." Yes, the smoking change was behavioral. But is this a good example? Scientists claim that smoking is directly harmful to nearby non-smokers via second-hand smoke. The smoke from a cigarette and its effect is direct and obvious when a smoker subjects us to this risk – we immediately see it, smell it, and feel it in our lungs. On this basis, health advocates were finally able to get policy-makers to ban indoor smoking, although even that took decades.

In contrast, online carbon counters help us estimate the impacts of our flying behavior, but they don't seem to be having much effect. For one thing, the impact of airplane emissions is not nearly as immediate and obvious as smoking next to someone. Indeed, I note that most of my environmentally aware friends and colleagues fly well above the average in terms of person-miles-traveled. Why? They are wealthier than the average person, they love to see the world, their friends and family are spread around the globe, and many of them (here's the rub) fly frequently to meetings and conferences dedicated to stopping climate change.

As a corporate leader having to deal with all people, not just the environmentally focused, Richard Branson, president of Virgin Airways, has put considerable thought into behavioral change when it comes to flying.

> I think it's impractical to start talking about people not being able to fly. What we need to do is come up with a technological solution to flying, which is to come up with a clean fuel so people can carry on flying but not actually damaging the environment, and that's what we're trying to do.[10]

Branson has always expressed a deep concern for the climate threat and he has backed his words with his wealth, investing millions in the development of biofuels to replace conventional jet fuel. Jet fuel from non-fossil fuel sources is now being produced and its use would dramatically increase if required by regulation, albeit with an increased cost for airline travel.

It can be revealing to monitor our behavioral change efforts. Sometimes our behavioral change reduces energy use or GHG emissions. But sometimes each choice involves a difficult trade-off. A friend of mine provides an example. He once explained to me that he was adopting a greener lifestyle to have less impact on the planet. This included his new-found passion for hot yoga.

When I mentioned this to my grad students, one of them, inspired by our Ms. Skeptic, could not resist. Soon he was browsing websites, calling hot yoga studios, and even visiting a few. Later, with a straight face, he recounted conversations with puzzled staff as they earnestly tried to answer queries about their building's insulation and heating system. Perhaps they assumed the new client had a furnace fetish. But when he asked to see their monthly utility bills, the staff at one studio showed him the door. Amazingly, another studio let him copy their bills. Some companies will do a lot to attract new customers.

According to his notes, the studios he tracked kept their hot yoga rooms at over 38 degrees Celsius (100 degrees F) during the day, with only a moderate reduction at night because the rooms needed to stay hot for early morning sessions. The studios were in older commercial buildings with poor insulation. He estimated the average annual energy consumption of a 7x7 meter (20x20 foot) hot yoga room as equal to 20 average-sized, moderately insulated houses in our climatic zone.

When I next saw my hot yoga friend, he again mentioned how he had changed his behavior to fight climate change. I am sure he is doing many good things, and I want to encourage that. I did not tell him about my grad student's surreptitious research.

* * *

The belief that we must change our behavior to succeed against climate change is a bad-news-good-news story. The bad news is that all but the most extreme behavioral changes (living like a monk in an abbey or like Diego in New Mexico) will have little effect while we still live within an energy system dominated by fossil fuels. The good news is that we don't need behavioral change to reduce GHG emissions. We only need technological change.

Humans aren't going to stop using electricity. So we know with certainty that we need to phase out coal in electricity generation. This is now happening in wealthier countries, in some faster than others, and we need the trend to spread to developing countries. We also need to phase out gasoline and diesel in transportation. Led by jurisdictions such as California and Norway, people in wealthier countries are shifting toward zero-emission vehicles. Even in a developing country like China, people are buying electric vehicles. Other countries may soon emulate China's new policies that accelerate the adoption of low- and zero-emission vehicles.

At the same time, behavioral change should be encouraged. Some people will consciously use less electricity than their neighbors, which reduces the amount of zero-emission electricity needed in the energy transition. Some people will use cars less, instead favoring public transit, cycling, and walking. But, if we are to succeed with the climate-energy challenge, the contribution from technological change will dwarf these efforts at behavioral change, just as our past successes with other pollutants were almost entirely attributable to technological change.

Although we should encourage behavioral change, we must guard against deluding ourselves and others that such efforts are effective. Take the example of our consumption choices. In recent decades corporations have figured out that labeling products as "green" helps sales. So most products now tout their greenness. Even fossil fuel marketers do it, as I explained in Chapter 5. If this labeling leads me to unconsciously assume that my consumption choices are making a difference with GHG emissions, this is bad news for the climate.[11]

Likewise, while the movement for ethical investment should be encouraged, we must not delude ourselves into assuming its effect will be significant. Think about the frequent claims by industries about their "corporate social responsibility" or "triple bottom line" – the idea that an ethical corporation simultaneously pursues profits, societal well-being, and environmental protection. How durable are such initiatives?

Compare the recent histories of British Petroleum and Exxon Mobil. During his 10 years as CEO of BP, from 1997 to 2007, John Browne promoted a socially responsible corporate stance on global warming by investing in renewable energy and pilot projects to capture and store carbon. With much fanfare, BP rebranded itself as "Beyond Petroleum," an agent of change in the energy transition. It even argued that shareholders would benefit in the long run, although that again begs the question of whether the goal was corporate social responsibility or long-run profits.

In contrast, its competitor, Exxon Mobil, took the opposite strategy, focusing on investments that benefited from the lack of regulation or pricing of GHG emissions. Not surprisingly, Exxon earned higher returns for its shareholders than BP did during Browne's tenure. After his departure, BP's management quietly backed away from his approach, no doubt to the relief of shareholders.

The fossil fuel industry and insincere politicians would like nothing better than to delay compulsory decarbonization policies by claiming that we need behavioral change. We must not play into their hands. Instead, we should prioritize the one behavioral change that can make a big difference: changing our behavior as citizens and voters to more forcefully pursue deep decarbonization policies. Annie Leonard, producer of the documentary, *The Story of Stuff*, put it this way.

> Instead of asking what we as consumers can do, let's ask what we as citizens can do. Our real power to reduce the environmental and health impacts of the energy we use lies not in convincing consumers to make different choices from a limited menu but in engaging as citizens to influence what's on the menu.[12]

Thirty, twenty, and ten years ago, zero-emission vehicles were not on the menu. I pursued behavioral change as best I could, almost always commuting by transit or bike (never buying a parking pass to ensure I would not lose my resolve during miserable weather). But I also had a gasoline car, which was our best option for getting kids to hockey practice and lugging home groceries. Now my partner and I have an electric car. The purchase price of such cars is still out of reach for many people, although we addressed that challenge by sharing the car's cost and use since neither of us drives much (and ours is a Nissan Leaf, not a Tesla!).

What a fantastic feeling to finally have a commercially available technological option for eliminating our vehicle emissions. But that option only materialized because of the compulsory policies I described in Chapter 6. With vehicles, the most important policy was the ZEV mandate California initiated in 1990, that gave vehicle manufacturers deadlines for innovating and then marketing zero-emission and near-zero-emission vehicles – leading to the development of hybrid, plug-in hybrid, electric, and hydrogen-fuel-cell cars. The successful push for climate-energy policies in California helped change the menu for citizens, enabling the kind of technological change that previously addressed smog, acid rain, and other environmental threats. And this is essential because people won't stop using vehicles in the next three decades, yet they must dramatically reduce their GHG emissions in that period.

Fifteen years ago, electric companies in North America were still building coal plants, so clean electricity was rarely on the menu, except where hydropower and nuclear power dominated. As I noted in Chapter 6, the British Columbia government in 2007 was finally convinced to implement a clean electricity standard, which prevented the construction of two coal plants and a natural gas plant. Because of this, the electricity I use in my electric car is zero-emission. Coal-plant phase-out regulations and carbon pricing in Canada, and state renewable portfolio standards and federal regulations in the US are decarbonizing the electricity sector. Various compulsory policies are also decarbonizing the electricity system in most European countries. Our citizen efforts to change climate-energy policy are changing what's on the menu so that now consumers can use near-zero-emission electricity in their homes, including for space and water heating which are the two main household energy uses.

These changes are technological, not behavioral. But this is not to deny the value of also changing our behavior. Drive less and you reduce electricity consumption. Use less hot water and turn off unneeded lighting and you reduce electricity consumption. Fly less and you reduce GHG emissions from the combustion of fossil fuel-derived jet fuel, but perhaps – if our policy efforts succeed – you will one day instead reduce the combustion of bio-jet fuel, produced in sustainable processes. These types of behavioral changes reduce total energy demand, which in turn reduces the aggregate investment required for the transition to a zero-emission energy system, making that transition easier and faster.

Speaking of what's on the menu, our food system is an important source of GHG emissions. Studies repeatedly confirm that a dramatic reduction in meat consumption would significantly reduce agricultural GHG emissions, while improving human health.[13] In developing countries, meat consumption is rising in step with incomes. But in wealthier countries, it is declining and this trend is accelerating with the growing awareness of delicious and healthy vegetarian recipes and the development of simulated-meat substitutes for those with continued carnivorous cravings. My bet is that agriculture-related GHG emissions will decline significantly over the next two decades on a per capita basis. Unfortunately, aggregate emissions might not fall, as this trend is offset by population growth. Still, this is an important behavioral change that should be championed, even if mostly for its human health benefits. People think of this as a behavioral change, and I accept that. I note, however, that switching from beef burgers to meatless burgers with an identical taste seems more technological than behavioral.

In any case, it's time to stop feeling guilty about ourselves as consumers and start feeling guilty about ourselves as citizens. As consumers, there is little we can do with the guilt in those cases where we have no realistic options to reduce GHGs. As citizens, however, there is a lot we can do. There is a lot we must do. But it won't always be comfortable.

The adoption of transformative climate-energy policy is a Herculean task. If we have sincere politicians, we need to push and support them. They can easily go off course. And, sadly, sincere politicians are rare when it comes to this challenge for reasons I explained in Chapter 4 (a global problem without a global government), Chapter 5 (the political power of incumbent fossil fuel interests), and Chapter 6 (the difficulty of enacting and sustaining effective domestic climate-energy policies). When these factors result again in the election of insincere politicians, we must especially challenge ourselves as citizens. For as Bill McKibben asks, "Planet Earth is miles outside its comfort zone; how many of us will go beyond ours?"[14]

In the final chapter, I explain the reasons why I left my comfort zone in 2012, leading to my arrest with 12 other people for blocking a coal train in Vancouver. For me, this was an enormous but unfortunately essential behavioral change as a citizen – one I and many other citizens may need to repeat before achieving climate success.

CHAPTER 9

We Can Be Carbon Neutral

The great enemy of truth is very often not the lie – deliberate, contrived and dishonest – but the myth – persistent, persuasive and unrealistic.

John F. Kennedy

KNOWING THAT I DO CLIMATE-ENERGY RESEARCH, MY friend Gurmeet asked me about carbon offsets. His interest was spurred when booking online his vacation at a Caribbean 'eco-resort.' He recounted for me his dilemma.

"I was almost finished when it asked if I wanted to fly carbon-neutral. I wasn't keen, but I clicked to see the cost. You plug in your flight number, and it tells you the amount that will offset your share of your flight's emissions. It was about \$20."

"That sounds cheap."

"I thought it would be more. I was going to skip past, but the low cost stopped me."

"What do you mean?"

"I'm an eco-resort kind of guy. I was feeling a bit guilty about flying, especially once the offset option popped up. Only \$20 for a guilt-free vacation. On the other hand, I already do a lot for the environment, so why pay extra?"

"What did you do?"

"I thought about the other guests. What if I met an interesting woman who had bought offsets, and she asked about mine? What if everyone had offsets except me? After all, it *is* an eco-resort. Maybe other guests would flaunt their receipts to show what good things they were funding. I bought the offset. Good thing too. As it turned out, everyone had purchased them, or so they claimed!"

It seems a simple concept. You pay someone to reduce their carbon pollution while you fly, as always, to your destination. The only difference is that you no longer feel responsible for global warming, no longer guilty about your lifestyle.

No wonder this industry is growing. Estimates suggest the global voluntary offset industry is above $10 billion in annual revenue. The industry feeds on image and guilt. Individuals keep it going. So do corporations, vying for a marketing edge as carbon neutral businesses. "For only $4.95 your website can be carbon neutral!" So do politicians. For his 2011 State of the Union Address, President Obama's motorcade traveled carbon neutral from the White House to the Capitol. (In 2017, Donald Trump did not.) Even some faith communities have gotten involved, with the US Presbyterian Church once urging its congregation to become carbon neutral.

Speaking of religion, offsetting will sound familiar to Christians. In the Middle Ages, the church sold indulgences to wealthy worshippers to expiate their sins. It rationalized this lucrative practice by claiming that its devout clergy, on a sure path to heaven, had done so many good deeds and acts of repentance that they had a surplus to sell to those less confident of their immortal prospects. The sins of the latter would be offset by purchasing the surplus good deeds from the clergy. Skeptics were ignored. The prospect of paying money to neutralize one's sins, without having to change one's lifestyle, was enticing.

Today, Christians no longer believe they can offset their sins by paying someone more pious. They see sin-offsetting as a delusion. But what about carbon offsets? Can we pay someone else to expiate our sins of emission? Can we buy our way to carbon neutrality? Or is this another myth that interferes with our ability to act effectively on the climate-energy challenge?

To address these questions, we should start by clarifying current and potential flows of carbon between the earth's crust (the 'lithosphere'), the atmosphere, and the biosphere. We extract fossil fuels from the lithosphere. We could capture the CO_2 emissions from burning these fossil fuels before they reach the atmosphere. It would be difficult to have a CO_2 capture device on the tailpipe of every gasoline car, but coal- and natural gas-fired power plants could have equipment that captured CO_2 from exhaust gases 'post-combustion,' or that converted coal or natural gas into hydrogen (for combustion to generate electricity), in this case capturing the CO_2 'pre-combustion.' That zero-emission hydrogen and electricity could then be used in vehicles.

If these captured emissions were injected permanently into underground storage, the coal or natural gas plant would be effectively carbon neutral. It would return to the earth's crust almost the same amount of carbon it had removed. Atmospheric GHG concentrations would not increase in this process of using fossil fuels to produce zero-emission electricity or hydrogen for use in vehicles, buildings, and industry.

Instead of taking carbon from fossil fuels, to prevent its flow to the atmosphere, we could extract carbon from the atmosphere. Carbon Engineering is a company, partly funded by Bill Gates, that has developed such a 'direct air capture' technology. The concept originator is David Keith.[1] Because it is located north of Vancouver, I have visited the company's development plant several times with my students. As humanity's climate predicament worsens, the CO_2 from direct air capture could be shipped by pipeline to a favorable place for geological storage. If this occurred, the technology would be carbon negative rather than carbon neutral, physically reducing the atmospheric CO_2 concentration. Because of our climate-energy policy procrastination, we will need technologies like this in the future (we need them now actually) to reduce atmospheric CO_2. As the harms from CO_2 intensify, we will gladly pay their cost.

Until such time, new technology developers like Carbon Engineering need a revenue stream for their funders, which they hope to earn by using the extracted CO_2 to produce a valued hydrocarbon product, such as synthetic diesel for sale to diesel-fueled technologies, such as trucks, farm equipment, industrial equipment, trains, and ships. When burned, this diesel would release CO_2 into the atmosphere. But this would be equal to the CO_2 that was initially extracted from the atmosphere to produce the synthetic diesel, making the process as a whole carbon neutral. Under the low carbon fuel standard flex-regs of California, this diesel would generate credits that Carbon Engineering could sell, meaning that it would earn the normal diesel wholesale price plus the low carbon intensity credits. And, of course, its product would be exempt from any carbon taxes. But a direct air capture system like that of Carbon Engineering needs energy to run its air capture process and its fuel production process. To benefit the atmosphere and earn credits under the low carbon fuel standard, that energy cannot be producing many GHG emissions, so it should come from wind, solar, hydropower, nuclear, or fossil fuels with carbon capture and storage.

Biomass energy is also a candidate for carbon neutrality. Except for the last 250 years, the human energy system has relied almost entirely on wood, brush, crop waste, and animal dung, and these have been essentially carbon neutral. As they grow via photosynthesis, trees, bushes, grasses, and crops extract CO_2 from the air to produce carbohydrates. When plants are burned or decay, this carbon is returned to the atmosphere, with no net increase in atmospheric GHG concentrations (although this is not precisely true if more of it returns as methane). Thus, with some caveats, the IPCC generally defines biomass energy as carbon neutral.[2]

If, however, the burning of wood and other forms of bioenergy at an electricity generation plant was combined with carbon capture and storage from the plant's flue gases, the underground storage of the resulting stream of CO_2 would cause the entire process to be carbon negative. This is referred to as 'bio-energy with carbon capture and storage' (BECCS). As with the direct air capture technology of Carbon Engineering, we may need a lot of BECCS in future to compensate for our procrastination on the GHG threat, as we desperately try to lower the atmospheric CO_2 concentration.[3]

Figure 9.1 summarizes these technologies and processes. On the left, it shows how our extraction and burning of fossil fuels emits CO_2 to the atmosphere, where its concentration increases. On the right, it shows how photosynthesis in growing plants extracts carbon from the atmosphere, but when those plants die and decay much of their embodied carbon returns to the atmosphere.

The figure also shows the options for preventing more CO_2 from getting to the atmosphere and for extracting it from the atmosphere. The thick dark line from 'combustion' down to underground carbon

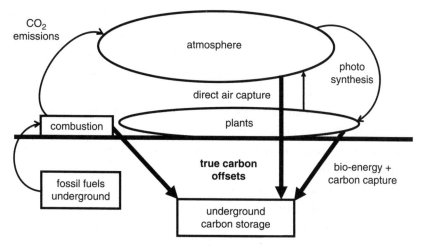

Figure 9.1 True carbon offsets

storage is a way of preventing CO_2 from reaching the atmosphere when using fossil fuels. As noted, this extraction of CO_2 is technologically feasible at large industrial plants burning fossil fuels, but not in smaller technologies like vehicles. The thick dark line in the middle from 'direct air capture' (DAC) down to underground carbon storage, as described above, is a way of reducing atmospheric CO_2 concentrations. If the energy used for DAC were zero-emission, this process would be carbon negative. The third option, the thick line on the right, denotes 'bio-energy with carbon capture,' which is also carbon negative if the CO_2 is returned to storage in the lithosphere.

In bold letters, Figure 9.1 associates 'true carbon offsets' with the box labeled 'underground carbon storage.' Since the CO_2 emissions we are trying to offset invariably come from the burning of fossil fuels extracted from the earth's crust, it stands to reason that the only way to *truly* offset them would be to put the equivalent amount of CO_2 back into the earth's crust that we removed when extracting fossil fuels. If we are to prevent atmospheric CO_2 concentrations from rising, we need to either prevent the emissions in the first place, via carbon capture and storage when we use fossil fuels, or capture CO_2 from the atmosphere and store it permanently underground using direct air capture technologies or biomass with carbon capture and storage.

Planting trees is not an offset for burning fossil fuels because when the trees die and decay (or are burned for energy), they release most of the carbon they extracted through photosynthesis back into the atmosphere, some of it as methane. Carbon flows between the atmosphere and the biosphere in an almost-closed loop. (Some carbon ends up in the oceans and soils, and some in sediments, to become fossil fuels after millions of years.) So it is incorrect to assume that planting trees somehow offsets the CO_2 released from extracting and burning fossil fuels.

The one exception is if we create a forest on barren land that would not have naturally returned to a forested state. And if that new forest became permanent (which we can never know for certain), it would represent an increase in carbon stored away from the atmosphere – in this case in the biosphere. But simply replanting trees on land that would eventually return to forest does not materially reduce atmospheric CO_2 concentrations. The carbon extracted from the atmosphere via photosynthesis returns with burning and decay of biomass, so it cannot be a legitimate offset for carbon that was extracted from the earth's crust and not returned.

In sum, for humanity to be truly carbon neutral, the carbon annually stored underground must equal the carbon the fossil fuel industry annually extracts from the earth's crust. For individuals, corporations, or government to be deemed carbon neutral, the carbon they return to the lithosphere must equal the carbon they extracted from it. We have all the technologies today to achieve this true carbon neutrality. But there's one catch. It doesn't cost \$20 to truly offset Gurmeet's flight. It costs more like \$100, or even \$200.[4]

* * *

The higher cost of truly offsetting GHG emissions explains why promoters of carbon neutrality have an alternative definition from the one I presented above. They say that an offset payment need not fund the actual extraction of carbon from the atmosphere and its burial. Instead, all the payment need do is "prevent emissions that would otherwise have occurred." Here are three examples of what they mean.

If someone intended to purchase a standard efficiency car but accepted an offset payment to purchase an electric vehicle instead, proponents claim that the alternative vehicle choice reduced emissions that would otherwise have occurred. The offset payment to the electric vehicle purchaser allows someone else to claim carbon neutrality without reducing their own emissions. If an electricity supplier intended to build a natural gas plant but accepted a payment to build a hydropower plant instead, carbon neutrality proponents argue again that this reduced emissions that would otherwise have occurred. If an owner of forested land intended to log some of it but was paid to keep it forested instead, carbon neutrality advocates argue that keeping carbon stored as biomass reduced emissions that would otherwise have occurred.

Note that in each example the concept of carbon neutrality depends on the assumed intended action: what would have occurred if the seller of the offset had acted as they apparently intended. This is critical. Presumably, *they* know what they intend to do now and in future with their choice of car or power plant or land. But we don't know. Thus, the carbon offset industry needs to build a hypothetical future that would otherwise have occurred in order to determine if the emissions reductions were truly 'additional' to that future. That future depends on intentions.

Enter the 'offset verification' industry. These are companies paid to verify that an offset is additional. In the early years of offsetting, they simply verified that what was claimed actually occurred: someone bought an electric vehicle, the electric company built a hydropower plant, and the forest was not logged. This was the full extent of offset verification.

Soon, however, skeptics noted that confirmation of the action (or non-action in the case of not logging) does not prove it was additional. Offset verifiers need to also prove that what happened when the offset payment occurred is different from what otherwise would have happened. But since they can't know the true intention of the offset seller, their best hope, 'gold standard verification,' is to gather evidence showing that the car buyer's cheapest option was a gasoline vehicle, the utility's best option was a natural gas plant, and the forest owner's most profitable option was to log the forest. They then presume that these agents would have taken these financially superior actions, if not for the offset payment.

But from whom does the offset verifier obtain cost and profit estimates? You guessed it, the offset seller. Of course, some information is publicly available: the cost of the electric vehicle, the cost of hydropower turbines, the market price for timber. But every economic decision has unique aspects. There will be cost and benefit information that only the seller knows: the use rate of the electric vehicle, future payments for flood control to the hydropower plant owner, future payments for forest use by local hunters. But we can only really know what the offset seller intended to do if he or she provides an honest disclosure of all possible decision factors. Full disclosure is not, however, in the offset seller's interest, since he or she would like the offset money regardless of original intent.

This self-serving bias of the offset seller is not the only problem. The incentives facing verifiers also favor distortion, since their income depends on the development of a thriving offset industry, with lots of offset payments to be verified. They have no incentive to question the offset seller's decision too deeply lest they dramatically reduce the likelihood that offset buyers and sellers will be active. And because we cannot ever know the true intent of the offset seller, no one can prove that the verifiers did a bad job.

What about the brokers who bring together offset buyers, sellers, and verifiers? No help here either. Since they get a commission on the transaction, their income too depends on the development of a thriving offset industry. The broker would be smart not to question too deeply the relevant decision information used by the offset seller lest they reduce offset sales.

What about the offset purchaser, like Gurmeet? Surely he is the one party to the transaction who wants certainty that his payment actually reduced emissions, that he has not wasted his money on a delusion. Or are his motives so simple? Christians purchasing indulgences from the church wanted to feel less guilty about their lifestyle. Gurmeet now feels less guilty about his lifestyle. And that good feeling was cheaply acquired.

* * *

Economists refer to Gurmeet's dilemma as an 'asymmetric information problem.' Gurmeet and everyone else has less information than offset sellers about their costs and benefits. Because of this, he risks paying excessively for a legitimate offset or, even worse, one that doesn't reduce GHGs.

Governments face a somewhat similar challenge when they want a private company to provide a public good or service. The company, being privy to details about costs and benefits, might pad its cost estimate to extract additional funds from government. In most situations, however, what is provided is tangible – a fighter jet, a bridge, food delivered to the elderly. Government can ask for competing bids so it can compare the offers of firms vying to provide a tangible good or service. But with offsets, what is provided is hypothetical. There is no physical product or service for comparison, so the information asymmetry persists. As Mark Schapiro said in a 2010 *Harper's* article, "the offset market is based on the lack of delivery of an invisible substance to no one."[5]

The offset purchaser cannot know all the decision factors considered by offset sellers. Perhaps the seller likes the eco-status of owning an electric car and would have paid extra to get one, without the benefit of the offset payment. Perhaps the electricity supplier was intending to build the hydropower plant, which would cost more but earn extra revenue by timing water releases to benefit downstream irrigation users. This information asymmetry is a fundamental problem with carbon offsetting. And, contrary to offset industry talk of 'rigorous verification,' it can't be completely eliminated. Uncertainty is *unavoidable* in a verification process that requires assumptions about a hypothetical future that never happens.

To illustrate with a racy analogy, some skeptics once created a (presumably) mock internet service where you could purchase offsets for sexual infidelity. They claimed that if you have a secret affair, your feelings of guilt increase the "concentration of sexual guilt in the atmosphere." These high concentrations are bad for the planet, "raising temperatures with unhealthy clouds of suspicion and regret." While the website was still live, you could log in to Cheat-Neutral and pay someone not to have an affair, so that their fidelity offsets your infidelity. The motto said it all: "helping you, because you can't help yourself."[6]

For a small commission, Cheat-Neutral would help you find the offset seller who makes a fidelity commitment and receives your payment. You pick them from a catalog of cheery, innocent-looking individuals and couples eager to accept money for not having an affair. Bob and Pria are one such couple. An accountant, Bob admits that the word sheets makes him think of spreadsheets. Pria dotes on her four cats. If you're worried these people might take your offset payment and then secretly renege, you can pay extra for "gold standard verification" – 24-hour video-surveillance.

Why are you suspicious? Cheat-Neutral and carbon neutral both depend on something we can't prove. It does no good to pay people who are celibate, and will remain so in future, so you must find someone in a relationship who was about to have an affair, an outcome that changed only because of your payment. But you can't be sure the person you paid would have had an affair were it not for your payment. You can't be sure of their initial intention, although you might gather information to help you guess. (Bob and Pria look suspiciously like people who don't have affairs, but looks can be deceiving.)

Perhaps you learn that one was previously a compulsive adulterer. This improves the chances that your offset payment (in concert with 24-hour surveillance!) will reduce the global total of infidelity-guilt. But perhaps they recently experienced a spiritual awakening, and renounced forever their promiscuous lifestyle. All you can do is hope that they would have secretly broken their vow and continued to cheat (a warped thought), just as we must hope that the electric vehicle purchaser would have bought another gas-guzzler, the electric company would have built another natural gas plant, and the forest owner would have clear-cut her land.

We can extend this analogy to the entire verification apparatus. As with carbon neutrality, all parties in the Cheat-Neutral transaction have an incentive to argue or believe that the offset payment caused the future to unfold differently than it otherwise would have. Offset sellers like Bob and Pria only make money if they can convince someone they were sure to have an affair, regardless of the truth. Cheat-Neutral only makes money if trans-actions occur, so it needs to find people claiming to be imminent cheaters, even if uncertain of their true intentions. Finally, the offset purchaser wants to avoid guilt as cheaply as possible, but lacks the time and motivation to investigate the likelihood that the offset seller was going to cheat.

Claiming to neutralize atmospheric guilt from sexual infidelity may sound bizarre, but it is no different than claiming to neutralize our emissions without returning to underground storage the carbon we removed from the earth's crust. In both cases, we cannot be certain a given offset-funded project is additional, since we cannot verify a hypothetical future that never happens.

When we mix together the ubiquitous nature of GHG emissions, financial self-interest, human imagination, and the propensity to delude, we have a potent cocktail. Little wonder that today you can pay to offset your emissions from drinking a beer, racing Formula 1, or changing diapers. And you can do this by paying someone to capture cow farts in Montana, plant trees in the Sahara, or shoot camels in Australia. As actor Ed Begley Jr. put it, "If you're going to drive around in a big old Hummer and then buy carbon offsets to mitigate that, that's like getting drunk and throwing some money through the window of an AA meeting."[7]

"Don't worry, we've purchased carbon offsets."

Figure 9.2 Cartoon by Jacob Fox

But should we write off the entire offsetting business? Are all carbon offsets a sham? Perhaps there is a way to estimate the percentage of offsets likely to be additional.

While carbon offsets are relatively new, offset-like schemes have a long history. For decades, researchers have assessed the effectiveness of government and voluntary programs that pay people to provide something of public value, many with strong similarities to offset payments. These include payments by electric utilities for improved energy efficiency and payments by governments and charitable organizations for reforestation, forest conservation, and afforestation (foresting an area that never was forested). I and my research team have contributed to assessments of electric utility efficiency payments and forest payments.[8]

From 1985 to 2000, US electric utilities spent over $20 billion in subsidies and information programs to induce consumers and businesses to acquire energy-efficient devices. These subsidies are effectively the same as offset payments. The utility pays someone to buy an efficient device who otherwise, presumably, was going to buy an inefficient device. Because some jurisdictions had subsidy programs while others didn't, this provided an opportunity to estimate if the offset-like payments made a difference, by comparing the two jurisdictions.

The challenge is illustrated by the following example. At any given time, some consumers buy high-efficiency fridges, while others buy medium- and low-efficiency models. When a utility offers a $50 rebate to purchasers of the efficient models, its program would be completely successful if all subsidies went to people who were not intending to buy these. If, in contrast, all subsidies went to people who would have bought the efficient models anyway, this program would be a complete failure, with zero additionality. (Economists call it 'adverse selection' when a program benefits the wrong people because only they possess information on their true intentions.)

Researchers have tried to detect an efficiency improvement in those jurisdictions with subsidy programs compared to those without. As it turns out, the last two decades have witnessed many of these studies on electric utility efficiency programs. While there is not complete agreement on the rates of additionality, there is agreement that it is rarely above 50%. In other words, at least half of the offset-like subsidy payments did not increase efficiency, instead going to people for buying what they would have bought anyway.[9]

Another offset-like subsidy with a long history is the practice of paying for forest conservation and reforestation, especially payments from governments and private donors to conserve forest land in developing countries. Independent research has generated results the offset industry would not want widely known. Researchers at *Resources for the Future* noted that in some cases, such as a program in Costa Rica, offset-like payments were less than 10% effective because almost all the land receiving money was ill suited for other uses.[10] Thus, forest land owners received money for not cutting down forests they weren't going to cut down anyway.

The Kyoto Protocol in 1997 created two offset mechanisms. One of these, called Joint Implementation, allows companies in developed countries to subsidize GHG-reducing investments in other developed countries. A 2015 hindsight analysis by the Stockholm Environment Institute estimated that 75% of the funding paid for actions that would have happened anyway.[11] The other Kyoto offset program is called the Clean Development Mechanism, which allows companies in developed countries to subsidize reductions in developing countries. A popular offset is to pay for 'reduced emissions from deforestation and forest degradation' (REDD). Hindsight research has shown that it too is much less effective than its promoters promised, with 85% of funded projects unlikely to be additional.[12] To Lisa Song, the reduced effect of forest preservation offsets is "an even more inconvenient truth."[13]

These are a few examples of independent research that assesses the likely additionality of offset-like mechanisms, whether private or institutional. Such research finds, unsurprisingly, that offsets are vulnerable to the same flaws found with previous subsidy programs for energy efficiency and forest conservation: additionality is almost impossible to prove with individual projects, while the aggregate effect is less than claimed. This is bad news for the offset industry – although only if widely publicized and understood.

* * *

Maybe it doesn't matter if some people are misled about carbon neutrality. Why should Gurmeet be prevented, even if there is little effect, from voluntarily increasing his airfare by $20 to transfer money to a forest owner in Costa Rica? One can hardly prohibit offsetting just because it's not all additional. And we don't want government, in a bizarre perversion of roles, to stop people from voluntarily taxing themselves for the environmental harm they cause, just because the tax is too low.

But the point of carbon offsets and carbon neutrality is to effectively address the climate-energy challenge. If offsets are often ineffective, yet its proponents convince themselves and others that they are effective, we have a problem. We risk further delaying a truly effective effort if claims of carbon neutrality enable insincere politicians to delay the essential but difficult regulatory and pricing policies. This concern explains why Kevin Anderson, a leading researcher at the UK Tyndall Centre, claims that, "offsetting is worse than doing nothing."[14]

If we are to get past carbon offsetting, we should understand why it emerged. I've described previously the successes we've had in addressing environmental threats from acid, lead, smog, and ozone-depleting emissions. We succeeded because we implemented regulations and sometimes pricing. Never have we pursued acid offsets, lead offsets, smog offsets, or ozone-depletion offsets. The terms sound fanciful.

The carbon emissions story is different. For reasons I've described in previous chapters, national governments have been far too slow in implementing effective climate-energy policies, which is why individuals, groups, organizations, and businesses are exploring voluntary actions, like the behavioral change I described in Chapter 8. Carbon offsetting has emerged in this context. Even those who understand that strong national policies are essential may look to carbon offsetting to show that immediate action is possible as an alternative to only railing about government.

There is also the 'glass half-full' argument. If 50% of offset recipients are not additional, this means that 50% are. If their actions accelerate the market penetration of low-emission technologies, like wind turbines, solar panels, and electric cars, the costs of these technologies may fall faster thanks to greater economies of scale from mass production. From this perspective, even partially effective carbon offsetting may contribute to the solution.

Also, not all offsets are equally bad. Some subsidies to afforestation might develop a vibrant forest on land that would have remained barren indefinitely, storing carbon on the earth's surface that would otherwise be in the atmosphere.

Proponents also point out that offsetting provides a means of reaching GHG emissions that are difficult to regulate or price. In agriculture, changes in tilling practices, animal feed, and the storing and treating of animal waste can reduce GHG emissions. Imagine the reaction of farmers to an onslaught of regulations and taxes on these activities. Offset payments, so the argument goes, increase farmer awareness of the climate-energy challenge, preparing them for more exacting policies in future.

Thus, advocates sometimes argue that carbon offsetting complements and facilitates the compulsory pricing and regulatory policies that governments must enact. This sounds good. But the experience doesn't match this image. To understand why, we must distinguish between the trading of carbon offsets, and the trading of carbon permits in a comprehensive cap-and-trade system. These two forms of carbon trading differ fundamentally, yet are often conflated in the eyes of proponents, the public, politicians, and the media.[15]

In a comprehensive emissions cap-and-trade policy, all emissions would require a permit and all permits would sum to the total allowed emissions. Under this policy, there would be no such thing as carbon offsets, no such thing as carbon neutrality. Some people might have high emissions. Some might have low or even zero emissions. But no one would pretend that buying someone's permits makes them carbon neutral. This is why no one promoted 'acid offsets' when the US government implemented its ambitious acid emissions cap-and-trade program in 1990. Nor would anyone promote 'carbon offsets' if government implemented a similar policy for reducing carbon emissions.

Or so one might think. However, carbon offsetting has inculcated itself into the very design of climate cap-and-trade policies. Lobbyists have convinced politicians that difficult-to-regulate emissions in farming and forestry can be addressed in the cap-and-trade system with a win-win mechanism that lowers the cost of emissions reduction and induces climate policy buy-in from farmers and forest land owners. Under this approach, those whose emissions are capped would have the option to buy offsets from those whose emissions are not. A factory that has permits for only 80% of its current emissions would now have three options instead of two. Initially, its two options for achieving the 20% reduction were to reduce its own emissions or buy permits in the permit trading market. Now, its third option is to buy offsets from a farmer or other entity whose emissions are not capped.

From a political perspective, allowing offsets in a cap-and-trade system is attractive. By lowering the cost of achieving the government's emissions target, offsets increase political acceptability. The factory is better off if offsets are cheaper than buying permits or reducing plant emissions. The farmer is happy to get paid for something that she was perhaps going to do anyway, and to avoid new complicated regulations. For the whole economy, offsets add another low-cost option, which decreases the permit trading price and thus everyone's compliance costs. (Of course, if the offsets are not additional, the low compliance cost is explained by the fact that emissions are not actually declining.)

With these apparent cost advantages, political negotiations to develop cap-and-trade regulations in a given jurisdiction tend to expand the role of offsets to overcome stalemates. The various interests clamoring for offsets drown out the few economists and environmentalists frantically arguing that including offsets increases the likelihood of replacing real with fictive reductions.

This is the dilemma for climate policy, both within and between countries. Even if governments one day acknowledge that carbon neutrality is a myth, the practice of carbon offsetting is not easily expunged. This does not mean we must resign ourselves to perpetual climate policy failure. But we do need to severely restrict the offset loophole. Here's how.

First, governments should only recognize a strict definition of carbon neutrality. A carbon offset must physically remove carbon from the atmosphere and store it, preferably underground, as I showed in Figure 9.1.

Second, governments should not allow carbon offsetting to undermine their compulsory climate energy policies. Whether using flex-regs, carbon pricing, or a combination of these, government should restrict the contribution of offsets to 10% of total reductions. And the claimed quantities of 'permitted' offsets should be discounted by 50% to reflect their likely additionality flaws. Thus, a factory would have to hold 200 tons of carbon offsets to get credited for 100. This is not a new idea; some early drafts of US cap-and-trade bills discounted offsets by 25%.

Third, governments should assign sunset clauses to offset provisions in their cap-and-trade policies. While agricultural emissions might initially be exempt from an emissions cap, but available for offsets, the cap would gradually extend to tillage practice, animal waste handling, and so on, while gradually diminishing the offset contribution.

Fourth, at the international level, developing countries would be eligible for offsets from developed countries, but their eligibility would be tied to domestic implementation of effective climate-energy policies – either stringent regulations or a rising carbon price or both that were guaranteed to phase-out coal plants in electricity and gasoline and diesel in transportation.

With these four conditions, governments would undermine the myth that one can achieve carbon neutrality by buying offsets and would prevent offset programs from weakening otherwise effective climate-energy policies. But the offset problem started because most governments are unwilling to implement effective policies. The carbon neutral delusion suits many political leaders just fine, which returns us to where we started, trying to help Gurmeet decide what to do.

At least by now it's obvious Gurmeet is not helping anybody by sustaining the myth of carbon neutrality. He needs to do something else. He could use the funds he would have spent for offsets to directly reduce his own emissions, especially by an action he would otherwise not yet have taken. Thus, he might put the money toward an electric car or electric heat pump or solar panels.

Perhaps he could use offset money to pay extra for goods and services in order to reward companies that commit to use these funds for additional emissions reductions, without buying and selling offsets. An example is to pay a higher rate to a natural gas supplier for blending more biomethane into its gas supply. If this is a high-cost option, Gurmeet can be confident that it would not have occurred without his offset payment, potentially meeting the additionality test.

Finally, Gurmeet needs to recognize that if his fellow citizens are not also reducing emissions, his individual efforts don't mean much. He might take the money he would spend on offsets and instead donate it to organizations and politicians pursuing the essential compulsory policies that regulate energy and technologies or price carbon emissions. If he finds climate-sincere politicians willing to champion and implement these strategies, helping elect them is the best use of his offset money. Success with the climate-energy challenge requires action from everyone, not just the small number of people willing to voluntarily tax their pollution.

CHAPTER 10

Energy Efficiency Is Profitable

Nothing is so difficult as not deceiving oneself.

Ludwig Wittgenstein

MY NEIGHBOR MING RECENTLY DESCRIBED HER PARTICIPATION in an energy-saving contest of her local electric utility. It started when two college students on a summer work placement convinced her to enlist in the company's promotion.

According to the eager students on her doorstep, reducing her electricity demand would save money and help the environment. As a bonus, if she cut her average electricity use by 15% in six months, relative to the previous year, she would win $100. What sold Ming were the brochure testimonials in which parents described the contest's family-bonding benefits. With parents feeling guilty about their kids' devotion to texting, internet browsing, TV watching, and gaming, the prospect of a successful family project was appealing. Ming's kids, Tania and Sam, were 13 and 15 at the time.

From the utility's pamphlets, Ming and her husband Dave learned that efforts to cut energy use entail either 'efficiency' or 'conservation.' Efficiency involves replacing your appliances, lights, and other devices with higher efficiency models. These tend to have a higher purchase price than less efficient devices, but they should save money over time through lower electricity consumption. Conservation involves changing behavior or lowering one's expectations for energy services. Examples include switching off unused lights and computers, taking shorter showers, washing clothes with cold water and drying them on the line, and accepting a slightly lower indoor temperature in winter and a slightly higher temperature during air-conditioning season.

The brochures advised Ming and Dave to start with easy measures that didn't require a focused behavioral change: washing laundry with cold water, lowering the temperature setting for the hot water tank, and reprogramming the thermostat down to 11 degrees Celsius (52°F) from 11 pm to 6 am, and to a maximum of 20 degrees Celsius (68°F) during winter days. Although the last action saved natural gas rather than electricity, their electric utility's strategy was to promote a non-discriminating 'culture of energy saving.'

So far so good. These conservation efforts might be thought of as lifestyle changes, but they didn't require a conscious effort to act differently on a daily basis, nor any cooperation from their kids. That challenge came next.

Turning off lights in unused rooms is a no-brainer when it comes to reducing energy use, but it does require a conscious effort. Ming and Dave discussed this with Tania and Sam, and they resolved to try. Ming even detected a note of enthusiasm, which made her appreciative of the family-bonding angle in the promotional brochures.

Hanging clothes on the line instead of using the dryer sounded doable, but involved tricky planning for her and Dave. Since both had full-time jobs, she wondered how to match laundry chores to sunny weekend days.

Dave purchased power bars for all electrical devices. By remembering to switch off the power bars, the family could eliminate vampire load from idle TVs, DVD players, audio systems, microwave ovens, wireless transmitters, coffee machines, cell phone rechargers, computers, and so on. Everyone promised to click the power bars after finishing with a device.

Six months later, I asked Ming how it was going.

"Well, at first everyone was enthusiastic, but in the end it kind of unraveled."

"How so?"

"It was harder than expected to change our habits. We made some progress at first, including hanging clothes outside."

"Yes, I noticed – or, at least, for a while."

"Exactly! Drying clothes outside is *complicated.* You have to have a sunny day; you have to do the laundry in the morning; you have to stay home to put it out after washing; and you have to be ready to pull it in if the weather changes, even if still wet. That means lugging wet laundry back downstairs to rehang in the basement or toss in the dryer, which we increasingly did.

"Couldn't you delegate the hanging and removal of clothes to the kids?"

"We tried. But they were unreliable unless we nagged them. And that's just the half of it. Pretty soon they were forgetting to turn off lights in unused rooms and switch off the power bars. What started out as a fun family challenge broke down into increased bickering between the kids about who was to blame for failures."

"And the results?"

"Not great. There are just too many other things to think about. It's like regularly flossing your teeth. Over time, good intentions dissipate."

"Weren't you also going to switch to more efficient appliances? That's supposed to be the easier way to save energy since it only depends on a one-time decision rather than constant behavioral monitoring."

"But how many of these decisions do you make in six months, let alone six years? All our major appliances are less than five years old."

"There was nothing you could replace?"

"Actually, we did make one new acquisition. Dave and the kids were at the mall when they stumbled on an "unbelievable" sale of wide-screen plasma TVs. After they brought it home, we realized it uses eight times the power of our previous TV!"

"Ouch."

"It gets worse. For our anniversary, my mother bought us a new device for the kitchen counter. It's a digital picture frame which continuously scrolls through illuminated photos of my parents, us, and the kids. Since my mother drops by unexpectedly, I can't risk unplugging it during the day, although I try to remember at bedtime."

"What about lighting? Conventional light bulbs don't last more than a year or two. And because they're cheap you can replace even the ones that are still functioning."

"We did switch several. But even that wasn't as easy as the college kids said it would be. In some light fixtures, the new lights looked ugly, although it took us some time to admit this. That meant an extra trip to the store to return them. And some of the new lights don't give the warm glow we're used to, so we brought them back too. Some bulbs, which one store refused to take back, now sit in a drawer. I guess our efficient lights save electricity, but what value do you put on all the time we killed learning what worked for us?"

* * *

I didn't tell Ming that her stories rekindled memories of my pioneering experiences 30 years earlier as one of the first adopter of efficient lights. A new professor and homeowner, obsessed with energy efficiency since my teens, I dazzled my grad students and wife with calculations of the monetary and environmental benefits of energy efficiency, with lighting as the example.

Back then, the efficient bulbs were compact fluorescents. At $20 to $30 each, they presented a serious financial commitment. But I had done my homework. While my wife's interest in my calculations quickly faded, tuning out was not an option for my captive grad students. My numbers showed that though an efficient light bulb would cost 10 to 20 times more than an inefficient incandescent bulb, this extra investment would eventually be compensated by the annual savings from buying less electricity. But how much less electricity depended on how long the lights were illuminated. They needed to be lit an average of three hours a day over the year to earn sufficient bill savings to compensate for the higher cost. Only a few lights in high use areas of the house reached the profitability threshold of averaging three hours a day. My wife cheekily offered to leave lights on in empty rooms to improve my benefit-cost calculation.

I remember the day in 1988 when I brought home my first efficient lights. I and my students had calculated that my $160 investment in eight of these for the highest use fixtures would achieve payback in the ninth year from electricity bill savings, just in time, since their rated life expectancy was 10 years. But on arriving home, I opened the end of one package before realizing that earlier in the store, to view my treasure, I had opened the other end.

After sweeping up $20-worth of broken glass, I dutifully re-calculated my payback, this time incorporating the bulb's untimely demise. As feared, to recover the initial investment, all remaining light bulbs now needed to survive twelve years. Chastened, but undeterred, I installed the surviving bulbs, neglecting to mention the mishap to my devoted students, or my wife.

Eventually I realized that what had first seemed like a hiccup on the path to profitable energy efficiency was symptomatic. My initial calculations failed to include the standard risk of which any sound investor, indeed any prudent householder, is all too aware: the greater likelihood of premature failure with new technologies, and the greater financial risks of higher-cost technologies.

Research shows that new technologies typically experience a higher failure rate than tried-and-true technologies, and this was no different with efficient light bulbs. Within a year, two new lights inexplicably stopped working, one turning an ominous dark shade in its final days. And my calculations didn't include the probability of accidental breakage, in spite of my traumatic first day. This error became obvious when, near the end of the second year, my rambunctious kids and our dog toppled two lamps in a birthday bash. Breaking two $20 bulbs is different than breaking two $1 bulbs, which explains why people instinctively gravitate to devices with lower up-front costs, even if these have higher operating costs.

It was during this period that another problem emerged. I returned from an energy efficiency conference to find that two of my cherished lights had disappeared. My wife sheepishly confessed to removing them during my absences. She needed respite, however briefly, from the "night-of-the-living-dead ambiance they gave to the living room." On this occasion, she had forgotten to re-install them before my return.

Finally, the light switched on – the one inside my academic head – and my students and I began to probe the literature. As it turns out, there is an extensive technical literature assessing the failure rates of new equipment and devices. New technologies have a higher failure rate, making them riskier. There is also a business literature assessing how consumers and corporations value new products and equipment that may differ in the quality of service they provide (like lights with a different hue). New technologies are rarely perfect substitutes for conventional ones.

Some researchers combine these factors to estimate the full financial and intangible costs of new energy-efficient technologies. Since these technologies are rarely perfect substitutes, and since their newness and high cost make them riskier, my initial calculation failed to tell the full story about the likely profitability of energy efficiency investments. Many consumers and firms instinctively suspect this problem, hence their wariness of claims by energy efficiency advocates.

The compact fluorescent lights are today much cheaper and more dependable than 25 years ago when I was an early adopter. That's because they're no longer new. After almost three decades of trial-and-error by manufacturers and consumers, it's easier to convince people to buy them, especially since their price has fallen 80% and their reliability and hue are much improved. Today, though, compact fluorescents are being overshadowed by highly efficient LED lights. Now it's this technology that faces concerns about long-term performance, attractiveness, and the economic value of its higher up-front cost, especially if installed in low-use fixtures or where there is risk of accidental breakage. Healthy consumer skepticism remains a challenge for new energy-efficient technologies.

In a cruel irony, some students visiting my house castigated me for still having some compact fluorescent lights instead of LEDs, the latter being more efficient and higher quality. They were a bit more understanding when I pointed out that I was still trying to recoup some of the losses from my initial foray into home energy efficiency.

As for Ming, her family reduced their electricity use 5%, far short of the 15% needed to win the $100 incentive. She has not checked if their consumption increased afterwards. Like most ratepayers, she only looks at the dollar amounts of her monthly bills, if at all. But the experience cured her of the notion that energy efficiency is easy and profitable.

* * *

Governments and utilities have promoted energy savings for more than three decades. They've done it with advertising, labeling, contests, promotions, and subsidies. A dominant narrative is that saving energy is the first step in deep decarbonization because we reduce emissions *and* make money. It's the "low-hanging fruit."

In 2011, then US Secretary of Energy, Stephen Chu, said, "For the next few decades, energy efficiency is one of the lowest cost options for reducing US carbon emissions."[1] In 2012, Exxon Mobil's website stated, "Energy efficiency is one of the largest and lowest cost ways to extend our world's energy supplies and reduce greenhouse gas emissions."[2]

Statements such as these were reinforced by widely circulated studies of the McKinsey management-consulting firm.[3] These estimated the potential for profitable energy savings and reduced carbon pollution throughout the US, using the same simplistic method with which I had calculated my expected profits from switching to efficient lights. In other words, their studies ignored the hidden risks and costs of untried technologies that require long payback periods and consumer acceptance. McKinsey concluded that the US could reduce energy use 45%, which would also reduce GHG emissions 30%, and all of this at a profit.

With reports like these, it's no wonder that politicians and opinion leaders claim that reducing carbon pollution is easy and profitable because saving energy is easy and profitable. But what happens when we enrich the analysis of McKinsey with real-world evidence about the hidden costs and risks that Ming and I discovered? In Chapter 5, I described how the Energy Modeling Forum at Stanford University conducts collaborative studies in which multiple teams of researchers address the same set of energy-related questions. In its EMF 25 study, completed in 2011, all research teams estimated the US energy efficiency potential based on technology and cost.

In our contribution to EMF 25, my grad student at the time, Rose Murphy, used our US model to produce two scenarios.[4] One scenario reproduced the McKinsey results by assuming that newer, higher-cost efficient technologies were perfect substitutes with no additional risks. The other scenario accounted for the hidden costs and risks estimated in the research literature and incorporated them in the parameters of our US model. Like all the other EMF 25 modelers, our results indicated a dramatically smaller potential for profitable energy efficiency.

This is where things stand today. On one side, energy efficiency advocates, sometimes supported by high-profile consultants, argue that saving energy is cheap and easy. On the other, most independent researchers, like those assembled by the Energy Modeling Forum, find evidence contradicting the claims of a large potential for profitable energy saving. But politicians and other opinion leaders are more attracted to the former than the latter, for obvious reasons. It is easier to argue that saving energy offers a win-win path to reducing carbon pollution.

This inaccurate view of energy efficiency's profitability might seem harmless. But it isn't if it could inadvertently delay the carbon pricing and regulations that should have been implemented decades ago. Its advocates need to vigorously champion these compulsory policies if they are to avoid inadvertently assisting the opponents of deep decarbonization. A brief history of energy efficiency explains this point.

The two decades prior to 1970 were heady times for energy companies, as energy demand and economies grew in lock-step. Energy supplies were plentiful, corporate profits strong, and no one worried about wasting energy. But the oil price spikes in 1973 and 1979 alerted people to the possibility of a different future, one in which sudden and perhaps sustained energy price increases could become the norm. Wasting energy might no longer be okay. That's when a physicist named Amory Lovins published the book, *Soft Energy Paths*, in which he popularized the method of calculating energy efficiency benefits that I later used for my light bulbs and McKinsey for its studies.[5] With this method, he estimated that the US could profitably reduce its electricity use by a whopping 75%. (He coined the term 'negawatts' to describe the reductions in demand due to energy efficiency.) This means that investments in more efficient energy-using devices in industry, buildings, and transportation would make profits and obviate the need for three quarters of the stock of US electricity plants, oil refineries, and so on.

His case for the benefits of energy efficiency gained prominence thanks to a string of exceptional events around 1980. When President Ronald Reagan chose to fight inflation with tight monetary policy, interest rates rose to unprecedented levels, deepening what was already an economic recession. This happened just as many US utilities had built up massive debt to fund new nuclear plants. With electricity demand suddenly stagnant, the new plants would not have enough sales and therefore revenue to cover debt payments. Regulators allowed utilities to raise tariffs to make these payments, but the rate increases caused the electricity demand to fall even further, erasing the need for many of the plants. Pundits labeled this cycle of rising tariffs and falling demand a "utility death spiral." The resulting fleet of idle and unfinished nuclear plants, plus widespread utility bond defaults, taught investors that the electricity market can be risky.

With demand no longer predictable, electric utilities warmed to the idea of managing electricity demand to reduce financial risk. This new focus transformed Lovins from an anti-growth pariah to an industry savior. At conferences and in corporate boardrooms he explained how utilities could stabilize their balance sheets and reduce risk with energy efficiency programs. Thus, through the 1980s and 90s, US electric utilities pursued energy-saving programs like the one offered to Ming, a combination of enticing information and monetary inducements.

I played a small role in this process, serving from 1992 to 1997 as Chair of the British Columbia Utilities Commission. Working in parallel with states like New York and California, we ordered our electric and gas utilities to prioritize energy efficiency, mandating millions of dollars in information programs and subsidies to consumers and businesses to acquire high-efficiency equipment. Eventually the evidence, which I described in Chapter 9, convinced me that these subsidies had little effect on energy demand. And the experience of leading a quasi-judicial institution, involving evidence, testimony, and cross-examination, opened my eyes to how people fixate on the evidence that supports their interests and desires, and ignore the counter-evidence.

The slower growth of North American electricity demand seemed to vindicate the energy-saving programs. But economists noted that electricity prices also rose during this time, and higher prices motivate savings. Skeptics also noted that the structure of the US economy changed, with more energy-intensive industries moving offshore, reducing electricity demand. Demand also fell because of more stringent efficiency regulations. Consumers and industry had to buy more efficient models, regardless of whether that increased efficiency was profitable.

Interest in energy efficiency faded in the late 1990s and early 2000s, as energy prices moderated and utilities focused on deregulation of electricity markets. But rising oil prices after 2000, in conjunction with concerns about global warming, rekindled interest in saving energy. And because efficiency advocates again promise profits while reducing carbon emissions, energy efficiency is often portrayed as the first step in climate-energy success.

* * *

Even if much evidence contradicts the belief in energy efficiency's profitability, presumably the evidence at least confirms that energy efficiency reduces energy demand. Not so fast. Humans use energy to get things they value, starting with the increased security and comfort our cave-dwelling ancestors enjoyed thanks to their mastery of fire. Today, that use of energy can be direct, when we burn wood in caves or gasoline in cars, and indirect, when firms use energy to provide non-energy goods and services, like a chair or insurance.

Direct and indirect energy use usually rise with income. The richer we are, the more we use energy in airplanes, hot tubs, vacation homes, and so on. The richer we are, the more goods and services we consume, leading to more energy consumption by manufacturers, retailers, internet servers, restaurants, truckers, and so on. With few exceptions, poorer people use less energy because they are constrained by their limited incomes. This relationship is found between richer and poorer citizens within one country, and between richer and poorer countries.

Of course, per capita energy can differ between individuals with the same income, and between countries of similar incomes. One country may use more energy because of low prices thanks to low-cost hydropower or fossil fuels, or because of cold winters that increase space heating needs, or because of a disproportionate share of energy-intensive industries like steel and cement.

Lower energy prices encourage greater energy use. But even with stable energy prices, the acquisition of a more efficient device will decrease operating cost. A more efficient car decreases the fuel costs for driving a given distance, which may increase the willingness to commute further or take a long-distance trip with the family.

In other words, the reduction in energy costs resulting from an efficiency improvement may induce increased demand for a given energy service, such as the number of miles driven each year, even *without* a decrease in the price of energy. Energy analysts call this feedback the 'rebound effect.' Thus, while a more efficient car should have reduced annual gasoline consumption by say 400 liters (100 gallons), because of the rebound effect the net reduction might be only 300 liters.

Analysts on all sides of the issue generally agree that the rebound effect for most direct energy uses is modest. Even a significantly more efficient car is unlikely to dramatically change someone's driving patterns. Certainly, for energy services like cooking, home heating, hot water, and lighting, the lower operating costs due to efficiency are unlikely to cause major increases in demand. Acquiring a more energy-efficient stove won't motivate me to cook more at home.

However, at an aggregate level, the energy rebound effect is likely significant.[6] Economists have long noted that as the cost of an input to the economy falls, humans innovate new ways to use more of it. The input could be energy, skilled and unskilled workers, or material resources like wood, minerals, and water. If the cost of the input falls relative to the value it can produce, then the economy in aggregate uses more. This is sometimes called the 'productivity rebound.'

William Stanley Jevons first explained this concept in his 1865 book, *The Coal Question.* He claimed that England should not bank on efficiency improvements in coal boilers and steam engines to spare it from depleting its domestic coal supplies.

> It is wholly a confusion of ideas to suppose that the economical use of fuel is equivalent to a diminished consumption. The very contrary is the truth ... Every improvement of the engine, when effected, does but accelerate anew the consumption of coal.[7]

Our historical demand for lighting provides an example of what is today referred to as 'Jevons' paradox.' In a 2006 paper, Roger Fouquet and Peter Pearson tracked the evolution of lighting in the United Kingdom from 1800 to 2000, a period during which the population grew five-fold and GDP fifteen-fold.[8] While this growth in people and economic output would certainly increase the use of lighting, it alone can hardly explain the astounding 6,500 times increase. The more obvious explanation is that over the same period the cost of lighting plummeted to 1/3,000th its earlier level, as measured in $ per lumen. (Lumen is the lighting measure displayed on today's light packages; an older term is candlepower.) While some of this cost decrease resulted from lower energy prices, it was driven by dramatic improvements in the efficiency of lighting, as technologies evolved from the almost complete reliance on candles to oil lamps in the early 1800s, to gas lamps in the late 1800s, and to electric lights in the 1900s. As Jevons would have predicted, tremendous improvements in the productivity of lighting greatly contributed to a decrease in cost of use, and an explosion in demand.

If we compare the uses of artificial lighting today to those of 1800, we begin to understand the scope of the productivity rebound. Two hundred years ago, artificial lighting was expensive and so there was little of it. All but the very richest households had to carefully husband their candles, mostly relying on light from the fire as they gathered near the hearth. As the cost of lighting services fell, people increased their use of lighting for traditional purposes, mainly interior illumination in the evening, while also developing a multiplicity of new lighting services: security, decoration, safety, entertainment, and information among others. The aggregate effect was a huge increase in energy used for lighting in spite of, or more likely because of, an equally huge increase in energy productivity. At the end of the day, these gains in lighting efficiency did not lead to reduced energy use for lighting. As Thomas Edison said about his cost-reducing innovations, "We will make electric lighting so cheap that only the rich will burn candles."[9]

Refrigeration has seen a similar productivity rebound. Half a century ago, domestic fridges were small, extremely inefficient devices by today's standards. Again, rising incomes and falling energy costs were key in the widespread adoption of this appliance by all households in wealthier countries. At the same time, cooling devices became significantly more efficient, with a dramatic reduction in operating costs. The result? An explosion of demand for all manner of cooling services and devices. A suburban house in North America today could well have air conditioning, a large fridge, a freezer, a water-cooler, a wine and beer cooler, and a desk-top fridge. The family might also have a portable electric cooler for travel.

And this is just at the level of direct energy use. Refrigeration now provides an abundance of once-unimaginable goods and services. Food stores have extensive frozen and cooled food and drinks, often stored in coolers without doors to seal them from the heated interior of the store. Frozen and fresh food is transported long distances in refrigerated trains, trucks, boats, and planes, a non-existent service 50 years ago. Moreover, the amount of refrigerated food that we eventually waste has grown significantly – by some accounts we now discard 40% of the food that at some point was frozen or maintained at a cool temperature. Hotels and motels have small fridges in each room, often running with nothing in them, or cooling beverages that no one uses.

In addition to food, refrigeration devices now provide other services, as Ming pointed out at a neighborhood barbecue.

"I sometimes wish I had never entered that energy contest."

"How's that?"

"I didn't save much energy, but I sure notice things now."

"Like what?"

"Take my local gym. In the past, my work-out was thirty minutes on the treadmill, listening to my iPod. I decompress as my thoughts drift with the music. Lately, instead of relaxing, I notice all the crazy ways the gym uses energy, especially all the new devices. They've got water coolers everywhere, which is pretty bizarre since our tap water is cold. Also, they keep getting more treadmills, exercise bikes and ellipticals. People used to jog or lift weights for a workout. Now, these plugged-in machines are running exercise programs, heart monitors, timers, music, TV. They could be self-powering if they tapped into the energy of the exerciser – like those old mini-generators on bikes that used the spinning wheel to power the light."

"Now you're talking."

"Last year they installed a small TV monitor on every jogging and cycling machine. These are on all the time, although no one seems to be watching. Like me, everyone just listens to their iPod. And now they have a fan in front of every machine. Everyone turns these on, but no one turns them off. Some days I've seen all twenty fans whirring away, with only me

"And now we can monitor all our energy savings on our new 70-inch flatscreen TV."

Figure 10.1 Cartoon by Jacob Fox

on a machine. You should see the looks I get as I turn them all off. I'm starting to feel obsessed about this energy waste."

"Careful. Soon they'll be coming for you."

"There's more. They just installed six mini-fridges in the work-out room. Three of these are for drinks, so the fridge door is constantly being opened and closed. And three are for – wait for it – cooling your towel while you exercise. I'm not making this up."

"Did you speak to the manager?"

"I did! He gave me a speech about how they compete with other gyms, and these things are worth the cost. When I asked for proof, he gave me a weird look and made some excuse to get away. I wish I'd never entered that damn energy contest!"

Fearing I might fan the flames, I didn't dare tell Ming Ed Begley Jr.'s story about a typical member of his local gym. "There's this guy who drives his BMW 10 or 15 miles to the gymnasium. He walks inside, and what does he do? He gets on a bicycle and pedals, going *nowhere*. And what do we do with that energy? *Nothing*."[10]

* * *

Former US Environmental Protection Agency Administrator Lisa Jackson reflected a common view when she said, "We're showing people across the country how energy efficiency can be part of what they do every day ... confronting climate change, saving money on our utility bills, and reducing our use of heavily-polluting energy can be as easy as making a few small changes."[11] Yet the evidence of the last two decades has shown that energy efficiency is rarely cheap, involves much more than a few small changes, and can actually increase overall energy use. Why, then, do so many opinion leaders still argue that energy saving is key to our climate challenge? Why do politicians, environmentalists, and corporate heads say it? And why are physicists and engineers such ardent efficiency promoters?

As it turns out, each of these groups has its own motives for claiming that conservation and energy efficiency are critical. By their training, physicists and engineers are sensitized to the fact that humans could use much less energy to attain a given amount of goods and services. Physicists know how little energy is required to heat a room or transport someone from point A to point B. Engineers know about technologies that are far more efficient than the equipment people typically acquire.

But neither of these professions have expertise in human behavior, and therefore on the hidden costs and risks that economists find in any prospective investment, or on the feedback effects that drive increased use as energy costs decline. Time and again, narrowly focused studies of energy-saving potential are produced by physicists and engineers, always concluding that energy savings are profitable, always ignoring evidence from economists, behavioral psychologists, and market experts about the hidden costs, risks, and rebounds.

But what about other key players? Why do environmentalists embrace the idea that saving energy is cheap and easy?

A key factor is the wishful thinking bias that I described in earlier chapters. Those concerned about environmental threats are especially conscious of the wastefulness of human economies that I described in Chapter 7. They see that energy efficiency and conservation will reduce wastes and help transition to a less harmful economy. Unfortunately, when we hope for such changes we are susceptible to the seductive argument that reducing waste is win-win because of its profitability. If correct, this might increase our chance of motivating fellow citizens to act. Telling someone they can make money while saving the world is a lot easier than telling them they must spend money to save the world.

What about industrial leaders? Why do they parrot the call for energy efficiency as the leading climate strategy? Perhaps you can guess. The clamor of physicists, engineers, and environmentalists for a greater effort on energy efficiency lets polluting corporations off the hook. It delays the day when governments finally acknowledge that we must apply regulations or carbon pricing to quickly phase out the burning of fossil fuels. When governments finally do this, life gets trickier for corporations. They must navigate an uncertain period of accelerated technological change in which some firms will thrive while others fail. Will most vehicles be electric, biofuel, or hydrogen? How will homes be heated and cooled? What energy will industrial plants use? Corporations struggle already with uncertainties, and many are nervous that climate-energy policies will amplify these.

What about politicians? While some are sincere about climate change, they also need to get re-elected. They instinctively gravitate to beliefs that are politically saleable, like the serendipitous story that saving energy is profitable. If true, there is little need for compulsory policies. Non-compulsory policies, like information programs and a few subsidies, sound awfully attractive when your goal is re-election in four years.

While we might feel cynical about the energy efficiency jingoism of some political and corporate leaders, especially if these same people are not aggressively pushing for pricing or regulation of GHG emissions, we must recognize that most advocates of energy efficiency also want effective climate-energy policies. And although the evidence may not support their belief in the widescale profitability of energy efficiency, it does support their view that reducing our energy consumption will reduce not just GHG emissions, but also other negative impacts from the production and use of energy. By reducing the size of the energy system, energy efficiency provides multiple benefits.

The global demand for energy grew 12-fold in the last century. With over a billion people still having restricted or no access to electricity and modern fuels, and the global population slated to reach 9 or 10 billion by mid-century, the global demand for energy will grow. Even if people in wealthier countries dramatically cut their energy use, the global use of energy will grow significantly to better the lives of people in the developing world. If much of that energy is provided by the burning of fossil fuels, without carbon capture, GHG emissions will grow.

The only viable strategy is to push hard for a rapid transition to zero-emission energy. But the best chance for this transition is if energy efficiency is rapidly improving at the same time. If accelerated gains in energy efficiency can reduce by 10% or even 20% the size of the global energy system from what it otherwise would be, this improves our chances with the decarbonization task. But this efficiency improvement, to be sustained and substantial, needs rising energy prices. Compulsory decarbonization policies, even if flex-regs rather than carbon taxes, will increase the cost of energy, which improves the prospects for energy efficiency. But to push for energy efficiency first is to put the cart before the horse.

As summarized in the text box, claims for the profitability and ease of energy efficiency can inadvertently help those who oppose effective action on climate by giving climate-insincere politicians an argument for weak or no decarbonization policies. If energy efficiency advocates instead integrate their pursuit of efficiency with the campaign for stringent regulation or pricing of GHG emissions, they improve the prospects for both energy efficiency and success with the climate-energy challenge.

Deep decarbonization requires policies that price carbon or regulate technologies.

These compulsory policies will cause fuel switching to low-emission energy and dramatic improvements in energy efficiency.

The wishful thinking claim that energy efficiency is profitable undermines the argument for compulsory decarbonization policies, because insincere or reluctant politicians can argue energy efficiency will happen from market forces without needing climate policy.

Energy efficiency advocates help the planet and their cause by focusing their policy campaigns on compulsory decarbonization policies.

CHAPTER 11

Renewables Have Won

What a man believes on grossly insufficient evidence is an index into his desires – desires of which he himself is often unconscious.

Bertrand Russell

RECENTLY, I HAD A THREE-WAY CONVERSATION WITH a leading environmentalist and a cabinet minister. For me, it was *déjà vu*. Almost 20 years ago I had the same conversation with a different leading environmentalist and a different cabinet minister.

Politician: "At the next cabinet meeting we'll be discussing policies to advance clean energy. This is a rare opportunity and I don't want to mess up. What arguments should I make for a stronger renewable energy policy?"

Environmentalist: "Point out that renewables are already cheaper than fossil fuels and attracting more investment, so pushing renewables has no cost for the economy."

Me: "Did you say renewables are cheaper than fossil fuels? If true, why should government do anything? If renewables have won the economic competition, then government can take credit for falling GHG emissions without lifting a finger."

Politician (with a smile): "Exactly my thoughts as I heard that."

Environmentalist: "Well, it's true. Renewables are the cheapest option. But subsidies to fossil fuels are unfair. If we get rid of these, we'll accelerate the transition to zero-emission energy. Argue this to cabinet."

Me: "Good luck. I don't think you'll get far trying to eliminate subsidies. They're difficult to determine, and many economists dispute what some people call subsidies. But I guarantee that the cabinet will fix on your argument that renewables have won. This justifies its delay of politically difficult decarbonization policies. If you want renewables to rapidly replace fossil fuels, you need cabinet to implement more stringent pricing or regulatory policies, and you need them to do that now."

The conversation dragged on, but you get the point. Statements by renewables advocates and environmentalists that renewables are now cheaper than fossil fuels sound encouraging. But if they let politicians off the hook from enacting stringent climate policy, then they inadvertently slow the energy transformation. We can't afford that.

Stories about the economic victory of renewables are decades old. With hindsight, we know with certainty that the earlier claims, like the one I encountered 20 years ago, were overly optimistic. Today, some renewables are much cheaper, with falling costs and a promising growth rate. But often that growth is because of compulsory government policies that require a growing market share for renewable electricity (the renewable portfolio standard), provide a subsidy (feed-in tariffs and tax credits), or require minimum blending of ethanol and biodiesel into conventional gasoline and diesel (biofuel mandates). If we inadvertently convince politicians they don't need strong policies to reduce the burning of fossil fuels, we contribute to the continued failure against the climate threat. Politicians need a push because, as I explained in Chapter 6, all effective climate policy is politically difficult.

For an academic, I have had my share of experiences in the policymaking arena, including the occasional direct window into cabinet decision-making. Cabinet members (or secretaries in the US) are like most of us – sincere, wanting to do right. But to survive in the rough and tumble world of politics, they must have sensitive antennae for anticipating and avoiding policy decisions that cause a strong negative reaction from some quarters. When such opposition appears, or can be foreseen, the cabinet conversations are intense, but decisions may be evasive.

One raconteur of cabinet decision-making is Pat Carney, Canada's former energy minister in the 1980s Conservative government. Between my undergrad degree and the start of my masters, I worked for the small economic consulting firm she ran before entering politics. We became friends. Years later, when I was a professor and she no longer in parliament, although still an appointed member of Canada's Senate, she gave annual guest seminars in my graduate energy course. To the students' bewilderment, her only required advance reading was a chapter from the book version of the British TV sitcom, *Yes Minister*.[1] In one memorable passage, the deputy minister explains to the inexperienced junior advisor how to discourage their cabinet minister from pursuing a particular policy. What they should say is, "Bravo Minister. You are *very* courageous to pursue that policy." Then wait a few days.

The policies that are essential to transform our energy system are not politically easy. They require leadership. Politicians who sincerely want to contribute need to be told this inconvenient truth, and guided to policies that have a lower political cost per ton reduced, as I described in Chapter 6. Otherwise, they will delay, waiting for renewables to outcompete fossil fuels.

* * *

I am frequently asked by non-experts why they never hear about how to transform our energy system to prevent climate change. People are shocked at my response: energy analysts have publicly reported on this transformation with great fanfare since the 1980s. Of course, in the daily deluge of news, why would they remember this particular topic?

It was the so-called oil crisis of the 1970s that launched the field of 'energy system transformation.' The first major studies explored how humanity might wean itself from fossil fuels, given the widespread concern about imminent oil scarcity. At the time, several major institutions touted nuclear power as the obvious replacement for diminishing fossil fuels. But an alternative, renewables-focused future was sketched by some researchers, notably Amory Lovins of energy efficiency fame, as I explained in the previous chapter.

In Chapter 3 I noted that the highest-profile studies into transforming the global energy system are the assessment reports of the Intergovernmental Panel on Climate Change (IPCC), with its five comprehensive assessments since 1990.[2] In these reports, energy-modeling teams explore multiple paths for achieving dramatic GHG emissions reductions over several decades. Each path has a different contribution from the major GHG-reducing options: energy efficiency, nuclear power, renewables, land-use change, and carbon capture and storage when using fossil fuels or extracting CO_2 directly from the air. When these multiple paths are combined with a range of assumptions on population and economic growth, global income equity, and key technological uncertainties, the graphed results looked like a downward sloping mass of intertwined spaghetti.

These studies produce a consistent takeaway message. First, we need several decades to fully transform the energy system for significant GHG reductions. Second, this can occur without major technological innovations, although cost-reducing innovations will continue as commercialized technologies increase market share. Third, the cost is manageable if we prioritize the lowest cost options and transform the energy system at a pace that reflects the replacement rate of electricity plants, industrial plants, vehicles, and buildings. This is the consensus view from assessments prepared by experts crafting a compromise summary of the leading evidence. Outside of these collaborative assessments, there are of course some disagreements among individual researchers.

The prolific energy writer Vaclav Smil is known for emphasizing the inertia of energy systems, hence the long time required for system transformation. In the 2017 edition of his book, *Energy Transitions*, he takes aim at researchers and studies that in his view are too optimistic about the possible rate of change.[3] He argues that changing an energy system depends on multiple interrelated developments, each with its own countervailing inertia. A wholesale switch to electric cars requires more than just innovating long-lived batteries and convincing people to buy this unfamiliar device, which in itself takes time. It also requires growth of zero-emission electricity generation to power the cars, installation of a network of domestic and public rechargers, reinforcement of the electricity grid and building electrical systems to handle the higher load, and development of widespread expertise in electric vehicle maintenance and repair.

Smil and most other system researchers note that the feasibility and cost of energy system transformation is lower if we are open to the widest possible set of GHG-reducing options. Examples of major studies supporting this claim are the 2012 *Global Energy Assessment*, in which I participated, and the 2015 *Deep Decarbonization Pathways Project*.[4]

People who believe renewable energy is the only decarbonization option worth pursuing (alongside energy efficiency of course) follow the research of Mark Jacobson of Stanford University. In recent studies, he argues that humanity can switch quickly and completely to a sub-set of our renewable energy options without any effect on GDP.[5] He claims that a transition to 100% renewables will not increase the cost of electricity, home heating, industrial production, and mobility of people and goods. Moreover, he claims that this can be achieved while meeting the rapidly growing demand for energy services by people in the developing world. And, all of this while restricting the renewables options to wind, water, and solar – the 'WWS path.'

In support of this scenario, Jacobson highlights the dramatic decreases in the cost of electricity from wind and solar. Figure 11.1 shows that the average price of electricity from wind in the US fell from 6 cents per kilowatt-hour in 2010 to 2 cents in 2017, while photovoltaic electricity fell from 14 cents to 4 cents. This is a truly remarkable development, especially considering all of the speeches I've heard over the years from entrenched fossil fuel defenders, who confidently predicted that the cost of renewables would never decline.

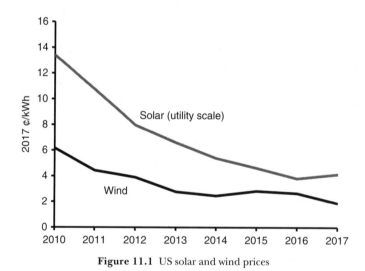

Figure 11.1 US solar and wind prices

Jacobson's water, wind, and solar scenario deserves serious consideration. But, as with the earlier work of Lovins, his findings have provoked significant criticisms from other researchers who argue that his limited reliance on wind, water, and solar will be much costlier than he claims.[6] Several experts went so far as to publish a 2017 paper in the Proceedings of the National Academy of Sciences which directly critiqued Jacobson's analysis.[7] He responded with a defamation lawsuit against the publisher and authors. But he later dropped it.

To an economist like me, the idea that it will be costlier if we exclude some low-emission options from competing to replace the burning of fossil fuels seems obvious. A decade ago, in *Sustainable Fossil Fuels*, I explored a decarbonization scenario in which renewables gradually came to dominate the global energy system, but some jurisdictions still retained a modest role for nuclear power and others relied on some carbon capture and storage to continue benefiting from their endowment of high-quality fossil fuels.[8] (This is why we must distinguish the high-emission burning of fossil fuels from the near-zero-emission use of fossil fuels when integrated with carbon capture and storage.) If the goal is decarbonization, why spend more than necessary, especially when the developing world can use any money it saves for welfare-improving schools, hospitals, housing, and infrastructure?

* * *

When we look more closely at the "renewables have won" claim, perhaps it is no accident that Lovins is a physicist and Jacobson an engineer. Researchers can agree with them that it is physically and technologically feasible for the global energy system to become 100% renewable. But to most economists, their cost estimates for quickly achieving that 100% renewable future seem tainted by wishful thinking bias. They also seem to downplay the social challenges to fully transforming a global energy system that is currently dominated 80% by fossil fuels, and in which most energy demand growth is occurring in the developing world, as more of the planet's poorer people gain access to electricity and modern fuels produced primarily from fossil fuels.

When we shift from the technological feasibility perspective to economic feasibility, four factors challenge the "renewables have won" paradigm. The first is energy quality. (Physicists have specific terms like 'energy density' and 'power density.') When it comes to energy quality, fossil fuels are amazing. A half cup of gasoline has enough energy to lift a car to the top of the Eiffel Tower. Most renewables, as found in their natural state, don't have nearly that punch. Solar energy reaches the earth at a low power density, measured in watts per square meter. If that energy is converted into electricity using photovoltaic panels, a lot of land and equipment is required. To produce the same amount of electricity as a 1,000 megawatt coal or natural gas plant, a solar facility in a sunny location would require 100 times more land. There is room for reducing the land cost by covering rooftops with solar panels wherever possible. But the amount of investment per unit of energy provided is still usually greater for the solar option because of its lower energy quality.

Growing wood, straw, and grains to produce ethanol, biodiesel, bio-methane, and perhaps bio-jet fuel also requires a lot of land. This leads to concerns that an effort to dramatically increase biofuels requires land that could otherwise grow food crops or sustain biodiversity in forests and grasslands. Researchers like Jacobson are aware of this problem, which is why his renewables scenario focuses on wind, water, and solar. But this means excluding the potential, as demonstrated in Brazil, to produce ethanol from sugar cane as a relatively low-cost substitute for gasoline.[9] While we should not rely on biofuels for wholesale replacement of gasoline and diesel, the use of forestry, agricultural and urban bio-wastes, and some marginal lands to produce an array of biofuels offers low-cost opportunities without major impacts.[10]

Wind, like solar, has a low power density. A lot of land must be covered with wind turbines to produce a significant quantity of electricity. Fortunately, the extra land needed for wind parks can usually be shared with other users, such as cattle grazers and grain growers. To avoid land-use conflicts, large-scale wind parks are increasingly located offshore. But throughout the world there is still an enormous amount of land available for wind turbines.

The second important factor when assessing the cost of scaling up renewables for electricity generation is 'capacity utilization.' (Electrical engineers refer to 'capacity factor.') This is the annual output of a facility compared to the output it could produce if running at full capacity every hour of the year. A coal or natural gas power plant can operate at full output almost all year, shutting down perhaps 5% of the time for maintenance – a 95% capacity utilization rate. In contrast, solar panels don't produce electricity at night. And because sunshine is less direct near dawn and dusk, solar power's optimal capacity utilization doesn't exceed 30–40%, and that only in the sunniest locations.

Wind also has a capacity utilization challenge, in this case because the wind is not always blowing at an optimal speed, and sometimes not at all. Nonetheless, I note that critics who decades ago argued (as I remember clearly) that a wind turbine's capacity utilization could never surpass 25% have been proven wrong. Today, with new turbine designs, the most favorable sites can reach 50%.

Conventional medium- and large-scale hydropower has reservoirs that in many regions can hold enough water to achieve 60% capacity utilization on an annual basis. But constructing more of these plants would entail major environmental impacts, which limits their potential role in a water, wind, and solar future. Smaller hydropower (run-of-river, micro-hydro, pico-hydro), because it lacks substantial reservoirs, is more acceptable. But since such facilities rely on natural stream flows, which in most locations vary seasonally, their capacity utilization rates are usually much lower.

The lower capacity utilization rates of these key renewable electricity sources means that much more capacity must be installed to generate a given amount of electricity. Vaclav Smil has shown that replacing 100,000 megawatts of fossil fuel generating capacity requires 150,000 to 300,000 megawatts of renewable capacity, depending on the mix of renewable sources. When we consider replacing all existing fossil fuel capacity with renewables, plus constructing all the new generating capacity for the growing electricity needs in the developing world, plus constructing all the new capacity needed for electrification of transport, industry, and buildings, the investment and construction per decade is astronomical. And this massive financial outlay is just to generate the extra electricity, before adding the additional financial resources involved in electrifying almost all energy end-uses in industry, transport, and buildings.

The third key factor in estimating the cost of increased renewables is that wind, solar, and small hydro, often the lowest cost renewables, are 'intermittent.' (Electricity operators use the term 'non-dispatchable.')

Electricity generation and consumption must be instantaneously balanced at all times and all places on the grid to avoid brown-outs and black-outs. Natural gas and coal plants are fully dispatchable, meaning that they can produce electricity at full capacity when it is needed and therefore most valuable. For some renewables this can also be true – wood-burning plants, geothermal plants, and large hydropower plants with reservoirs. But solar, wind, and small hydro can only produce electricity when nature cooperates – the sun shines, the wind blows, and precipitation and melting snow cause water to flow. For these non-dispatchable sources to dominate the energy system, they must be integrated with energy storage of some kind. This investment should be considered part of their cost, but when making comparisons with conventional electricity plants, advocates of these forms of energy often forget to include the full costs of storage.

They make this error when they compare electricity-generating options by a single metric – cents per kilowatt-hour (c/kwh). The figure above showed how much the costs of solar and wind have fallen when measured in cents per kilowatt-hour. This is great news. But it is a mistake to compare these costs of non-dispatchable electricity with the costs of electricity from dispatchable sources, and then conclude on this basis that these renewables are economically superior to dispatchable sources like fossil fuels and nuclear.

This is tantamount to comparing the costs of a dispatchable and a non-dispatchable ambulance service. The first is continuously staffed with paramedics. It can respond immediately to all emergency calls. The second has the same number of paramedics, but their work is unscheduled. Sometimes no one is available to respond to an emergency call. This non-dispatchable ambulance service has lower annual costs because the paramedics, being unscheduled, demand less pay since they can come and go as they please. But this non-dispatchable service saves far fewer lives. To focus only on the cost side of the ledger would rightly be seen as lunacy by the people reliant on this emergency service.

To make a valid economic comparison, whether with ambulance service or electricity service, we need to compare the value provided by each option next to its costs. In a 2012 article Paul Joskow compares the full costs and benefits of dispatchable and non-dispatchable electricity sources.[11] He uses the price of electricity in wholesale and retail trading markets to indicate its value at a given time. Like other leading analysts, he finds that dispatchable electricity sources can sometimes be 10 times more valuable than non-dispatchable sources. It depends on how the demand profile in a given jurisdiction (the configuration of peak and off-peak hours) correlates with the production profile of a given non-dispatchable renewable source, and on the relative shares of dispatchable and non-dispatchable sources. In brief, we cannot conclude that wind, water, and solar are economically superior to fossil fuels for generating electricity based solely on their relative costs per kilowatt-hour. Our comparison must include the value of their production or the cost of adding backup storage so that their output is dispatchable.

When we do include storage costs with wind and solar, the cost per kilowatt-hour is higher. In addition to batteries, energy can be stored as natural gas (to provide reliable backup from a gas-fired turbine), as compressed air, or as solid biomass, biomethane, or hydrogen. This storage adds to the cost per kilowatt-hour, but in most jurisdictions, electricity prices will increase less than 1% per year over the next two decades as GHG emissions fall, thanks to a rapidly growing output from renewables.

The fourth important factor when assessing the cost of scaling up renewables is to recognize that the prices of resources like fossil fuels are subject to feedback effects. (Economists refer to 'market dynamics' or 'general equilibrium responses.') I notice that renewables advocates often assume that fossil fuel prices will stay the same or rise, but won't fall. This makes it plausible for them to *predict* the year when the falling cost of renewables, as depicted in Figure 11.1, descends below the costs of using fossil fuels, and hence the time when renewables win.

But as I explained in Chapters 5, 6, and 7, an understanding of how markets work leads to a different assumption. Like the prices of other commodities, fossil fuel prices rise and fall depending on the interplay of supply and demand, the appearance of cost-changing innovations and discoveries, and shifting consumer and firm preferences. When most people thought we were soon running out of fossil fuels, there was upward pressure on their price. When most people acknowledged that fossil fuels are plentiful, and innovations were lowering their production cost, there was downward pressure on price. At one time, markets were predicting rising coal prices. Today, markets recognize that coal prices will trend downward over the long term. Natural gas prices are historically low and unlikely to rise in the coming decades. Because of the shale gas innovations, there is still a huge amount of gas available at moderate to low costs. And these historically low prices are more likely to fall if humanity reduces its reliance on coal and to a lesser extent natural gas.

While the price of oil has some uncertainty today, when our GHG efforts are mostly ineffective, the price will trend downward if humanity gets serious about reducing GHG emissions. When the global transport industry is shifting away from gasoline and diesel toward electricity, hydrogen, ethanol, and biodiesel, the price of oil will be falling. When demand declines for a product, its price falls as high-cost producers are eliminated. It is easy to imagine the price of oil falling below $20 per barrel when humanity is seriously reducing GHG emissions. But at that low oil price, we won't be seriously reducing GHG emissions without high carbon prices or high stringency regulations. Renewables won't win without these.

These market dynamics should be accounted for by those calculating the costs of switching to renewables. Their analysis should show the prices of coal, oil, and natural gas falling in response to falling demand. Yet, I have not seen this in studies by those who claim that a transition to 100% renewables has little or no cost. Because of these normal market dynamics, the image that fossil fuels will soon be defeated by renewables should be replaced by the slap-stick comedy routine of a clown trying to pick up a ball – accidentally kicking it ahead each time she stoops to grab it. Small progress by renewables in taking market share from fossil fuels leads to lower fossil fuel prices, which frustrates efforts to take more market share.

* * *

While I agree with the criticisms leveled at Lovins, Jacobson, and other renewables advocates that their economic analysis may be biased, I part company with those who argue the analysis is flawed simply because humanity is not following the path they present. For example, I have read works of Smil in which he refers to past visionary studies as long-term energy forecasts, which failed because they got it wrong.[12]

To me, this is to confuse scenarios with forecasts. A forecaster says, "This is my prediction for how the energy system is likely to unfold, given my judgment on the key determining factors." A scenario analyst says, "This is my scenario for how the energy system *could* be transformed, if society takes the necessary actions. This is not a prediction of what will happen, but rather a roadmap for what is feasible *if* society makes the necessary effort."

This distinction is important because past societies have rarely been interested in deliberately transforming their energy systems, and never on a planetary scale. We transitioned from the wood age to the fossil fuel age not by deliberate collective effort, but rather from the self-interested decisions of agents at all levels in society in response to discoveries, inventions, and shifting preferences. As societies industrialized, industries switched from burning wood to using coal-fired steam, then diesel engines, then electric motors because each option was superior to its predecessor. People switched from horses to trains, then cars, then planes for mobility, and from wood to fuel oil, then natural gas and electricity for heating buildings. There was no collective intentionality driving these transitions. The new options performed better. Governments neither selected technologies nor restricted environmental impacts, focusing instead on providing the legal and regulatory framework, financial backing, and infrastructure to help powerful economic interests develop these advantageous and profitable new technologies and processes.

Scenarios of what is feasible can play an important role in helping societies change direction. And in today's Anthropocene epoch, in which human actions have global impacts, it is important to develop global scenarios of alternative feasible paths. Certainly, it is important to critique such scenarios if we believe they are unfeasible for technical, economic, social, or political reasons, as Smil often does so convincingly. But I have never heard developers of future energy scenarios claim to be making a prediction. Criticizing their scenarios because society didn't follow the path they provided seems unfair and misleading.

Perhaps I am sensitive to this issue because it parallels some of the criticisms of my 2005 book *Sustainable Fossil Fuels*. In the book, I was careful to explain at length that I was combining prescription and prediction. My *prescription* was that, based on the science and economics, humanity should quickly reduce GHG emissions. This was a normative statement about what humanity *ought* to be doing. My *prediction* was that if society quickly reduced GHGs, carbon capture and storage would be important in regions endowed with quality fossil fuel resources.

In spite of this explanation, a few readers later argued that my "prediction" was incorrect because no region was fully committing to carbon capture and storage. But, as I explained, my prediction was contingent on society following the prescription that we rapidly reduce GHG emissions. I was not forecasting that humans would do this. If anything, I devoted the policy section of the book to explaining why acting on the climate risk is so difficult (as I also explain in Chapters 4, 5, and 6 of this book). To say I was wrong because so little carbon capture and storage happened in the last decade is to confuse my prescription with my prediction. There has not yet been a serious global effort to reduce GHG emissions.

In any case, we should focus on the technical and economic feasibility, and ultimately the social and political feasibility, of the alternative deep decarbonization scenarios. Whether we are talking about the wind, water, and solar scenario of Jacobson or the all-hands-on-deck scenario of other deep decarbonization studies, the issue of technical and economic feasibility is associated with the issue of innovation. How much innovation is required and how does it happen?

* * *

In a TED talk a few years ago, Bill Gates explained why the planet needs a 'technology miracle' to avoid a climate disaster.

> If you gave me only one wish for the next 50 years – I could pick the president, I could pick a new vaccine, or I could pick a technology miracle that provides energy with no CO_2 emissions at half the cost of fossil fuels – this is what I would pick. This is the wish that would have the greatest impact. If we don't get this wish, the lives of the two billion poorest on the planet will be far worse ... When I say a miracle, I don't mean something

impossible. The micro-processor is a miracle. But most miracles don't have a deadline. This is a case where we have to get a miracle in a pretty tight timeline. We need to get to zero emissions by 2050.[13]

What might that miracle look like? Gates short-listed the candidates. Two of these would dramatically lower the cost of electricity from solar energy: a breakthrough innovation in photovoltaic cells; a dramatic cost-reduction in concentrated solar power (parabolic mirrors that reflect sunlight to heat water into steam for generating electricity). Another candidate would link wind power with energy storage to provide cheap, reliable electricity when needed, instead of just when it's windy. Another would be a safe and low-cost design for nuclear power.

For Gates, innovation is not manna from heaven; we *make* our miracles. As Gates said, "What do we need to do? We need to go for more research funding. You would be stunned at the ridiculously low levels of funding on innovative approaches." But while Gates calls for more public and private R&D, he has stepped up to the plate with his own millions, working on a new type of nuclear plant requiring no fuel enrichment, producing no radioactive spent fuel, and generating electricity at a much lower cost than current designs.

The development of a carbon-free energy source cheaper than fossil fuels would indeed be a game-changer. It would drive emissions reduction without needing an international agreement, or to change the minds of climate skeptics. As Gates said, "If you can make it economic and meet the CO_2 constraint, then you can say to the skeptics, 'at least this is saving you money and saving the planet'."

If only more wealthy people were like Bill Gates. He has assessed the great challenges facing humanity, and focused his talent and wealth on developing solutions, while using his personal influence to rally other influential people, educating the public and pressuring governments. In a world where so few influential people seem to care, he tries to make a difference, and he does.

But his focus on innovation returns us to the question of the technical and economic feasibility of our deep decarbonization options. Do we need a carbon-free energy source that is cheaper than fossil fuels? And how big should be our innovation effort?

In an influential 2010 article in *Foreign Policy*, Ted Nordhaus and Michael Shellenberger of the Breakthrough Institute in California argued that, "Solving global warming's technology challenges will require not a single Apollo Program or Manhattan Project, but many." This is required because, "fossil fuels are remarkable sources of energy – cheap, energy dense, and widely available – [that] will not be easily displaced by present-day renewable energy technologies."[14]

Nordhaus and Shellenberger argue that without the kind of massive public commitment to research that occurred under the 1960s Apollo Program to put a man on the moon in just eight years and the 1940s Manhattan Project to build the first nuclear bomb in just three years, policies to price or regulate carbon pollution will not succeed in shifting us to a deep decarbonization path. A massive public R&D effort is essential to addressing the climate threat.

This position of Nordhaus and Shellenberger might be motivational for some people. But it's probably depressing for others like me. Most of us recognize that the climate threat thus far lacks the motivational attributes of the nuclear bomb race against fascist Nazi Germany and the space race against the communist Soviet Union. In World War II, Nazi Germany was an immediate global threat (like an asteroid coming straight at us), as it conquered Europe and invaded Africa and the Soviet Union. Given that many of the world's leading nuclear physicists were still in Germany, the Allies feared it would quickly develop a nuclear bomb. So President Franklin Roosevelt launched the Manhattan Project to build one first. With strong public support for the war, the US government was able to incur massive debt and impose rationing as it marshaled people and resources to defeat Nazi Germany. The top-secret Manhattan Project was quietly funded in this context.

The Apollo Space Program had similar motives. With the US and Soviet Union locked in the Cold War, each threatening the other with nuclear annihilation, the Soviets launched the first rockets into space, shocking America and its NATO allies. Fearing the Soviet Union would achieve nuclear supremacy through its mastery of outer space, President John F. Kennedy launched the Apollo Program – using the moon-shot as a symbol to rally public support for the space race, and its thinly veiled implications for the arms race.

In both cases, a massive public R&D effort was motivated by an immediate, acknowledged national threat. Both Japan and Germany declared war on the US, leaving it no option but to fight a war in which survival required being first to develop a nuclear bomb. The threat was national, and the solution was national. In this context, a public-financed R&D effort to make the nuclear bomb was unquestioned by the country's political leaders. Likewise with the space race. The Soviet Union's suddenly demonstrated lead in rocketry science during the Cold War presented the US with the threat of nuclear annihilation from a missile attack. The threat was national, and the solution was national. The US could act alone in using the moon landing as the symbolic goal for its massive R&D effort in the space race.

The climate change threat is different. By its own actions, the US government cannot win the climate-energy challenge. It needs other countries to help. It can develop cheaper batteries to operate with solar and wind in electricity generation or with electric vehicles in transportation. But Chinese or Indians or Indonesians or Pakistanis might still opt for coal-fired power and gasoline vehicles, as these will remain – in the absence of global pricing or regulatory policies – low-cost energy options, ones whose costs will keep falling as modest innovations free-up more fossil fuel resources.

Fortunately, we don't need a massive R&D program to decarbonize the global energy system. We already have the technologies we need. As we implement the key decarbonization policies I described in Chapter 6, modest innovations will make these options even better. Wood has been used for centuries, hydropower and geothermal for a century, and modern forms of biofuels, wind, and solar for decades. Even electric and biofuel vehicles have been around for decades, as have nuclear power and carbon capture and storage, should we also rely on these.

All of these options provide energy with negligible carbon emissions. All are commercially available today. All play an important role in part of the energy system in at least one jurisdiction. All can be more widely disseminated at moderate cost in virtually all jurisdictions. And while each of these technologies would certainly benefit from more R&D, their widespread deployment doesn't need breakthrough innovation. What they absolutely require, to overcome the high energy quality, widespread availability, and incumbent position of fossil fuels, is the adoption of compulsory policies that either price or regulate GHG emissions or the technologies that cause them.

Such policies have two important effects. First, as noted, they drive the market dissemination of commercially available technologies that would otherwise not occur. If fossil fuels are cheaper – and they usually are – low-emission technologies capture niche markets at best, even though they could play a much larger role if market prices were corrected by a rising carbon price, or if GHG-emitting technologies like coal power plants and gasoline cars were phased out by flex-regs of increasing stringency.

Second, as regulations and carbon pricing cause the wider deployment of these technologies, they also stimulate private R&D, as manufacturers compete with each other to capture market share by finding design efficiencies and innovating small adjustments to technologies that make them more attractive to customers. While public R&D is important when a major technological breakthrough is needed, private R&D tends to be narrowly targeted and more effective once a specific technology is disseminating in a competitive market.

Today, private corporations are putting their R&D money into improving photovoltaic cells, wind turbines, electric vehicles, batteries, and biofuels because these low-GHG options are already established in the market. Government R&D has certainly also played a role in reducing their costs through innovation. But the California vehicle flex-regs were instrumental in stimulating private R&D leading to hybrid, plug-in hybrid, electric, and hydrogen vehicles, along with complementary battery and fuel cell innovations. And the US state renewable electricity flex-regs, along with subsidy and regulatory policies in the US and other countries (tax rebates, feed-in tariffs), played a role in the falling costs of wind and solar, and could do more if their stringency were tightened.

The key point is that a massive public R&D effort on the scale of the Manhattan Project or the Apollo Program is not necessary for rapid decarbonization. Opponents of decarbonization are happy when climate-concerned activists and sincere politicians assume that massive public R&D is essential, as this myth sustains our procrastination on the climate-energy challenge.

* * *

The following examples illustrate cases where government policies caused rapid energy system change and GHG reduction, while relying on commercially available technologies. Although the prime motive wasn't always GHG reduction, that doesn't matter. What matters is that the GHG reduction happened quickly, without waiting for a massive government R&D effort to produce a game-changing innovation. But compulsory policies or direct government action were essential.

From 1950 to 1980, France's CO_2 emissions from electricity generation grew in step with its electricity output. While the country had some hydropower facilities, it mostly produced electricity from coal or oil. Then, in response to the oil crisis of the 1970s, the French government decided to quickly switch its electricity system to nuclear power. Its motives included energy security, but especially a strategic bet that it could become a global leader and major exporter of nuclear power technology.

Figure 11.2 tracks the implications of this policy for CO_2 emissions. (For ease of comparison, I set both electricity generation and CO_2 emissions from electricity generation at 100 in 1975.) Over the period 1980 to 1990, electricity generation grew dramatically as France increased domestic consumption in buildings and industry, while increasing exports to its European neighbors. At the same time, CO_2 emissions from electricity generation fell 80%, thanks to the sequential construction of a series of near-identical nuclear plants.

The French government achieved this rapid energy substitution by directing its state-owned corporation, *Électricité de France*, to switch to nuclear power. Had this been a private utility, the government would have had to mandate the energy substitution. Although the government and the utility funded R&D to help this development, each nuclear plant was similar to the previous, a technology that was well established by the late 1970s.

The French development of nuclear power has a great deal of complexity that I am glossing over. Yes, electricity was a monopoly market.

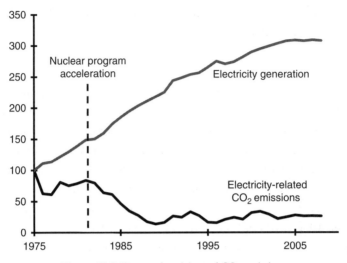

Figure 11.2 France electricity and CO_2 emissions

Yes, the government subsidized the nuclear industry by providing low-interest public loans, assuming all safety-related risks, and taking responsibility for recovering and reprocessing radioactive wastes and spent fuel. But these factors do not detract from the critical point that within just two decades, the French government reduced GHG emissions in its electricity sector by 80% through adoption of existing commercial technology.

My second example is the development of biofuels in Brazil. From 1960 to 1975, Brazil's CO_2 emissions from vehicles increased in step with the growth of vehicle stocks, as in all other countries. But the Brazilian government responded to the 1970s oil crisis by promoting domestic production of ethanol from sugarcane to reduce its oil imports. Figure 11.3 shows that, over the next three decades, vehicle-related CO_2 emissions climbed at less than half the rate of vehicle stocks. (Again, I have converted the values to equal 100 in the same year – 1971.) Today, about 50% of the fuel used by personal vehicles is from ethanol, meaning Brazil's vehicles produce half the fossil fuel-related CO_2 emissions of a country with a similar-sized fleet.

The government achieved this transition using fuel and vehicle mandates, alongside fuel taxes and some financial support for the ethanol industry, all without a major R&D effort and major innovation. (Vehicle

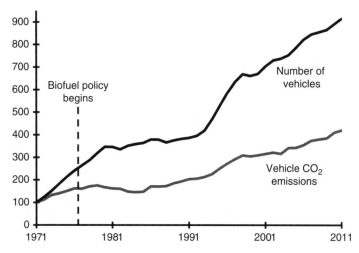

Figure 11.3 Brazil vehicles and CO_2 emissions

manufacturers have known how to run vehicles on biofuels since the introduction of the automobile.) This transition required the conversion of less than 1% of Brazilian arable land with ethanol as a co-product of sugar production for export. As noted in the *Global Energy Assessment*, the Brazilian example provides a model of rapid GHG reduction in transportation for the many tropical and sub-tropical countries with potential to produce sugarcane.[15]

My third example is the phase-out of coal-fired power in the Canadian province of Ontario in the decade 2004–2014. In 2003, coal plants met 25% of Ontario's electricity demand. But over the next decade, the 7,500 megawatts of coal-fired power were replaced by biomass used in a former coal plant, increased output from the province's nuclear plants, expanded small-scale renewables, new natural gas plants, and increased imports of hydropower from the province of Quebec.

The prime motivation for the coal plant phase-out was local air quality. Nitrous oxide emissions from the Ontario electricity sector fell 85% and sulfur dioxide emissions 99%. But GHG emission reduction was also an important objective. Electricity-sector CO_2 emissions fell 85% in just one decade, as Figure 11.4 shows.

This transformation was not costless. Electricity rates increased by about 15% during this period, which created problems for elected

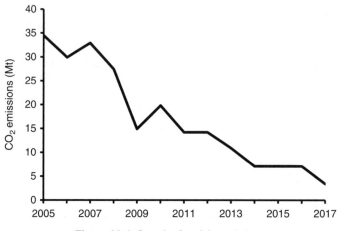

Figure 11.4 Ontario electricity emissions

officials. But some of the price increases were recognized by voters as attributable to the inefficient procurement policy (feed-in tariffs) that paid much more than necessary for solar and wind power and the relatively high management costs of the publicly owned corporation. Again, this significant transformation and rapid GHG reduction happened without waiting for a massive R&D effort to produce a major innovation, nor did it cause astronomical energy prices that are often given as the reason to delay deep decarbonization.

My fourth example is the rapid phase-out of fossil fuel use to heat Swedish buildings in the period 1985 to 2000. Prior to the 1980s, Swedish buildings were mostly heated by oil. About half of the heat was distributed in urban areas by district heating: a network of underground pipes delivering hot water from centrally located boilers, some of which co-generate electricity. The oil crisis of the 1970s triggered a brief switch to coal by many district heat facilities, but by the late 1980s government policy focused on GHG emissions. During the next decade, district heating boilers switched to a diversity of zero-GHG energy sources, including biomass, municipal solid waste, industrial waste heat, electric boilers, electric heat pumps, and geothermal. At the same time, smaller suburban and rural buildings not connected to district heating switched from oil to electricity and biomass. The net effect was an 85% reduction in GHG emissions from Swedish buildings in just 15 years.[16]

The climate-energy challenge was the prime motive for this rapid reduction of GHG emissions in the buildings sector. The government achieved its goal with a combination of new directives to publicly owned electric and district heat utilities, tighter regulations on building efficiency, and higher fossil fuel prices with the introduction of a carbon tax in 1991.[17] The buildings fuel switch was made easier by the fact that Sweden has no fossil fuels itself, but this reality hadn't stopped it previously from importing coal, oil, and some natural gas to heat buildings. The decision to phase out fossil fuels led to slightly higher heating costs, but there was no major innovation, as the fuel switch was achieved with commercially available technologies.

My fifth example is the rapid shift to electric vehicles in Norway since 2012. Although an oil producer, Norway's domestic energy consumption produces little GHGs. Its electricity system is dominated by hydropower, and this electricity is used intensively in buildings and industry. But, as in other countries, personal vehicles mostly use gasoline and diesel. In 2001, however, Norway exempted zero-emission vehicles from its hefty car purchase tax, which can be as high as $20,000, and gradually introduced a suite of other policies including lower road taxes and parking fees, a publicly funded network of vehicle recharging stations, and increases to its carbon tax.[18] From only a small percentage of vehicle sales as recently as 2013, electric and plug-in electric vehicles grew exponentially to 22% of sales in 2015 and 50% in 2018. The government has now committed to 100% of sales by 2025 at the latest.

As I mentioned earlier, the California flex-regs and other policies played a key role in the early development of low- and zero-emission vehicles. Certainly, there was also substantial government-funded R&D. But the regulatory requirements also motivated significant private R&D, such as research by manufacturers like Toyota to develop electric motors and regenerative braking (the Prius) and by Tesla to develop long-range batteries. Of course, one should not attribute the innovations of Tesla solely to government policy. Like Bill Gates, Elon Musk is a visionary who saw where the world needed to go and figured out a winning strategy on that path, that being the development of a luxury, status vehicle to entice high-income purchasers as early adopters. In Norway, compulsory policies did the rest, proving to the world that transportation sector transformation can happen in a decade if we elect sincere governments.

These five examples illustrate that we can change components of our energy systems to rapidly reduce GHG emissions if we have the political will. While the climate-energy challenge was not the prime motivator in the case of Brazilian vehicles and the French and Ontario electricity sectors, it was with Swedish buildings and Norwegian vehicles.

In all cases, government caused the rapid change by applying the compulsory policies I described in Chapter 6 (and sometimes issuing directives to state-owned corporations). These drove the transition from fossil fuel-using technologies to commercially available low-GHG technologies.

In all cases, the policies had an upward effect on the cost of energy services (electricity, heating, vehicle mobility). Had many countries been acting simultaneously in a global effort to rapidly reduce GHG emissions, the prices of coal and oil would have fallen substantially, which is why the pricing of carbon pollution or the regulation of technologies and energy are an essential element of deep decarbonization.

In all cases, the transformation happened without massive public R&D funding on the scale of the Manhattan Project or Apollo Program. While those opposed to quick action on the climate-energy challenge happily repeat the argument that success is impossible without a massive R&D program, the reality is otherwise. The adoption of compulsory policies signals to industry the seriousness of the government's intent, rewarding those firms that invest in R&D to improve existing technologies, and perhaps innovate new ones. Innovation is gradual, driven by emerging challenges as commercial low-emission technologies and energy forms penetrate the market.

As summarized in the text box, the claim that renewables are now cheaper than fossil fuels to provide energy services is inaccurate and potentially counterproductive. Yes, the costs of some renewables have fallen substantially, meaning that deep decarbonization will not greatly increase the cost of energy services. But because the price of fossil fuels will fall in step with GHG reduction, regulations or carbon pricing are essential. Renewables advocates need to ensure that their enthusiasm does not inadvertently slow the rate of deep decarbonization by providing politicians with an excuse to further delay the essential compulsory policies.

Renewable forms of energy can play the lead role in deep decarbonization because they are plentiful and their costs are falling, as are the costs of energy storage.

The lowest cost approach to decarbonization would allow for other low-emission and negative emissions options depending on the jurisdiction – nuclear power, fossil fuels with carbon capture and storage, bioenergy with carbon capture and storage, and direct air capture.

While ongoing cost-reducing innovations with renewables are desirable, they are not an essential pre-condition for decarbonization, as case studies of past, rapid energy transitions have shown.

Regulations and/or carbon pricing are essential for deep decarbonization.

1. It ensures expansion of renewables, which in turn fosters cost-reducing innovations.
2. It ensures that falling fossil fuel prices do not hinder the growth of renewables.

Wishful thinking claims that renewables have won and now outcompete fossil fuels undermine the rationale for regulations and/or carbon pricing, yet these are essential and must be applied with rising stringency.

CHAPTER 12

We Must Abolish Capitalism

What gets us into trouble is not what we don't know, but what we know for sure that just ain't so.

Mark Twain

A FEW YEARS AGO, THE EDITOR OF THE LITERARY REVIEW OF Canada, Bronwyn Drainie, asked me to review Naomi Klein's book *This Changes Everything: Capitalism vs The Climate.*[1] I immediately declined.

My reason for declining had nothing to do with the author or the book. As is often the case, I was overcommitted in my academic duties, which include reviewing research papers submitted to academic journals. Reviewing a non-academic book on energy and climate was of interest, as I am increasingly concerned about how to reach a wider audience with the urgency of climate-energy action – the very purpose of this book. But I knew that thoroughly reviewing Klein's work would require considerable time, and I had none to spare.

However, like many review editors, Bronwyn is tenacious. Soon after I declined, an advanced copy of Klein's book arrived with a note that said, "I know you can't do the review. But please read a few pages and suggest an alternate reviewer with sustainable energy expertise." I should have described Bronwyn as tenacious – *and* clever.

Klein is an engaging writer. She makes it easy for readers to zip through the pages as she mixes personal anecdotes, evidence, and logical argument with cameo appearances by interesting characters. Pretty soon, as I'm sure Bronwyn predicted, I was committed to the book, folding page corners, attaching yellow stickies, taking copious notes. It took only a couple of days to read the book, but much longer to write the review. As is often the case with reviews, I had far more to say than allowed by the 2,500-word limit.

Klein's thesis looks simple. On pages 21–22, she says, "our economic system and our planetary system [are] now at war," and "climate change [is] a battle between capitalism and the planet." This presents humanity with "a stark choice: allow climate disruption to change everything about our world, or change pretty much everything about our economy to avoid that fate."

But these simple statements beg some complicated questions. Why is Klein sure that our only way to prevent climate disruption is to change everything about our economy? And what does it mean to change everything? If we are getting rid of our capitalist economy, what will be its non-capitalist replacement? And how will this change occur?

To address these questions, I devote much of this chapter to recapping my review of Klein's book. I do this because the thesis she presents in her book provides a perfect example of the important point I made at the end of Chapter 6 – that humanity's failure thus far with the climate-energy threat has provided an opportunity for people to attach their agendas to the solution, and in the process render it more complicated and difficult than necessary.

Klein isn't the only person to do this, not by a long shot. And I discuss some of these other agendas at the end of this chapter. But the argument that climate success requires the abolition of capitalism is seductive to some of the same people who accept the climate science and the need for quick action. The fossil fuel industry benefits most when those who recognize the threat fail to coalesce around the most effective and efficient strategy for success.

And while anyone can issue dramatic statements that we must change everything about capitalism, and many people do, it's not so simple to explain what changing *everything* actually means, nor how that would happen in democratic countries where most voters keep demonstrating a strong preference for capitalism relative to its alternatives. After poring carefully over the book, here is my best effort to summarize what Klein wants to see happen, why she claims that abolishing capitalism is our *only* choice, and why I think that pursuing her prescription increases our likelihood of continued failure with the climate-energy challenge.

* * *

Klein argues that because the powerful elites in capitalist countries benefit greatly from our economic system, they are biased to downplay its severe environmental disruptions and its concentration of harm on poor and oppressed people. We are reaching a crisis level because the rampant economic growth under global capitalism intensifies these disruptions, with climate change now the most threatening of all. Yet preventing climate change is impossible under capitalism because this economic system concentrates economic and political power in the hands of the very people who get the benefits but don't pay the costs of its destructive growth. Deep decarbonization must happen quickly, but these people cannot allow this because their power is inextricably tied to the fossil fuel energy system.

The only way for humanity to diverge from this suicidal path is for people concerned for social justice and environmental sustainability to join forces with oppressed and marginalized people in mass activism that uses legal and political means, as well as civil disobedience where necessary, to block construction of new fossil fuel projects – what she calls 'blockadia.' At the same time, cooperatives, aboriginal bands, local governments, farmers, homeowners, and family businesses should develop small-scale renewable energy to replace fossil fuels.

Although Klein repeatedly says we must change everything about the capitalist system, she never actually names the system that would replace it. My best-guess candidate is 'energy-autarkic communalism.' By 'energy-autarkic,' I mean that Klein believes most energy consumed in a given location should be produced near that location, thus freeing communities and regions from dependence on global energy trade dominated by large corporations. Energy autarky is possible because renewable energy in some form is found everywhere on the planet. Some regions might have more sunlight, others more wind, others more capability to sustainably produce bioenergy, and others greater hydropower or geothermal potential. Decentralized, smaller-scale energy production is empowering for local communities and previously oppressed peoples because it enables them to attain greater control over their energy system and its local impacts.

By 'communalism,' I mean that Klein believes most of the renewable energy in a given location should not be produced by global-scale or even national-scale private corporations. Instead, it should be produced by smaller entities that are not driven by the profit motive. Examples include consumer cooperatives, municipally owned utilities, non-profit companies, corporations owned and controlled collectively by aboriginal peoples, community-controlled trusts, and some larger state-owned companies if control is shared between local and higher levels of government. The key benefit of communalism is that critical energy-producing assets would not be owned and managed by powerful, profit-driven corporations, but instead by locally responsive entities focused on serving community interests.

From the energy-autarkic communalism perspective, deep decarbonization strategies that do not entail changing everything about capitalism are doomed to failure. Thus, Klein argues that environmental groups, like the Environmental Defense Fund, are wrong to collaborate with the fossil fuel industry and other corporations in lobbying for market-based climate policies like carbon taxes and cap-and-trade. Likewise, people are fools to believe that Richard Branson, Bill Gates, Elon Musk, and other billionaires can solve the problem by funding technological innovations, like 'biofuel for jet airplanes' and 'safe nuclear power,' or by voluntarily 'greening' their corporations. And we should not expect salvation from geoengineering technologies, like shooting sulfur into the atmosphere to block sunlight, as these are too dangerous.

In essence, any policies that attempt to reduce GHG emissions, like carbon pricing or regulations on technologies and fuels, will not succeed if they do not also change everything about capitalism such that it is no longer capitalism. These policies will not succeed because capitalist elites, the fossil fuel industry, and our current political decision-makers are inseparable.

I can agree with Klein that the fossil fuel industry has far too much influence in our imperfect political processes. But how does Klein convince me and others that her abolish capitalism prescription is essential?

How do we know that abolishing capitalism is not simply her personal preference rather than, as she claims, our *only* choice for succeeding with the climate challenge?

To make her argument, Klein reports on her observations of climate science deniers in the US. After infiltrating some of their meetings, she notes that these people are motivated to deny climate science because they see that reducing GHG emissions will destroy capitalism. They don't want that because they ideologically prefer capitalism, so they deny the GHG threat.

For Klein's purposes, these people have a convenient cognitive duality. On one hand, they are delusional and not at all evidence-based when it comes to climate science. On the other, they are prescient and evidence-based when it comes to their conclusion that deep decarbonization means the end of global capitalism. As you may have suspected, this is where Klein's logic goes awry. She wants readers to believe that these people are delusional when they disagree with her on climate science, but not delusional when they agree with her that deep decarbonization spells the end of capitalism. Klein knows, however, she is on thin ice, so on page 58 she admits, "I am well aware that all of this raises the question of whether I am doing the same thing as the deniers – rejecting possible solutions because they threaten my ideological worldview."

Yes, that is indeed the question it raises. And her response on the next page? "But there are a few important differences to note. First, I am not asking anyone to take my word on the science; I think that all of us should take the word of 97% of climate scientists and their countless peer-reviewed articles . . ."

Agreed. But the question she posed was not whether we should trust her on climate science. It was whether we should trust that her ideological worldview has not biased her reading of evidence when it comes to her conclusion that we *must* abolish capitalism to prevent climate change. Thus, I was expecting something like, "Second, just as I rely on the IPCC's Volume I for the climate science, I rely on its Volume III, with its summary of evidence on the technological, economic and policy dimensions of GHG reduction, for supporting my capitalism-versus-the-climate thesis. Unlike those self-deluding climate science deniers, I don't ignore the evidence from leading researchers on the effectiveness of various policies and approaches to reducing GHG emissions."

But Klein doesn't say that. Instead of explaining the "important differences" which would demonstrate that she is not rejecting other solutions because they are inconvenient to her worldview, she says on page 59, "What I am saying is that the climate science forces us to *choose* how we want to respond."

Wait a minute. It forces us to choose how we want to respond? Earlier in the book (page 22), she said that the *only* choice was between climate chaos and abolishing capitalism – meaning that the *only* path to climate success is to "change everything" about capitalism. Now, however, she tells us (page 59) that we must *choose* how we respond. And her choice is to change everything about the economy so that it is no longer capitalist. But we knew that was her choice before opening the book, because an ideological agenda to abolish capitalism motivates every one of Klein's books.

This is why I titled my book review "I *Wish* This Changed Everything."[2] To me, this is a more honest title for a book devoted to Klein's wish that humanity respond to the climate-energy challenge, and any other major challenge for that matter, by replacing global capitalism with an autarkic, communalistic economic system.

* * *

Even though Klein has hitched her abolish capitalism agenda to the climate-energy challenge, is that reason enough to dismiss her evidence and arguments? While she admits that abolishing capitalism is her *preferred* choice rather than what she initially called the *only* choice, maybe abolishing capitalism, even if extremely difficult in just three decades, is nonetheless the least-difficult path. Since we have failed for several decades under global capitalism, we cannot dismiss *a priori* Klein's agenda.

But quickly abolishing capitalism is a tall order. While many people like me are deeply disturbed by the environmental harms and social inequities of our modern capitalist economies, we can't ignore evidence that such economies have had considerable success in reducing other energy-related pollutants, including emissions of acid gases, ozone-depleting chemicals, lead, and particulates. Globally, effective action on GHG reduction has been slow, but that doesn't prove it can't happen under capitalism. And we don't want to encumber an already difficult task with what seems to be a dramatically more challenging agenda, unless it's essential for success.

To fairly consider this possibility, I read carefully through the rest of the book. As I mentioned earlier, Klein accepts the work of climate scientists as reported in Volume I of the IPCC reports. But she does not seem interested in Volume III. Having served as an IPCC lead author in Volume III, which I am involved in yet again, I know this report reflects the consensus or near-consensus positions of leading engineering and economic researchers and a wide array of social scientists, all focused on reducing GHG emissions.[3]

In fairness to Klein, the IPCC's focus is too politically constrained for its members to consider abolishing capitalism as one option for GHG reduction. But the Volume III reports for each of the major IPCC assessments are full of real-world cases of jurisdictions and policies that reduced GHG emissions for a variety of reasons in various sectors, a few cases of which I summarized in Chapter 11. Working through Klein's book, I was surprised she would ignore this evidence. Why, if she were truly interested in finding the fastest feasible way to reduce global GHG emissions, would she not carefully examine instances where jurisdictions have succeeded in significantly reducing GHG emissions and other energy-related pollutants? After reviewing that evidence, she could then more credibly explain why abolishing capitalism is essential, and explain how to quickly convince a majority of voters in all democracies around the world to agree almost immediately to abolish capitalism in their countries and thus globally.

Since, like me, Klein lives on the west coast of Canada, I was surprised she never mentioned the climate-energy policies and GHG reductions of our neighbor, California. As I noted in earlier chapters, and return to in Chapter 13, California committed in 2006 to decarbonize its economy and its progress has been substantial, especially compared to the high-emission path it was on. As I showed with Figure 6.3 in Chapter 6, it has achieved its reductions mostly with flexible regulations on electricity, transport, and other sectors, backed by an economy-wide cap-and-trade policy. It has done this while remaining among the largest capitalist economies in the world. Over a decade after Arnold Schwarzenegger launched this ambitious energy system transformation, voters in California are still committed to world leadership in deep decarbonization. Yet they've shown no interest in electing politicians who promise to abolish capitalism.

I explained in Chapter 6 that cap-and-trade can be politically challenging relative to regulations because opponents propagate misinformation that the policy is a form of carbon tax and that carbon taxes are harmful to the economy. But in her discussion of cap-and-trade (her Chapter 6), Klein misrepresents this policy. She complains that its adoption in individual jurisdictions may be associated with government freely allocating some or all emission permits to trade-exposed industries. She sees this as an equity problem within a given jurisdiction, but never addresses the equity challenge if these industries move to other jurisdictions that lack policies of comparable stringency. The application of different stringencies of GHG policies in different jurisdictions is a problem that will not disappear if we abolish capitalism. As I explained in Chapter 4, GHG reduction is a global collective action problem, which it remains whether the global economic system is capitalist, anarcho-syndicalist, communist, fascist, or autarkic communalist.

Klein also confuses cap-and-trade with carbon offsets. In Chapter 9, I explained why climate-energy policy experts agree that carbon offsets achieve less than is often claimed. Thus, I concur with Klein's distrust of offsets. But Klein dismisses cap-and-trade as an ineffective policy simply because it includes some offsets. In this regard, she refers to the Waxman-Markey cap-and-trade bill that failed to pass in the US Senate in 2010 as "a narrowly dodged bullet" since it included a provision for offsets. She fails to mention the critical fact that the bill allowed only a small percentage of GHG reductions from offsets, which is why policy experts like me could support the bill and yet oppose carbon offsets. Depending on the jurisdiction, cap-and-trade policy has been successful in reducing acid emissions, smog-causing nitrous oxide emissions, water pollution, and GHG emissions. Klein never mentions these successful applications of a market-consistent policy that is inconvenient to her anti-capitalist narrative.

Klein seems misinformed about technologies, yet each error conveniently works in favor of her agenda. For example, if humanity gets serious about GHG reduction, some fossil fuel-rich regions, like Norway and the Canadian provinces of Alberta and Saskatchewan, may pursue carbon capture and storage, which they already do. IPCC reports estimate a significant potential to store captured CO_2 in deep salty aquifers.[4] For decades, though, CO_2 has also been pumped into aging oil reservoirs to increase oil extraction rates, Texas being an example. This is not a GHG-reduction strategy because the extracted oil gets burned and releases CO_2. Yet Klein mistakenly assumes (her Chapter 7) that enhanced oil recovery is what people mean by carbon storage, so she summarily rejects a technology that has made inroads in meshing the profit-seeking interests of the fossil fuel industry with the goal of deep decarbonization.

Klein likes small-scale development of renewable energy as this fits her energy autarky ideal. Thus, she links the increase in solar and wind generation in Germany with that country's partial allowance of local participation in electricity planning and ownership. She overlooks the fact that mass investment in renewable electricity in jurisdictions like Germany is possible because of centrally controlled and owned, integrated grids, in concert with large generating plants and long-distance electricity trade. In Germany's electricity system, major corporations work together with multiple small suppliers and municipal distribution companies. This kind of relationship has existed in different capitalist economies, including the US, throughout the history of the electricity industry. Klein portrays it as a radical economic departure from capitalism. It is not.

Klein argues (her Chapter 2) that a transition to renewables will take a long time since it involves "building vast new electricity grids and transportation systems, often from the ground up." This is not true. One of the advantages of renewable electricity and low-emission vehicles is their ability to develop with existing electricity grids and road networks, these being gradually reinforced in step with the switch to renewable electricity and electric vehicles.

On the flip side, Klein argues that we can "quickly" reduce energy use via "policies and programs that make low-carbon choices easy and convenient for everyone, ... public transit, ... energy-efficient housing, ...

cities planned for high density living, ... land management that discourages sprawl, ... urban design that clusters essential services like
schools and health care along transit routes." But this is simply
a portrait of modern Scandinavia, with its capitalist economy. Energy
experts know that this transformation of urban form, certainly a valid
pursuit, took decades – much longer than it takes to transition to renewable electricity and low-emission vehicles, as my real-world examples in
Chapter 11 showed.

Using the Canadian province of Ontario as an example, Klein claims
(her Chapter 2) that the free trade rules of global capitalism block GHG-
reducing policies. This is incorrect. Trade rules did prevent Ontario from
requiring manufacturers of solar panels to locate their plants there in
order to have the right to sell equipment. But, as I showed in Chapter 11,
they did not prevent Ontario from closing all its coal-fired power plants
and replacing these with low-GHG alternatives, reducing GHG emissions
85% in just a decade. And although Klein lives in British Columbia, she
avoids mentioning the world-leading, clean electricity policy this
Canadian province implemented in 2007 – a policy I helped design – to
force the cancellation of coal and natural gas projects and cause
a flourishing of renewables in a near-zero-emission electricity system.
Again, international trade rules could not block deep decarbonization
successes like these.

In other chapters, Klein provides a biased sample of evidence for her
caricature of fossil fuels as bad while renewable energy is good. She slams
fossil fuels for harming people and nature, citing the BP oil spill, the
smog in Chinese cities, and unhealthy conditions for people living near
Nigerian oil wells and Albertan oil sands projects. Had she read with an
open mind the IPCC reports and the Global Energy Assessment, she
would have acknowledged that one of the greatest benefits to human
health has been the 'energy transition,' the shift from indoor combustion
of wood, brush, and crop residues to the use of fossil fuel-derived kero-
sene, butane, and propane. Today, indoor air pollution still kills over
two million people a year, mostly the world's poorest women and children in Asia and Africa who have not yet attained the energy transition.
Klein never mentions huge health benefits like these that help explain
the historical allure of fossil fuels for humanity.

Figure 12.1 Cartoon by Scott Willis

Nor does she explain why the former planned economies of the Soviet Union and its East Bloc allies, as well as communist China from 1950 to 1990, relied on state-owned companies rather than profit-seeking corporations to develop fossil fuels for domestic consumption. And while blaming capitalism for the harms from fossil fuels, Klein fails to explain why most assets of conventional oil today belong to state-owned companies that were nationalized long ago.

With her anti-capitalism agenda, Klein ignores the main reasons why humanity is having so much trouble with the climate-energy challenge, reasons that exist irrespective of the type of economic system. While I have discussed these throughout this book, four warrant highlighting because they severely undermine Klein's thesis.

First, fossil fuels present a Faustian dilemma for humanity. As I highlighted in my book *Sustainable Fossil Fuels*, they have brought fantastic benefits for over 200 years, and still offer the lowest cost energy option in most places on the planet, which is especially important to the poorest billion people who have little access to the modern forms of energy that are healthier to use.[5] Yet, we now know that with these benefits comes a day of reckoning because of the GHGs emitted when we burn them. Indigenous people living in the Canadian Arctic provide an example of this dilemma between fossil fuel benefits and costs. Their per capita fossil fuel consumption is high because of cold winters and isolated communities that require substantial energy for livelihood (hunting and fishing) and for transporting goods and people within the region and in exchange with southern regions. With temperatures rising fastest at the poles, they are already experiencing significant effects of climate change. But they have the highest comparative benefits from using fossil fuels produced in distant lands since low-emission alternatives like bioenergy, wind, solar, and hydropower are extremely costly and sometimes technically unviable in the arctic. Arctic energy autarky is prohibitively expensive. Dilemmas like this result from the high energy quality and low cost of fossil fuels, not capitalism.

Second, unlike some environmental threats, such as smog, GHG emissions are invisible, and their effect is distant in time and space (albeit becoming more immediate every year!). They cause increases in temperatures, sea levels, and the probability of extreme weather and catastrophic events like wildfires, hurricanes, and floods. But since these phenomena are variable on a daily, seasonal, or annual basis, the change is difficult to personally detect. Psychologists note that our ability to recognize threats is related to personal physical experiences. This helps explain why humans can quickly focus on a terrorist attack, a disease outbreak, or an economic crisis, yet have difficulty focusing on climate change.[6] This threat perception bias is not caused by capitalism.

Third, as a global-scale threat, GHG emissions present a global governance challenge for which humanity is ill equipped. As I explained in Chapter 4, a *voluntary* international agreement that includes mandatory compliance mechanisms is unattainable because of the diversity of national interests. Poorer countries want wealthier countries to bear significant costs to help them reject the Faustian pact with fossil fuels. Wealthier countries agree they need to provide significant help. But each side has dramatically different views of what 'significant help' means. These irreconcilable differences are not the fault of global capitalism, just as the inability of the communist Soviet Union and the capitalist US and UK to act pre-emptively against Hitler was not the fault of global capitalism. Success with a global effort on the climate threat requires that countries, individually or in climate clubs, enact carbon tariffs to change the incentives for some countries to free-ride on the efforts of others. Changing everything about capitalism won't change the tendency for citizens and their national governments to have self-interest biases. Success with the climate-energy challenge requires that we recognize this.

Fourth, as I explain throughout this book, humans are good at self-deception when evidence is inconvenient to their lifestyle and income, or contradicts their worldview. Klein accurately observes this with right-wing climate deniers, yet claims they are only delusional when denying the science, not when agreeing with her that deep decarbonization inevitably spells the end of capitalism. Klein's biased selection of the available evidence on GHG-reducing technologies and policies suggests that she too is guilty of motivated reasoning based on her political preferences, in effect using the climate threat to advance her agenda. Paul Krugman of the *New York Times* summed up the counterproductive influence of such biased views when noting, "If we ever get past the special interests and ideology that have blocked action to save the planet, we'll find that it's cheaper and easier than almost anyone imagines."[7]

"Changing everything" in the global economy in just a few decades requires convincing a majority of people in a majority of countries to dismantle global capitalism and replace it with something that Klein never clearly explains or even names. Fortunately, this profound revolution is unnecessary for deep decarbonization, as individual jurisdictions are already showing. But vested interests within key countries and radically divergent views on international fairness make the task ahead daunting. We need to push past a tipping point for both the energy system within countries, and the international system for GHG governance. This is difficult. Attaching adventurist agendas like Klein's only makes it more so.

* * *

As I noted earlier, Naomi Klein is not alone in hitching her agenda to the climate-energy challenge. It's a common occurrence. Indeed, the longer humanity procrastinates on deep decarbonization, the greater the cacophony of solutions. While Klein argues that success requires abolishing capitalism, others argue it requires zero economic growth or zero population growth or global income equity or universal vegetarianism or banning air travel or banning cars from cities or saving all rainforests or gender equity.

When strung together, these solutions suggest that only a global utopia, with universally accepted values and behavior, can solve the climate-energy challenge. Yet, if considered individually on their merits, one can understand, and in some cases sympathize with, the proponents of these agendas.

Each would likely reduce emissions. We know that plane travel, car use, and eating meat in a fossil fuel-dominated energy system increase GHG emissions. Likewise, economic and population growth in a fossil fuel-dominated energy system increases GHG emissions. More equitable incomes and opportunities, between and within countries, are desirable goals in themselves, but one wonders how essential each of these actions is for deep decarbonization and, more importantly, how politically and diplomatically difficult each is relative to the essential energy system transformation.

In this book, I explain why we must focus our efforts on phasing out coal to generate electricity and gasoline to move people and goods. Fortunately, we already have the necessary zero-emission options and we know that this energy transformation will result in electricity and transportation costs not much higher than today. Cost increases will be especially modest if our policies are dominated by economically efficient carbon pricing or flexible regulations.

Slower rates of population and economic growth, along with conservation actions like reduced energy use, less meat consumption, and less air travel, would no doubt make the transition easier. A global energy system that is smaller because of these actions will require less investment in zero-emission energy to achieve the deep decarbonization transition. As long as the energy efficiency and energy conservation actions are not too difficult or expensive, this would result in a lower cost for transforming the system.

I am not arguing that advocates should abandon these various pursuits. Hopefully, however, they can recognize that these pursuits, if not combined with simultaneous pressure on politicians to enact the essential pricing or regulatory policies in electricity, transportation, and other key sectors, inadvertently help those who want to maintain the fossil fuel status quo. And when we succeed in decarbonizing electricity, transportation, and other sectors, as we must, then some of these solutions diminish in importance for success with the climate-energy challenge.

A politically difficult to implement city-wide ban on vehicles will not reduce GHGs when virtually all vehicles are zero-emission. A ban on air travel will not reduce GHGs when most aviation fuel is biologically derived. A behavioral shift away from meat consumption may have health and societal benefits, but will be less important for GHG reduction once the farming and food industries use zero-emission energy and organic fertilizer.

It is neither likely nor desirable that people hold identical views when it comes to our personal choices for activities like travel and diet, or the balance between collective and private ownership of the means of production in our economic system. While there is nothing wrong with trying to convince others of the benefits of one's particular preferences, we should not let the pursuit of these hinder or distract us from our essential task of quickly decarbonizing critical sectors of the energy system, where we have the capability to do so at a reasonable cost, regardless of the economic system. Many jurisdictions have already demonstrated how to do that – without abolishing capitalism.

While I see nothing wrong with Naomi Klein and fellow travelers trying to convince most of humanity to vote to abolish capitalism over the next decade, I resist when they propagate the myth that their low-likelihood agenda is *essential* for success with the climate-energy challenge. We cannot afford to make it more difficult than it already is.

CHAPTER 13

The Simple Path to Success with Our Climate-Energy Challenge

I say the debate is over. We know the science. We see the threat. The time for action is now.

Arnold Schwarzenegger

O N AUGUST 6, 2003, ON JAY LENO'S TONIGHT SHOW, ARNOLD Schwarzenegger announced his decision to run for governor of California. Later, in a public interview, he explained how he made such a momentous decision during his trip to Leno's TV studio.

> I thought this will freak everyone out. It will be *so* funny. I'll announce that I am running. I told Leno I was running. And two months later I was governor. What the fuck is that? ... It was the most difficult decision in my entire life – except in 1978 when I decided to get a bikini wax.[1]

Whatever your feelings about The Governator or The Terminator or Mr. Universe, you have to marvel at Arnold's multiple A-list lives. Born in a small town in Austria, he dreamed of playing professional soccer, but was more likely destined for a tradesman's life, as his mother hoped. Instead, his exceptional drive meshed with a teenage interest in body-building, and as a 20-year-old in 1967 he overcame enormous odds to capture his first Mr. Universe title, becoming world famous overnight. A great plot for one of those overcoming-the-odds Hollywood movies.

But realizing a Hollywood-style achievement was not enough for Arnold. Why not *become* a Hollywood movie star? Although his initial movie roles, including the *Terminator*, were fodder for acting critics, he again beat the odds. Decent performances in more challenging roles, like

Junior, earned him grudging respect as an actor, and a lot of money. After marrying Maria Shriver of the Kennedy clan, the Austrian hulk with the excruciating accent was now entrenched among America's rich and famous. Again, a great Hollywood plot. Again, not enough for Arnold.

To those fixated on politics, his decision to enter their arena produced derision and despair. Surely he would flop as governor, making a laughing stock of California in the process. Surely he would achieve nothing of lasting significance. As a Republican, though married into an iconic Democratic family, Schwarzenegger's prior political commentary followed the standard conservative line. "Government should reduce taxes, cut red tape. Environmentalists exaggerate, as do advocates for the poor and the disadvantaged. People should pull up their socks, unfetter the market, and let American ingenuity improve lives."

Schwarzenegger stuck to this script for his first two years as governor. With California's finances in trouble, he played the typical Republican governor, focused on spending cuts. Then the world changed. Hurricane Katrina struck in August 2005 and, along with other developments, created a policy window for serious climate-energy initiatives. Depending on various factors, politicians of similar political views may react quite differently. Some may show leadership. Some may appear concerned, but instead delay, waiting for the policy window to close.

No delay for Schwarzenegger. He was keenly interested in the claims of scientists, and once convinced the threat was real, morphed into the action hero for global warming commitment, becoming the overnight darling of environmentalists and Hollywood celebrities. The Democrat-dominated California legislature shared his concern. But he made global warming *his* issue, associated with his striking image and personality.

In the fall of 2006, Schwarzenegger signed the *Global Warming Solutions Act.*[2] This directed the California Air Resources Board, an arms-length regulatory agency, to consult interest groups, experts, and the public in developing a plan to reduce California's carbon pollution back to its 1990 level by 2020 – a 30% reduction from where emissions would otherwise be.

California has long relied on its air resources board to implement environmental policy, starting with its multi-decade battle with Los Angeles' infamous smog in the late 1960s. Like other non-legislative bodies, the air resources board lacks authority to tax carbon. But, as I described in Chapter 6, it can price it indirectly by implementing cap-and-trade, which it did in 2012, and can implement prescriptive and flexible regulations on different forms of energy, with its low carbon fuel standard, and on technologies, with its low- and zero-emission vehicle standards. In addition, the California Public Utilities Commission, which regulates electric utilities, controls the state's renewable portfolio standard, and the California Energy Commission implements regulations and incentive programs to increase energy efficiency as well as mandating technologies like rooftop photovoltaic panels.

The climate policy window closed in 2008. The global financial and economic meltdown took care of that. And in 2011 Schwarzenegger's term ended. Yet, even without its climate commander, California has soldiered on. Jerry Brown replaced Schwarzenegger as governor, showing the same climate concern and policy determination during his two terms. His replacement in 2018, Gavin Newsome, shares his priorities. Independent analysts say that California, one of the world's largest economies, is still on track with its ambitious emission targets for 2030 and 2050. While the climate efforts of many jurisdictions have waxed and waned, California's has been steadfast.

* * *

Deep decarbonization is a global collective action problem. Over the next decades, we need wealthier countries to rapidly decarbonize and developing countries to slow and then reverse the growth of their emissions. For this, we must have an international enforcement mechanism, probably carbon tariffs, to ensure that politicians in individual countries cannot win elections by promising to abandon their countries' efforts and free-ride on the efforts of other countries. Without such a mechanism, global decarbonization won't happen.

Since this mechanism is unlikely to result from consensus-based international negotiations, its emergence depends on leadership by a group of motivated countries – a climate club – that implement domestic decarbonization policies and together establish a system of carbon tariffs. Ideally, wealthier countries would transfer revenue from their tariffs to support adoption of low-GHG technologies in developing countries, but we can't bank on an increase in international generosity from the voters of wealthier countries.

Yet for almost three decades, international negotiators have pursued a voluntary agreement in which all countries agree on their reductions, and on the financial and technological transfers from wealthier to poorer countries. This approach's continued failure will most negatively impact the poorest people in the poorest countries. They and their governments are least able to withstand increasing droughts, wildfires, floods, diseases, crop failures, hurricanes, heat waves, ocean acidification, and sea-level rise. An intensifying global crisis, including mass migrations of climate refugees, awaits us if we cannot quickly replace international wishful thinking with international *realpolitik*. An enduring global effort is unachievable without enforcement mechanisms that will be objectionable to some countries, at least initially.

Politicians showing leadership in their own jurisdictions must also replace domestic wishful thinking with domestic *realpolitik*. They must understand that explicit carbon pricing favored by economists will rarely play the lead role in energy system transformation. Politicians who promote carbon pricing as lead policy are an easy target for opponents who deceive voters by promising lower gasoline and electricity prices and magically reduced GHG emissions.

Fortunately, carbon pricing is not essential for deep decarbonization. While many jurisdictions have carbon pricing, it is never used as lead policy. Instead, climate-sincere jurisdictions usually combine modest carbon prices with flexible regulations, prescriptive regulations, and subsidies. If designed well, these policy packages offer flexibility for consumers and producers, which reduces their economic efficiency disadvantage relative to pure carbon pricing.

When viewed from the perspective of political acceptability, flex-regs outperform carbon pricing, especially in the early stages of the energy transformation. But even flex-regs aren't easy to implement at stringent levels. They meet concerted resistance from fossil fuel companies, electric utilities, vehicle manufacturers and other interests. For a government trying to lead on climate-energy policy, however, it is less difficult to overcome these sector-specific corporate interests, which themselves are not particularly popular, than to survive the anger of voters in key electoral districts who succumb to lies trumpeting the punitive nature and ineffectiveness of carbon pricing.

Energy transformation is also difficult because its short-term costs are concentrated in regions that rely on fossil fuels for electricity supply, such as the US Midwest with coal-fired power, or regions whose economies are highly dependent on fossil fuel development and export, such as Texas. Some people in these regions experience climate action as an attack on their livelihood, and are therefore vulnerable to the argument that climate scientists distort evidence.

Challenging this myth with evidence and logic is difficult, as we are all susceptible to biases that align with our self-interest, especially when these are reinforced by well-funded misinformation campaigns. Over the last 20 years, advocates for climate-energy policies have tried various narratives to shift the views of the climate science skeptics. Will their views shift if we better explain the science? Or if scientists talk more about catastrophic outcomes? Or if we emphasize the co-benefits of GHG reduction, such as improved air quality? Or if we trumpet the innovation and jobs created by renewable energy? Or if we use carbon tax revenues to compensate fossil fuel-dependent regions and retrain workers in a 'just transition' strategy?

Unfortunately, no storyline has emerged as the silver bullet for countering climate science skepticism. As we know from the experience with smoking and lung cancer, myths based on our perceived self-interest and convenience are hard to undermine. Decades of accumulated scientific evidence slowly changed beliefs. Finally, public views on the risks of smoking passed a tipping point to reach wider acceptance. Climate science views may have reached a similar stage, in part because, as with smoking, some impacts are now obvious and immediate. But a significant percentage of people will still deny the science, or reject the need to act. If these action-resistant views align with political partisanship, as in the US, rising public acceptance still might not lead to effective economy-wide policies. Focusing on key sectors and less difficult policies is especially important in this context.

Even if most people in a fossil fuel-endowed region may accept the climate science, those whose financial interests align with expanded production are motivated to convince themselves and others to accept *their* project: it produces only a tiny percentage of global emissions; it is essential for our economy; it is cleaner than others; it will help the developing world. These rationales hinder people from 'connecting the dots' – realizing that the long lifespans of new fossil fuel projects far exceed the short timeframe for global decarbonization.

Fossil fuel-endowed regions would benefit if some of their trusted leaders questioned the prudence of doubling-down on coal, oil, and even natural gas. Such visionaries would argue that fossil fuel expansion increases their region's economic vulnerability to the future time when humanity finally accelerates on the decarbonization path. Unfortunately, such regions tend to produce political and corporate leaders who perpetuate the myth that they can thrive indefinitely on the fossil fuel path, simply by repelling attacks from environmentalists, foreign billionaires, Hollywood celebrities, and neighboring jurisdictions. This is why, sadly, sudden economic decline is the more likely future for most fossil fuel-dependent regions.

Fortunately, one myth that has kept humanity on the rising GHG path is fading. While some people still believe peak oil is nigh, it's now difficult to convince anyone that imminent oil exhaustion obviates the need for decarbonization policies. Technological advances of the last 15 years, notably the fracking and horizontal drilling that enable oil and gas extraction from shale rock, have greatly increased estimated global reserves. The price of oil may still jump at times, being a valued commodity vulnerable to geopolitical crises, and this may rekindle peak oil concerns. But we can now confront peak oil catastrophists with the crescendo of climate-related disasters to convince them that the priority must be stringent climate-energy policies. And we can note that such policies will, serendipitously, cause oil production to peak long before we run out – peak demand preventing peak oil.

As carbon pricing or regulations that phase out coal and gasoline increase in stringency, they spur behavioral change, energy efficiency, and renewable energy, and other policies can reduce inequities within and between countries. But our pursuit of these laudable objectives must not retard energy system transformation. If we argue, in spite of the evidence, that energy efficiency is cheap and easy, we inadvertently reduce the pressure on politicians to enact regulations or carbon pricing.

If we say consumer behavioral change is essential, we again let politicians off the hook, enabling them to claim that they are waiting for that behavioral change.

The same good intentions that motivate efforts to change consumer behavior also motivate the practice of offsetting. Feeling helpless with the ineffectiveness of climate policy, some of us purchase offsets. The sentiment is worthy, but the outcome is not, for many carbon offsets have little effect on emissions. We should instead consider contributing our offset money to the politicians and campaigns that demand the regulatory and pricing policies we know are essential. Deep decarbonization only happens if *every* polluter pays, not just the environmentally conscious.

Many people are rightly bullish about renewables, especially given the falling cost of wind turbines, photovoltaic panels, and the batteries, gas turbines, and other technologies that enable these intermittent sources to provide reliable electricity. But fossil fuels will not be swept away by market forces in the absence of rising carbon prices or stringent regulations. Renewable portfolio standards and tax credits in the US, producer subsidies and regulations in Europe, and government support in China have caused the dramatic growth in wind, solar, and other renewables. The stringency of these policies needs to increase because when they cause a declining demand for coal and oil, they also cause declining prices for these commodities, which slows the market penetration of renewables. This is why renewables advocates must demand stringent climate-energy policies. Proclamations that renewables are already cheaper are welcomed by fossil fuel advocates, helping them convince politicians that politically difficult policies can be avoided, thus slowing or preventing decarbonization.

While I am sympathetic to arguments that the global economic system should do much better in terms of equity within and between countries, attaching ambitious agendas to the deep decarbonization project only increases the difficulty of what is already an extremely difficult task. The resulting failure on climate makes global inequity even worse, since it is the poorest people who are most adversely affected, and this is already happening. Radical transformation of our economic system and our social relations, desirable as these may be for some, are not essential for deep decarbonization, as several GHG-reducing jurisdictions are demonstrating.

* * *

In my graduate seminar in sustainable energy, I ask students why California advanced its climate-energy policies from 2008 to 2013, while most jurisdictions halted their efforts and focused on the economic crisis.[3] This question triggers a bustle of evidence-gathering and speculation.

Prior to 2008, California was one of many US states and Canadian provinces negotiating a cap-and-trade system, which European countries had implemented the previous year for large industrial emitters. The idea was that this multi-jurisdictional initiative would eventually cover so much of the US economy that federal legislators would be compelled to implement a national policy, if only to reduce regulatory complexity for industry. Then came the financial crisis of 2008, followed by the global recession. While climate-energy policy initiatives were delayed or abandoned elsewhere, California soldiered on – tightening its renewable portfolio standard and vehicle emissions standards, initiating its innovative low carbon fuel standard, increasing the stringency of its energy efficiency regulations, and rolling out its cap-and-trade system.

The students offer several hypotheses for California's continued efforts: frequent wildfires making the climate threat real; Democratic political domination; influential Hollywood movie stars; conflation of LA smog reduction with GHG reduction; Schwarzenegger; etc. Perhaps all of these played a part. But as they investigate further, some students note how climate-energy policies are designed and implemented in California, in particular the lead role of the California Air Resources Board, with contributions from other state agencies like the California Energy Commission and the California Public Utilities Commission. These are quasi-judicial agencies to which the California legislature and governor delegate some regulatory authority.

Having chaired the British Columbia Utilities Commission for five years, I am familiar with the procedures of such regulatory bodies. They hold public hearings in a court-like setting, involving expert evidence, testimony, and cross-examination. Panel members are treated like judges. (I enjoyed the tradition of participants deferentially standing when the Chair entered the hearing room!) The California Air Resources Board is mandated by legislation to achieve the state's GHG targets using its regulatory powers, and to stay the course as long as that mandate has not changed. While the US government and other states have environmental protection agencies, only California has delegated to its agencies such powers to ensure GHG reductions.

Delegating climate-energy policy implementation to an arms-length regulatory agency is also beneficial if such institutions can better resist the inevitable push-back from some industries and voters. Since politicians hope to please everyone, they are vulnerable to lobbyists arguing that non-compulsory policies are effective. A regulatory agency, with the expertise to distinguish effective from ineffective policies, is less likely to succumb to this wishful thinking bias. And it may be more trusted than politicians, which researchers suggest is important when it comes to public acceptance of climate-energy policies.[4]

My students acknowledge that California's sustained leadership is not only a result of its policy delegation to regulatory agencies. But they believe such agencies may be helpful with a multi-decade task like deep decarbonization, especially given the partisan positioning and short attention spans of democratically elected governments. We must not bet the planet on every jurisdiction electing a steady stream of Arnold Schwarzeneggers.

* * *

People tell me they feel hopeless against the climate threat. They are horrified by the daily news of extreme events and dire scientific warnings. They want action. But they don't know what to do themselves or what actions to demand of leaders. They can't assess the personal or political implications from the activist campaigns that come and go – the 350 parts per million campaign, the 450 parts per million campaign, the 1.5°C target, the 2°C target, the youth climate emergency campaign of Greta Thunberg, and so on. People have trouble distinguishing effective from ineffective policies, and hence sincere from insincere politicians. They don't see how actions in their one jurisdiction can solve a global problem.

And they are overwhelmed by the myriad suggestions for changing their daily lives.

I have written this book for these people – citizens of countries, citizens of our planet.

My paramount message in this book is that climate-concerned citizens must concentrate on transforming a few key sectors of our economies, on focusing our politicians on a few key policies, and on changing a few key technologies. These simple tasks substantially improve our chance of climate success. Without them, climate failure is guaranteed. I now recap what we need to do, how to do it, and why each part matters.

The global nature of the problem complicates the decarbonization task. However, some sectors within our economies primarily provide domestic services. These include electricity generation, transportation, heating and cooling of buildings, firms for whom energy use is a small part of their costs, and our land-use practices in cities, agriculture, and forestry.

Electricity and transportation are especially important, and that's where we must focus. These two sectors are a major source of GHG emissions in developed and increasingly developing countries. Their decarbonization in a given jurisdiction will have negligible effect on the cost of producing goods that are subject to global competition, because near-zero-emission commercial technologies are already available at a reasonable cost.

In electricity, we need to regulate the rapid phase-out of coal plants (if lacking carbon capture and storage) while ensuring that natural gas plays only a modest, backup role for intermittent renewables. Canada has a regulation to phase out all coal plants by 2030, repeating the successful effort a decade ago in Ontario. The UK has a policy that combines carbon pricing, an emissions intensity regulation, and renewables subsidies for the same outcome. Many other countries are contemplating similar policies, and coal use is falling in most developed countries. Even in the US, in spite of promises from President Trump, coal-fired power plants are in decline thanks to a combination of renewable portfolio standards, tax incentives, tighter regulations, and low natural gas prices. This trend in wealthier countries to stop burning coal must extend to developing countries, albeit with a lag to reflect their reduced financial capacity and growing energy needs. China may have stopped growing its coal-fired power, but it needs a sustained decline, thereby providing an alternative model for other developing countries, like India.

In transportation, we need to regulate the phase-out of gasoline and diesel use in vehicles and other transportation equipment (buses, local delivery trucks, long-haul trucks, transit, trains, ships). Increasingly, electricity will play a dominant role with cars and some trucks, as governments at national, sub-national, and city levels commit to phase out sales of gasoline and diesel vehicles. Instead of carbon pricing playing the leading role, other key policies may include a zero-emission vehicle standard or a low carbon fuel standard, or both, as in California. Purchase subsidies and vehicle tax changes may also contribute, as Norway has demonstrated.

Long-haul trucks, buses, trains, and ships might switch to biodiesel, ethanol-gasoline blends, or hydrogen, perhaps in conjunction with electricity (plug-in hybrid trucks for example). These forms of energy must be produced in low-emission processes, with only minor impacts on forest and crop lands. A low carbon fuel standard, perhaps in conjunction with biofuel blending mandates, can achieve this shift, and is more likely than carbon pricing to play the lead role. But subsidies can contribute, since these improve the political acceptability of deep decarbonization policies, even if their GHG-reducing effectiveness is suspect.

Since unilateral decarbonization of electricity and transportation are the least-difficult actions, with the biggest impacts, citizens of wealthier countries must push their governments for a complete transition in these two sectors. They must also demand that this domestic progress be coordinated with a globalization effort to extend the transition to developing countries. The already-existing Powering Past Coal Alliance needs to add countries, and should be partnered with a new Driving Past Gasoline Alliance, the latter linking jurisdictions like Norway, California, China, and soon others on an accelerated gasoline phase-out.

This globalization of the energy transformation in electricity and transportation is essential because reducing developing country emissions is critical to climate success. The two pie charts in Figure 13.1 represent fossil fuel-caused CO_2 emissions in 2050 in a 'reference case' forecast of future emissions if we continue our procrastination. The

CO_2 emissions in gigatonnes in 2050

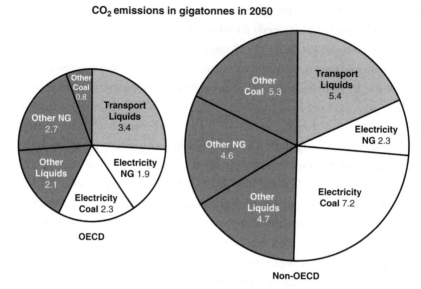

Figure 13.1 Global CO_2 emissions in 2050 reference case

emissions pie for developing and emerging-economy countries ('non-OECD') is more than twice that of wealthier countries ('OECD') – 30 billion metric tons per year versus 13 billion.

By 2050, fossil fuels in electricity generation, mostly coal and natural gas (NG), and fossil fuel transport liquids, mostly gasoline and diesel, will account for 50% of combustion emissions in non-OECD countries and more than 50% in OECD countries. Quickly decarbonizing these two sectors in wealthier countries sets a model for, and helps lower the costs of, a similar effort in developing countries. Significant decarbonization of these two sectors in OECD countries over the next 15 years, followed by a slowing of growth and then a downward trend in emissions in these sectors in non-OECD countries after 2035, would cause declining global emissions after 2035, assuming modest progress in other sectors and with other GHGs.

My focus on fuel switching in electricity and transportation does not imply that we ignore other sectors. But Figure 13.1 demonstrates that the climate-energy challenge is simpler than often presented. Yes, we want more livable cities, greater energy efficiency, and behavioral change like reduced meat consumption and more use of public transit. Yes, we want to preserve rainforests and adopt more sustainable agricultural practices. Yes, we want significant GHG reductions in emissions-intensive industries.

But we know with certainty that we must quickly decarbonize electricity and transportation, which individual countries can do without waiting for a global agreement. We know that decarbonization in these two sectors are linked, since zero-emission electricity is a key input for decarbonizing transportation. We know that if carbon pricing is politically constrained as the lead policy, there are sector-specific flexible regulations that are less politically difficult, with only a modest loss of economic efficiency. And we know that success in these two sectors puts us on the deep decarbonization trajectory, creating a tipping point within countries and globally for the consolidating next step of implementing economy-wide policies. Success in these two sectors has the greatest spillover potential for the global effort. We must think globally when deciding how to act locally.

In contrast with electricity and transportation, decarbonization of emissions-intensive trade-exposed industries requires a different strategy. Shifting to near-zero-emission production of steel, cement, aluminum, and petrochemicals will increase their production costs. But while the costs for primary materials (steel ingots, aluminum slabs, polyethylene) may rise by as much as 40% when switching to low-emission processes, the costs of intermediate products (metal brackets, aluminum frames, plastic molding) won't increase more than 10%, and that of most final products (vehicles, buildings) no more than 3%. My former student, Chris Bataille, is an expert on decarbonization of emissions-intensive industries, and publications from his collaborative research show an encouraging potential for these sectors.[5]

Even though these costs of decarbonizing emissions-intensive trade-exposed sectors are reasonable for humanity on a global scale, a unilateral effort in just one jurisdiction would be political suicide. Industries facing substantial decarbonization costs would threaten plant closures because of unfair competition from industries in countries with less stringent policies. This 'emissions leakage' could even increase global emissions if plants in these free-riding jurisdictions have higher emission intensities. So unilateral decarbonization is unlikely without major cost-reducing innovations for near-zero-emission production processes.

But the inability to quickly decarbonize these industries should not give them a free ride. When implementing its cap-and-trade system for industry in 2005, the European Union granted allowances to industries based on their historical emissions, but ensured that the policy included the incentive to reduce emissions, since doing so would generate surplus permits that could be sold to other industries. Another approach is the 'output-based pricing system' which was initiated in the province of Alberta and is now a nation-wide policy in Canada. In this system, companies pay a carbon price only on the amount by which they exceed emission-intensity targets, such as CO_2 per ton of steel. This incentivizes investments to reduce emissions without significantly raising production costs. My former student, Nic Rivers, explained the benefits of the initial Alberta policy in a 2010 paper.[6]

Governments can also use carbon pricing revenues to subsidize GHG reductions in emission-intensive industries. And if they implement what are called 'border carbon adjustments,' they could use revenue from tariffs on the imports from high-emission jurisdictions to offset their domestic industry's policy-induced cost increases.[7] But this approach is only necessary if domestic industries are forced by policy to significantly decarbonize, which governments have not been willing to require of their domestic trade-exposed industries. As an alternative strategy, leading jurisdictions would together pursue single-industry globalization agreements, such as a global steel-GHG pact, a global cement-GHG pact, and so on. While still difficult to negotiate, single-sector international agreements would be less difficult than the current process, which futilely pursues a voluntary international consensus covering all sectors of all countries.

For decarbonizing electricity and transportation in developing countries, wealthier countries should provide financial support. But there is no evidence the taxpayers in wealthier countries will suddenly become more generous, so we can't depend on this. And because some wealthier countries will elect climate-insincere leaders, the sincere governments must combine their domestic efforts with the real threat of carbon tariffs. Ideally, some of the revenue from carbon tariffs would be transferred to developing countries to help with decarbonization costs. But I would not bet the planet on that level of generosity.

Fortunately, low-emission electricity and urban transportation provide important co-benefits by improving air quality, and this is highly valued in the smog-choked cities of developing countries, which also happen to be where political leaders and their families live. It is thus encouraging, but not entirely a surprise, that with rising wealth China has suddenly become the leading producer and consumer of electric vehicles. Other developing countries may follow.

The following text box situates this 'focused deep decarbonization strategy' within the major themes of this book. Several jurisdictions are starting to pursue key elements of this strategy.

Decarbonizing the global energy system is a global collective action problem, but humanity lacks global governance mechanisms for allocating costs and ensuring compliance. A voluntary global agreement is unattainable because national interests differ greatly (poorer vs wealthier; fossil fuel-rich vs fossil fuel-poor).

National governments need to recognize the constraints of this situation and develop a strategy that has the greatest chance of a global impact. The strategy includes the following.

1. Apply regulations and/or carbon pricing to decarbonize domestic electricity and transportation, and work with other leader countries to globalize this effort.
2. Apply carbon tariffs on imports from climate-laggard countries and work with other leader countries to form climate clubs that globalize this effort.
3. Assist poorer countries in adopting low-emission energy, especially where this meets air quality and other co-benefit objectives.

In selecting domestic decarbonization policies, jurisdictions should be prepared to trade off economic efficiency against the likelihood of implementation. Although this exercise will depend on numerous jurisdiction-specific factors, such as public trust in

---

government, electoral system, and institutional arrangements for policy-making, the guiding principle should be to not let perfection be the enemy of good. Carbon taxes are particularly problematic if proposed as the sole lead policy for deep decarbonization.

* * *

In Chapter 1, I described how each year I make the new graduate students in my sustainable energy seminar argue convincingly for and against our technological options on the deep decarbonization path. With practice, this exercise enables them to see the pro and con complexity of our options. It undermines the comfort of seeing the world as black and white. But it improves their ability to compromise, an essential condition for climate success. It is consistent with my theme that we must not let perfection be the enemy of good in the pursuit of climate success. This means that it's time to consider carefully questions like the ones below.

What will be the role of natural gas in a decarbonized energy system? It can make a significant contribution in backing-up solar and wind, and perhaps a modest contribution in transportation. But our coal phase-out policies should not allow natural gas to play significantly more than a supportive role, unless used with carbon capture and storage. For while natural gas can contribute to decarbonization, it is not the 'bridge' to a decarbonized future, an issue my former student Stephen Healey explored in a recent paper.[8]

What will be the role of nuclear power? I don't have a strong preference. I worry, however, that climate-concerned people will waste time and energy battling each other over nuclear power. If a jurisdiction wants nuclear power as part of its GHG-reducing effort, it will have to overcome the well-known challenges of plant siting, permitting, safety, storage of radioactive wastes, cost overruns, and public opposition. Expanding nuclear power in a wealthy country is a long shot if that country has zero-emission options for dispatchable electricity at reasonable cost. Some observers note that nuclear power has better growth prospects in countries ruled by autocratic governments, where siting is easier because public opposition can be suppressed. But is it advisable that governments with poor records on civil rights, freedom of information, and safety standards build and operate a fleet of nuclear plants?

What will be the role of carbon capture and storage? Again, I am indifferent, and I ask other people to consider the merits of being neutral about this. If a particular fossil fuel-rich region wants to continue using its resources by converting them to electricity and hydrogen without causing GHG emissions, why oppose it? Recent IPCC reports note that because we have already put too much CO_2 into the atmosphere, we now need to extract it and return it to the earth's crust – hence the increasing importance of bioenergy with carbon capture and storage in scenarios that prevent more than a 2°C increase. I ask climate-concerned people to keep an open mind about carbon capture and storage, whether matched with fossil fuels or biomass. With fossil fuels, it can help get buy-in for the climate effort from fossil fuel-endowed regions. With biomass, it can help reverse our mistakes of the past. Humanity has procrastinated too long for us to now rule out options that, while not perfect, could help accelerate the global decarbonization effort.

What will be the role of biofuels? Again, I ask climate-concerned citizens to avoid blanket rejection. Yes, a global-scale replacement of *all* fossil fuel-derived gasoline and diesel with biofuels will negatively affect food prices and biodiversity. But Brazil's sugar cane production of biofuels presents a low-cost model for gasoline phase-out and economic development that other tropical and semi-tropical countries can emulate. Biofuels will never be impact-free. Indeed, none of our energy options are completely green or clean in spite of the claims of promoters and politicians. But by carefully choosing our biofuel providers, whether domestic or imported, we can influence how biofuels are produced, which is the current strategy of the European Union. It would be tragic if, instead, we rejected all biofuels because of modest environmental harms in some locations, and thus inadvertently accelerated climate change that disrupts *all* environments in *all* locations.

What will be the role of geoengineering? It will be significant, whether we like it or not. We have dithered for so long that geoengineering options are now unavoidably in the climate toolbox. In the coming decades, we will extract carbon from the atmosphere, deflect solar radiation, neutralize ocean acidification, cause snowfall at the poles, and employ other unimaginable and risky technological fixes. We'll accept the risks of these and other options to avert the worst devastation from climate change, because we didn't act in time to avoid them.

Indeed, we cannot be rigid about solutions. We must pay attention to technical, economic, political, and social feasibility, and be willing to shift our preference for a particular action or policy if one of these factors presents an insurmountable barrier to its contribution.

Sadly, I all too often encounter arguments by experts and media commentators that *this* particular action or policy is essential for deep decarbonization, in spite of it being especially difficult for political, social, or psychological reasons, and not actually being essential. Some seem to revel in arguing that citizens must quickly accept a particular solution.

One frequent argument, for example, is that massive expansion of nuclear power is essential, and if citizens can't quickly accept living beside nuclear plants, then humanity will fail. But I sometimes wonder if people making this argument are simply expressing their own need to feel superior in their understanding of risk. Yes, researchers know that many people have an exaggerated view of the risks from a nearby nuclear plant, especially in comparison to the daily risks from our current energy system (a building gas explosion, vehicle exhaust, car fire, coal plant emissions, and fires, storms, and floods from climate change). And yes, researchers know that nuclear power could make a significant contribution to decarbonization. But to argue that nuclear power is essential is to deliberately ignore all of the sound research by the IPCC and other leading institutions showing decarbonization scenarios with little or no nuclear, albeit with slightly higher energy service costs. Arguing that nuclear is essential, while ignoring the challenges of getting people to accept a nuclear plant in their midst, presents a take-your-medicine-or-else myth that only hinders our progress with the climate threat.

While arguing that nuclear power is essential provides an example of this attitude toward GHG-reducing *actions*, arguing that carbon pricing is essential provides an example of it with climate-energy *policies*. It is not true that carbon pricing is essential. Someone who says this is simply expressing their preference that we decarbonize in the most economically efficient manner, even if the single-minded pursuit of that approach results in continued policy failure, and thus climate failure. Again, this logic seems to be more revealing of its proponent than our policy choices. For if some people are unwilling or unable to accept the economic efficiency lessons from an Economics 100 textbook, does that really justify refusing second-best policies, even if these latter have a far higher likelihood of political, and therefore climate, success?

Our chances increase significantly if more of the people who claim to want climate success incorporate into their prescriptions the key lessons from research on human cognitive imperfections when assessing the relative risks of actions, such as nuclear power versus alternatives, or the relative efficiency and fairness of decarbonization policies, such as carbon pricing versus flexible regulations. I say it again. With the climate-energy challenge, perfectionist prescriptions are the enemy of success. Those advocating them need to look in the mirror when allocating blame for humanity's continued failure on this critical challenge.

* * *

This leaves one last task on the simple path to climate success. We must be able to detect and elect climate-sincere politicians, and then pressure them to implement a few simple policies, such that any citizen can detect procrastination and evasion. The nature of this task crystalized for me a few years ago during the question period after one of my talks. Someone in the audience asked, "Don't we need to better inform our political leaders about climate science and effective policy options? Some are skeptical of the science. Some acknowledge the science, but oppose carbon taxes and other strong policies. Don't we need to send politicians to remedial school for the climate?" Before I could respond, a woman waiting at the other mic engaged the questioner.

"There is nothing we can tell politicians they don't already know about the climate threat and GHG reduction policies."

"How can you be sure?"

"I spent years as a senior political advisor. Believe me, *they know*."

"Then what would cause them to act?"

"A policy window of the kind that influenced right-of-center politicians in the mid-2000s like Arnold Schwarzenegger, John McCain and Mitt Romney in the US, and Gordon Campbell in British Columbia."

"But how does a policy window happen? Do we need more devastating hurricanes, floods and wildfires?"

"Probably. Our political system is not configured to take difficult steps in the present to avoid great harm in the future. We don't reward politicians for thinking and acting that way."

"So that's it? There's no hope? Nothing that might change their minds before the calamity?"

"There certainly is. Politicians will abandon a position if the political costs are excessive. Simply put, if the political costs exceed the political benefits."

"But how can that happen with the climate threat?"

"We need to *create* the policy window. We need enough people to act in ways that catch the media's attention and pressure politicians. Easiest is to engage politically. Citizens active in the political process are important, although the effect is impossible to measure. Unfortunately, phasing out fossil fuels directly threatens powerful and wealthy people who have political influence. So creating a policy window may entail a bigger personal commitment as past successful social movements have shown, whether for civil rights, women's rights or opposition to war. Options include boycotts, protests, demonstrations, even acts of civil disobedience to alert fellow citizens to the importance of the issue."

"And then the politicians will do the right thing?"

"Maybe. But then you're still not out of the woods. Politicians have short attention spans. You probably need to convince them to create regulatory institutions that will sustain the policies regardless of the next distraction. Something like the California Air Resources Board. Tell the politicians this delegation of climate policy responsibility is in their best interests, since effective policies are not vote-getters!"

She had left nothing for me to say. But I really appreciated her response. It made me reflect on my responsibilities as a citizen. Until then, I was generally satisfied with my comfortable role as independent expert, helping sincere politicians with policy advice and analysis, exposing insincere politicians with my energy-policy modeling for think tanks, non-government organizations, and the media. But with the climate threat, was that enough?

When I later recounted this exchange to my research group, one grad student said, "You should produce a flow chart." He noted that engineers draw flow charts to guide them with contingent decisions – if A, do X; if B, do Y. That night I produced the diagram in Figure 13.2. While it might strike some as playful, it's not meant to be. It's my "guide to citizen behavior for climate success."

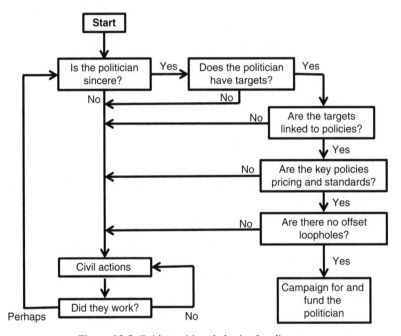

Figure 13.2 Guide to citizen behavior for climate success

Moving to the right along the top of the diagram, we see that finding a climate-sincere politician is just the first of many steps. Lots can go wrong. The politician must set targets. But even insincere politicians do that. The political benefit-cost ratio for setting targets while doing nothing is strongly positive, especially if these are distant targets beyond the politician's elected life expectancy. Mid-century is ideal, but 2030 is still pretty safe. (In my career, I have assessed GHG targets for the years 2000, 2005, 2010, 2020, 2030, 2050, and 2100. Do I sound jaded?)

The targets must be linked to policies. The danger at this stage lies in the policy-making process. A common avoidance strategy is to create a "citizen climate advisory committee." The politician selects members of the public (not policy experts) and gives them lots of resources and time – the longer the better. Eventually, the committee produces a melange of GHG-reducing actions and policies, such as "increased wind power" as one item and a "renewable portfolio standard" as another. But as I explained in Chapter 6, because policies cause actions, these cannot be mixed. A climate plan should *only* contain policies, because it explains the policies government will implement to cause GHG-reducing actions by citizens and corporations. It can include a forecast of the possible technological and behavioral actions caused by the policies – which should be produced by independent and credible policy forecasting experts. But the policies are all the plan should list and that list should be very small. It might be a single economy-wide carbon tax, but I would be happy with five or six flex-regs each applying to a different sector of the economy.

Instead, the ineffective climate plan (of which I have read over a hundred from jurisdictions around the world) will look like a long to-do list. In addition to actions that should not be in there, it will include numerous small-effect policies that would not be needed if the essential carbon pricing or flex-reg policies were implemented. These might include funding for electric vehicle rechargers, a tax-break for wind power, training for electric car technicians, grants for biofuel producers, climate research, adaptation planning, an educational kit for schools, a carpooling website, behavioral change information, a scrap-it program for old vehicles, a carbon offset program, subsidies for home insulation, incentives for efficient natural gas appliances, funding for urban transit feasibility studies, and so on.

Even if the politician sincerely intends to one day implement carbon pricing or regulations, it's easier to start with small-effect policies. In public speeches and media sound-bites, the politician rhymes through the list, ticking off achievements to show progress, noting that the regulations and pricing will happen, but these take longer to implement (which is not true). Later, the politician acknowledges that the year before an election is not a good time to impose carbon pricing or regulations (which is true), so more delay is needed.

After almost two decades of these delaying tactics in most jurisdictions, governments have finally been implementing some compulsory policies. Evidence against the ineffective policies became too obvious, as jurisdictions missed target after target. Now the issue is stringency. While flex-regs might be less difficult than carbon pricing, for a given amount of GHG reduction, both types of compulsory policy are difficult as we increase their stringency, as I illustrated with my "political difficulty of climate policies" Figure 6.5 in Chapter 6. This is why concerned citizens today must focus on the stringency of a few decarbonization policies in a few key sectors.

In this final chapter I've explained why those key sectors are electricity and transportation, and how to get higher stringency by targeting a rapid phase-out of coal plants and gasoline vehicles in wealthy countries. This transformation must extend to developing countries via falling costs of clean alternatives, transfers to support clean investment where wealthier countries are able to show some generosity, and carbon tariffs by a club of climate leaders that disincentivize other countries from free-riding. When a government sincerely advances along this policy and action trajectory, we must support it vigorously. Sadly, that is not always the case, as an example from my own country illustrates.

In the period 2015–2019, the Canadian government showed global leadership by rapidly developing policies to phase out coal plants, regulate methane emissions, implement national carbon pricing, fund transit, implement an output-based pricing system for emissions-intensive trade-exposed industries, and apply a clean fuel standard (a flex-reg like the low carbon fuel standard) to coal, oil, and natural gas. It also launched with the UK the Powering Past Coal Alliance to lead a growing movement of jurisdictions acting to phase out coal-fired power – the very strategic global spillover of national policies that I had been championing.[9] Yet, few environmentalists in Canada gave the government credit for these impressive efforts. Because the government leads a diverse country with conflicting regional interests, it also supported a new pipeline from the Alberta oil sands. To many environmentalists, this one decision equated this government with the previous Canadian government, which had faked it completely on climate for a decade. If we cannot support climate-sincere politicians, warts and all, they won't survive, and we further reduce our chances of climate success.

But what if our political leaders are insincere on the climate threat, as is so often the case? What should we do then? Descending the left side of Figure 13.2 leads to a box labeled "civil actions." This covers all types of public engagement, including social media, discussions with friends and neighbors, donations, volunteering with environmental organizations and their public awareness campaigns, letters to newspapers, calls to radio shows, boycotts, and demonstrations. We may take these actions to influence and support the decisions of sincere politicians too, just as protests against the Keystone XL pipeline facilitated its rejection by President Obama, a climate-sincere politician.

In this book I have often noted why success with the climate threat is so difficult: a global governance problem without a global government; phasing out the combustion of high-quality fossil fuels that have so benefited humanity and could still benefit the poorest among us; the combination of wealth and power seeking to continue the burning of fossil fuels for self-interest reasons; the inability of our national and sub-national democratic processes to initiate and sustain an effective decarbonization effort; and our human penchant for self-delusion in the face of inconvenient truths. In this light, our decades of failure are not surprising.

Moreover, with atmospheric CO_2 concentrations now well above 400 parts per million and rising rapidly, and the impacts of climate change increasing in intensity, reasonable people are seriously studying risky geoengineering options. What was for years seen as the 'climate threat' is increasingly recognized as the 'climate emergency.'

In this context, a growing number of otherwise law-abiding citizens are considering the option of peaceful civil disobedience. I am one of these. Civil disobedience takes me far outside my comfort zone. I believe we should obey laws created by our democratic institutions. To disobey a law, even as an act of peaceful protest, even with a willingness to take the legal and economic consequences, is to me a profoundly troubling act. The situation must be dire.

Until reaching my mid-50s, I never imagined engaging in civil disobedience. I had been lucky that my career as a climate-energy policy expert offered so many avenues for expressing my views and educating others, whether conducting policy effectiveness research, exposing faking-it politicians, advising sincere politicians, providing media commentary, or public speaking.

However, the situation in Canada and in my province of British Columbia around 2011 became especially desperate. Prime Minister Stephen Harper, who had defeated the Liberals under Stephane Dion in 2009 by campaigning against his "job-killing carbon tax," had just won a national majority. Now he was unconstrained in pursuing the rapid expansion of fossil fuels, although, of course, he maintained that he was also sincere on climate. In British Columbia, Premier Gordon Campbell, the politician who had implemented North America's first carbon tax, was gone and his replacement as premier had frozen the tax. National and regional media teemed with industry advertisements and statements by political and corporate elites focused entirely on the economic benefits of fossil fuel expansion. Much of the public seemed passive, overwhelmed by the pro-fossil fuel messaging.

After lengthy discussions with friends and colleagues, I finally agreed with one of my former students, Kevin Washbrook, an effective climate campaigner, that a civil disobedience action challenging the contradictory fossil fuel and climate-sincerity narratives of the Harper government might contribute to its defeat in the 2015 election. Our goal was to increase, even if only by a tiny amount, the number of Canadians suspicious of the government's climate sincerity, and thus their willingness to vote differently next time. So 13 of us blocked a coal train as a public wake-up action in May 2012.[10] We were arrested and jailed for a few hours.

I explained my actions to the media at the time, and later in an essay in Canada's premier magazine, *The Walrus*.[11] While I had thought a lot about this action in advance, it is difficult in hindsight to see our effort as entirely coherent. I preferred arrest blocking coal, as consumption of this fossil fuel must unequivocally be falling everywhere, as I have explained throughout this book. But this was metallurgical coal, bound for steel factories in east Asia. Even this type of coal should only be used with carbon capture and storage when making steel, but that's a complicated story for the media to convey. I also wondered if our message about the Harper government's climate insincerity would resonate with anyone.

The government was defeated in 2015, and this occurred in part because younger Canadians turned out in record numbers to vote for the Liberals and other climate-concerned parties. Polls showed that by the time of its defeat, the government was severely distrusted on the climate, a major concern for the 68% of Canadians who voted for the other parties. I cannot say if our action contributed to this changing view, but we got a lot of media attention. Imagine if there had been 100 similar citizen actions during the government's term, or even 1,000.

I hope that this first act of civil disobedience was also my last. But I can't be sure. As the flow chart suggests, our actions as citizens should be conditional, dependent on what is needed and likely most effective at any time. If we can elect climate-sincere governments, civil disobedience may not be necessary. In that regard, I could not bring myself to join others engaged in civil disobedience in 2017 in an effort to stop construction of the TransMountain Pipeline expansion from the Alberta oil sands to the coast at Vancouver. I was more concerned with supporting a government that was quickly implementing the effective climate policies I and others had been demanding for over two decades, especially with its leveraging of our domestic coal plant phase-out with a global multi-country initiative.

If I feel compelled to repeat this act, I think it should focus on vehicles, since we can and must quickly phase out sales of gasoline cars and trucks, following Norway's example. Perhaps chaining myself to the door of a luxury car dealership that sells gasoline vehicles?

For people who criticized me for the audacity of breaking the law, I have some understanding. We can all make excuses for why our particular act of civil disobedience is essential. But I cannot agree that civil disobedience is never an option, especially when it comes to protecting current and future generations from a global disaster that has climate scientists not only alarmed but many themselves opting for civil disobedience. I have sometimes responded to criticism of my arrest by reversing the accusation in asking, "Why are you not engaging in civil action, including perhaps civil disobedience? You know what I know about the seriousness of this threat and the inaction of our government. Will future generations agree that you did all you could with that knowledge? Or will they say you opted for a comfortable life, even while knowing that your actions could have made a difference?" As Albert Einstein purportedly once said, "Those who have the privilege to know, have the duty to act."

This dilemma on appropriate action reminds me of people in the 1930s, like Adam von Trott in Germany, who recognized early the threat posed by Adolf Hitler and urged fellow citizens to join them in active opposition. Von Trott and other early resisters understood the need to take actions that were judged as unlawful and unpatriotic by many of their contemporaries, but would be seen as justified and courageous by future generations. They also understood that those who did not act bore responsibility for the harm to come. We cannot absolve ourselves from responsibility by downplaying the importance of our actions as individuals. Social and political outcomes are the responsibility of all of us, and therefore of each of us.

The human propensity to delude has for three decades prevented us from effective action on the climate threat. But as more of us are willing to inconvenience ourselves in our actions as responsible citizens, we increase the likelihood of success against this grave threat. And for this we need to understand and overcome the myths that hinder our progress.

Notes

1 THE ROLE OF MYTHS IN OUR CLIMATE-ENERGY CHALLENGE

1. Boustany, N. 1991. Iraqi Leader Remains Defiant following US-led Air Attacks. *The Washington Post* (January 17).
2. Tavris, C. and Aronson, E. 2007. *Mistakes Were Made (But Not By Me): Why We Justify Foolish Beliefs, Bad Decisions, and Hurtful Acts*. Orlando, FL: Harcourt.
3. Haidt, J. 2012. *The Righteous Mind: Why Good People Are Divided by Politics and Religion*. New York: Pantheon.
4. Mooney, C. 2011. The science of why we don't believe science. *Mother Jones* (May/ June).
5. Bataille, C. et al. 2016. The Need for National Deep Decarbonization Pathways for Effective Climate Policy. *Climate Policy*. 16, S7–S26.
6. Le Quere, C. et al. 2019. Drivers of Declining CO_2 Emissions in 18 Developed Economies. *Nature Climate Change*. 9, 213–218.
7. Hastorf, A. and Cantril, H. 1954. They Saw a Game: A Case Study. *The Journal of Abnormal & Social Psychology*, 49, 129–134.
8. Kahan, D. 2018. Why Smart People Are Vulnerable to Putting Tribe before Truth. *Scientific American* (December 3).
9. Zito, S. 2016. Taking Trump Seriously, not Literally. *The Atlantic* (September 23).
10. Jaccard, M. 2005. *Sustainable Fossil Fuels: The Unusual Suspect in the Quest for Clean and Enduring Energy*. Cambridge: Cambridge University Press.
11. Jaccard, M., Nyboer, J., and Sadownik, B. 2002. *The Cost of Climate Policy*. Vancouver: University of British Columbia Press.
12. Simpson, J., Jaccard, M., and Rivers, N. 2011. *Hot Air: Meeting Canada's Climate Change Challenge*. Toronto: McLelland and Stewart (Doug Gibson books).
13. Gore, A. 2006. *An Inconvenient Truth: The Planetary Emergency of Global Warming and What We Can Do About It*. Emmaus, PA: Rodale Press. [Film. Hollywood. CA: Paramount.]
14. Stern, N. 2006. *The Economics of Climate Change*. Cambridge: Cambridge University Press.
15. United Nations Framework Convention on Climate Change. 2015. *Paris Agreement*.
16. Keys, D. 1982. *Earth at Omega: Passage to Planetization*. Wellesley, MA: Branden.

2 THE ART OF DELUDING OURSELVES AND OTHERS

1. Elliott, S. 2008. When Doctors, and even Santa, Endorsed Tobacco. *The New York Times* (October 6).

2. Brandt, A. 2007. *The Cigarette Century: The Rise, Fall, and Deadly Persistence of the Product that Defined America.* New York, NY: Basic Books.

3. Kluger, R. 1996. *Ashes to Ashes: America's Hundred-year Cigarette War, the Public Health, and the Unabashed Triumph of Philip Morris.* New York, NY: Knopf.

4. Oreskes, N. and Conway, E. 2010. *Merchants of Doubt.* New York, NY: Bloomsbury.

5. Michaels, D. 2008. *Doubt is their Product.* Oxford: Oxford University Press.

6. Wexler, B. 2006. *Brain and Culture: Neurobiology, Ideology, and Social Change.* Cambridge, MA: MIT Press.

7. Gilbert, D. 2006. *Stumbling on Happiness.* New York, NY: Alfred A. Knopf.

8. Festinger, L., Riecken, H., and Schachter, S. 1956. *When Prophecy Fails: A Social and Psychological Study of a Modern Group that Predicted the Destruction of the World.* Minneapolis, MN: University of Minnesota Press.

3 CLIMATE SCIENTISTS ARE CONSPIRATORS

1. Emanuel, K. 2005. *Divine Wind: The History and Science of Hurricanes.* New York, NY: Oxford University Press.

2. Horne, J. 2006. *Breach of Faith: Hurricane Katrina and the Near Death of a Great American City.* New York, NY: Random House.

3. Brinkley, D. 2006. *The Great Deluge: Hurricane Katrina, New Orleans, and the Mississippi Gulf Coast.* New York, NY: Harper Collins.

4. Fourier, J. 1824. Remarques générales sur les températures du globe terrestre et des espaces planétaires. *Annales de Chimie et de Physique,* 27, 136–67.

5. Tyndall, J. 1861. On the Absorption and Radiation of Heat by Gases and Vapours, and on the Physical Connexion of Radiation, Absorption and Conduction. *Philosophical Transactions of the Royal Society of London.* 151, 1–36.

6. Arrhenius, S. 1896. On the Influence of Carbonic Acid in the Air upon the Temperature of the Ground. *London, Edinburgh and Dublin Philosophical Magazine and Journal of Science,* 41, 237–275.

7. Callendar, G. S. The Artificial Production of Carbon Dioxide and its Influence on Temperature. *Quarterly Journal of the Royal Meteorological Society,* 64, 223–230.

8. Charney, J., et al. 1979. *Carbon Dioxide and Climate: A Scientific Assessment.* Washington, DC: National Academy of Sciences Press.

9. IPCC. 1990, 1995, 2001, 2007, 2014. *Assessment Reports.* Cambridge: Cambridge University Press.

10. Lontzek, T. et al. 2015. Stochastic Integrated Assessment of Climate Tipping Points Indicates the Need for Strict Climate Policy. *Nature Climate Change.* 5(5), 441.

11. *Real Time with Bill Maher.* 2005. Season 3, Episode 15.

12. Hansen, J. 2009. *Storms of my Grandchildren: The Truth about the Coming Climate Catastrophe and Our Last Chance to Save Humanity.* New York, NY: Bloomsbury.

13. I was an author on the 2nd IPCC Assessment Review, and am an author on the 6th.

14. Oreskes, N. and Conway, E. 2010. *Merchants of Doubt*. New York, NY: Bloomsbury.

15. Shulman, S., et al. 2007. *Smoke, Mirrors, and Hot Air. How ExxonMobil Uses Big Tobacco's Tactics to Manufacture Uncertainty on Climate Science.* Cambridge, MA: Union of Concerned Scientists.

16. Coll, S. 2012. *Private Empire: ExxonMobil and American Power.* New York, NY: Penguin.

17. Hoggan, J. and Littlemore, R. 2009. *Climate Cover-up: The Crusade to Deny Global Warming.* Vancouver: BC: Greystone Books.

18. Associated Press. 2012. Climate Change Fears Overblown, Says Exxon Mobil Boss. *The Guardian* (June 28).

19. Revkin, A. 2003. Politics Reasserts itself in the Debate over Climate Change and its Hazards. *The New York Times* (August 5).

20. Gleick, P. H., et al. 2010. Climate Change and the Integrity of Science. *Science*, 328, 689–690.

21. Mann, M. 2012. *The Hockey Stick and the Climate Wars: Dispatches from the Front Lines.* New York, NY: Columbia University Press.

22. *The Colbert Report.* 2012. Season 7, Episode 42.

23. McKibben, B. 1989. *The End of Nature.* New York, NY: Random House.

24. Flannery, T. 2005. *The Weather Makers: How Man is Changing the Climate and what it Means for Life on Earth.* New York, NY: Grove Press.

25. Diamond, J. M. 2005. *Collapse: How Societies Choose to Fail or Succeed.* London: Penguin.

26. Olson, R. 2009. *Don't be Such a Scientist.* Washington, DC: Island Press.

27. Baron, N. 2010. *Escape from the Ivory Tower: A Guide to Making your Science Matter.* Washington, DC: Island Press.

28. McKibben, B. 2010. *Eaarth: Making a Life on a Tough New Planet.* New York, NY: Holt.

29. Flannery, T. 2015. *Atmosphere of Hope: Searching for Solutions to the Climate Crisis.* New York, NY: Grove Press.

30. Mann, M. and Toles, T. 2016. *The Madhouse Effect: How Climate Change Denial is Threatening our Planet, Destroying our Politics, and Driving us Crazy.* New York, NY: Columbia University Press.

31. Hornsey, M. et al. 2016. Meta-analysis of the Determinants and Outcomes of Belief in Climate Change. *Nature Climate Change*, 6(6), 622–626.

32. Hulme, M. 2009. *Why We Disagree about Climate Change: Understanding Controversy, Inaction and Opportunity.* Cambridge: Cambridge University Press.

33. Marshall, G. 2014. *Don't Even Think About It: Why our Brains are Wired to Ignore Climate Change.* New York, NY: Bloomsbury.

34. Hoffman, A. 2015. *How Culture Shapes the Climate Change Debate.* Palo Alto, CA: Stanford University Press.

35. Hoggan, J. 2016. *I'm Right and You're an Idiot: The Toxic State of Public Discourse and How to Clean it Up.* Gabriola Island, British Columbia: New Society Publishers.

36. Farrell, J., McConnell, K. and Brulle, R. 2019. Evidence-based Strategies to Combat Scientific Misinformation. *Nature Climate Change.* 9, 191–195.

37. *Last Week Tonight with John Oliver.* 2019. (May).

4 ALL COUNTRIES WILL AGREE ON CLIMATE FAIRNESS

1. Hitler, A. 1925. *Mein Kampf.* Munich: Eher-Verlag.
2. Beller, H. 1992. *The Restless Conscience: Resistance to Hitler inside Nazi Germany* [Documentary film].
3. Churchill, W. 2012. *The Power of Words,* ed. Gilbert, M. Boston, MA: Da Capo Press.
4. Churchill, W. 2012. *The Power of Words,* ed. Gilbert, M. Boston, MA: Da Capo Press.
5. Churchill, W. 2012. *The Power of Words,* ed. Gilbert, M. Boston, MA: Da Capo Press.
6. Churchill, W. 2012. *The Power of Words,* ed. Gilbert, M. Boston, MA: Da Capo Press.
7. Victor, D. 2001. *The Collapse of the Kyoto Protocol and the Struggle to Slow Global Warming.* Princeton, NJ: Princeton University Press.
8. Gore, A. 2006. *An Inconvenient Truth: The Planetary Emergency of Global Warming and What We Can Do About It.* Emmaus, PA: Rodale Press. [Film. Hollywood. CA: Paramount.]
9. Rogelj, J. 2016. Paris Agreement Climate Proposals Need a Boost to Keep Warming Well Below 2°C. *Nature.* 534, 631–639.
10. Jaccard, M. and Wu, H. (co-chairs). 2009. *Report and Recommendations to Chinese Premier Wen on the Prospects and Policies for Sustainable Use of Coal in China.* Beijing: China Council for International Cooperation on Environment and Development.
11. Victor, D. 2011. *Global Warming Gridlock.* New York, NY: Cambridge University Press.
12. Nordhaus, W. 2015. Climate Clubs: Overcoming Free-riding in International Climate Policy. *American Economic Review,* 105(4), 1339–1370.

5 THIS FOSSIL FUEL PROJECT IS ESSENTIAL

1. Goodell, J. 2007. *Big Coal: The Dirty Secret behind America's Energy Future.* Boston, MA: Mariner Books.
2. Goodell, J. 2010. As the World Burns. *Rolling Stone* (January 7).
3. Orwell, G. 1949. *Nineteen Eighty-four.* London: Secker & Warburg.
4. Weyant, J. and Kriegler, E. 2014. Preface and Introduction to EMF 27. *Climatic Change,* 122, 345–352.
5. Krey, V., et al. 2014. Getting from Here to There: Energy Technology Transformation Pathways in the EMF 27 Scenarios. *Climatic Change,* 123, 369–382.
6. McCollum, D., et al. 2014. Fossil Resource and Energy Security Dynamics in Conventional and Carbon-constrained Worlds. *Climatic Change,* 123, 413–426.
7. IPCC. 2018. *Global Warming of 1.5°C. An IPCC Special Report.* Cambridge: Cambridge University Press.
8. Kamiya, G., Axsen, J., and Crawford, C. 2019. Modeling the GHG Emissions Intensity of Plug-in Electric Vehicles Using Short-term and Long-term Perspectives. *Transportation Research Part D.* 96, 209–223.
9. Rudd, S. 2012. Cost-effectiveness of Climate Change Policies for the United States. (Master's thesis) School of Resource and Environmental Management, Simon Fraser University.
10. Jaccard, M., Hoffele, J. and Jaccard, T. 2018. Global Carbon Budgets and the Viability of New Fossil Fuel Projects. *Climatic Change.* 150, 15–28.

11. Bertram, C. et al. 2015. Carbon Lock-in through Capital Stock Inertia Associated with Weak Near-term Climate Policies. *Technological Forecasting and Social Change.* 90, 62–72.
12. Shakespeare, W. 1605. *King Lear.*

6 WE MUST PRICE CARBON EMISSIONS

1. British Columbia Government. 2008. *News Release Balanced Budget 2008 – Greener Future, Stronger Economy.* www.bcbudget.gov.bc.ca/2008/newsrelease/.
2. Gore, A. 2006. *An Inconvenient Truth: The Planetary Emergency of Global Warming and What We Can Do About It.* Emmaus, PA: Rodale Press.
3. Stern, N. 2006. *The Economics of Climate Change.* Cambridge: Cambridge University Press.
4. European Commission. 2005. *EU Emissions Trading System.* Retrieved from https://ec .europa.eu/clima/policies/ets_en.
5. Beck, M. et al. 2015. Carbon Tax and Revenue Recycling: Impacts on Households in British Columbia. *Resource and Energy Economics.* 41, 40–69.
6. Olson, M. 1965. *The Logic of Collective Action: Public Goods and the Theory of Groups.* Cambridge, MA: Harvard University Press.
7. Achen, C. and Bartels, L. 2016. *Democracy for Realists: Why Elections do not Produce Responsive Government.* Princeton, NJ: Princeton University Press.
8. Kahneman, D. 2011. *Thinking Fast and Slow.* New York, NY: Farrar, Straus and Giroux.
9. Rabe, B. *Can We Price Carbon?* Cambridge, MA: MIT Press.
10. Bernauer, T. and McGrath, L. 2016. Simple Reframing unlikely to Boost Public Support for Climate Policy. *Nature Climate Change.* 6, 680–683.
11. Jaccard, M. 2012. The Political Acceptability of Carbon Taxes: Lessons from British Columbia. In Milne, J. and Anderson, M. *Handbook of Research on Environmental Taxation.* 175–191. Cheltenham: Edward Elgar.
12. MacKay, D., Ockenfels, A., and Stoft, S. 2017. *Global Carbon Pricing: The Path to Climate Cooperation.* Cambridge, MA: MIT Press; Metcalf, G. 2018. *Paying for Pollution: Why a Carbon Tax is Good for America.* New York, NY: Oxford University Press.
13. National Conference of State Legislatures. 2019. *State Renewable Portfolio Standards and Goals.* www.ncsl.org/research/energy/renewable-portfolio-standards.aspx.
14. Berry, T. and Jaccard, M. 2001. The Renewable Portfolio Standard: Design Considerations and an Implementation Survey. *Energy Policy.* 29, 263–277.
15. Vass, T. and Jaccard, M. 2017. Driving Decarbonization: Pathways and Policies for Canadian Transport. *Energy and Materials Research Group: Simon Fraser University.*
16. Upton, G. and Snyder, B. 2017. Funding Renewable Energy: An Analysis of Renewable Portfolio Standards. *Energy Economics.* 66, 205–216; Holland, S., Hughes, J., and Knittle, C. 2009. Greenhouse Gas Reductions under Low Carbon Fuel Standards? *American Economic Journal: Economic Policy,* 1(1), 106–146.
17. Vass, T. and Jaccard, M. 2017. Driving Decarbonization: Pathways and Policies for Canadian Transport. *Energy and Materials Research Group: Simon Fraser University.*
18. Jenkins, J. 2014. Political Economy Constraints on Carbon Pricing Policies: What Are the Implications for Economic Efficiency, Environmental Efficacy, and Climate Policy Design? *Energy Policy.* 69, 467–477.

19. Jaccard, M., Hein, M., and Vass. T. 2016. *Is Win-Win Possible? Can Canada's government Achieve its Paris Commitment … and Get Re-elected?* Energy and Materials Research Group, Simon Fraser University.

20. United States House of Representatives. 2009. *American Clean Energy and Security Act.*

21. Broder, J. 2009. Obama to Toughen Rules on Emissions and Mileage, *The New York Times* (May 18).

22. United States Environmental Protection Agency. 2015. *Clean Power Plan for Existing Power Plants.* https://web.archive.org/web/20160325042337/https://www.epa.gov/cleanpowerplan/clean-power-plan-existing-power-plants.

23. Grubb, M. and Newberry, D., 2018. UK Electricity Market Reform and the Energy Transition: Emerging Lessons. *The Energy Journal.* 39(6), 1–25.

24. Fairbrother, M., 2016. Trust and Public Support for Environmental Protection in Diverse National Contexts. *Sociological Science.* 3, 359–382.

25. Shmelev, S. and Speck, S. 2018. Green Fiscal Reform in Sweden: Econometric Assessment of the Carbon and Energy Taxation Scheme, *Renewable and Sustainable Energy Reviews*, 90, 969–981.

26. McAuley, J. 2019. Low Visibility. *New York Review of Books* (March 21).

27. Rhodes, K., Axsen, J., and Jaccard, M. 2014. Does Effective Climate Policy Require Well-informed Citizen Support? *Global Environmental Change*, 29, 92–104.

28. Caplan, B. 2007. *The Myth of the Rational Voter: Why Democracies Choose Bad Policies.* Princeton, NJ: Princeton University Press.

29. Rhodes, K., Axsen, J., and Jaccard, M. 2015. Gauging Citizen Support for a Low Carbon Fuel Standard. *Energy Policy*, 79, 104–114.

30. M.K. Jaccard and Associates. 2008. *A Quantitative Analysis of Selected Climate Policies in British Columbia.* Prepared for the B.C. Climate Action Secretariat; British Columbia Government, 2008. *Climate Action Plan.* Victoria: Government of B.C. (see especially the climate policy modeling appendix).

31. Rhodes, K. and Jaccard, M. 2013. A Tale of Two Climate Policies: Political-economy of British Columbia's Carbon Tax and Clean Electricity Standard. *Canadian Public Policy*, 39, S37–51.

32. Rabe, B. 2018. *Can We Price Carbon?* Cambridge, MA: MIT Press.

33. *National Survey on Energy and Environment.* 2019. http://closup.umich.edu/national-surveys-on-energy-and-environment/.

34. Stern, N. 2006. *The Economics of Climate Change.* Cambridge: Cambridge University Press.

35. Hulme, M. 2009. *Why We Disagree About Climate Change: Understanding Controversy, Inaction and Opportunity.* Cambridge: Cambridge University Press.

7 PEAK OIL WILL GET US FIRST ANYWAY

1. Moses, M. 2018. What Drives Doomsday Preppers? *The New Yorker* (November).

2. Howden, D. 2007. World Oil Supplies Are Set to Run Out Faster than Expected, Warn Scientists. *The Independent* (June 14).

3. Hubbert, M. K., 1956. *Nuclear Energy and the Fossil Fuel.* In: Meeting of the Southern District, Division of Production, American Petroleum Institute. Shell Development Company, San Antonio, TX.

4. Hirsch, R. L., Bezdek, R., and Wendling, R. 2005. *Peaking of World Oil Production: Impacts, Mitigation, and Risk Management.* Washington, DC: U.S. Department of Energy.

5. Rolling Stone. 2006. Kurt Vonnegut says This Is the End of the World (August 24).

6. Meadows, D. H. et al. 1972. *The Limits to Growth: A Report for the Club of Rome's Project on the Predicament of Mankind.* New York, NY: Universe Books.

7. Lomborg, B. 2001. *The Skeptical Environmentalist: Measuring the Real State of the World.* Cambridge: Cambridge University Press; Ridley, M. 2010. *The Rational Optimist: How Prosperity Evolves.* New York, NY: Harper Collins.

8. Hamilton, C. 2010. *Requiem for a Species. Why We Resist the Truth about Climate Change.* Sydney, AU: Earthscan; Wallace-Wells, D. 2019. *The Uninhabitable Earth: Life after Warming.* New York, NY: Tim Duggan Books; Rich, N. 2019. *Losing Earth: A Recent History.* New York, NY: Farrar, Straus, & Giroux.

9. British Petroleum. (annual report, all years) *Statistical Review of World Energy.*

10. Johansson, T. et al. (eds.). 2012. *The Global Energy Assessment: Towards a Sustainable Future.* Cambridge: Cambridge University Press.

11. Aguilera, R. and Radetzki, M. 2016. *The Price of Oil.* Cambridge: Cambridge University Press.

12. Yergin, D. 2011. *The Quest: Energy, Security, and the Remaking of the Modern World.* London: Penguin.

13. Krugman, P. 2008. *The Return of Depression Economics and the Crisis of 2008.* New York, NY: W. W. Norton & Company.

14. Stiglitz, J. 2010. *Freefall: America, Free Markets, and the Sinking of the World Economy.* New York, NY: W. W. Norton & Company.

8 WE MUST CHANGE OUR BEHAVIOR

1. Kinsey, A. C. et al. 1953. *Sexual Behavior in the Human Female.* Philadelphia, PA: Saunders; Hite, S. 1976. *The Hite Report.* New York, NY: Macmillan.

2. *Associated Press.* 2006. Shell Oil Chief: US Needs Global Warming Plan (September 23).

3. Natural Resources Defense Council. 2010. Simple and Inexpensive Actions Could Reduce Global Warming Emissions by One Billion Tons. *Energy Facts* (May).

4. Girrbach, C. 2012. 3 Ways IT Can Support Greener Behaviors. *GreenBiz* (March 20).

5. Schmidt, C. 2006. *Workers of the World Relax.* Vancouver, BC: WLP Publishing.

6. Frank, R. H. 2009. *The Economic Naturalist's Field Guide: Common Sense Principles for Troubled Times.* New York, NY: Basic Books.

7. Rees, W. 2010. What's Blocking Sustainability? Human Nature, Cognition and Denial. *Sustainability: Science, Practice and Policy,* 6(2), 13–25.

8. Groves, S. 2009. The Desire to Acquire: Forecasting the Evolution of Household Energy Services. Master's research project, Simon Fraser University.

9. Truby, J. 2018. Decarbonizing Bitcoin: Law and Policy Choices for Reducing the Energy Consumption of Blockchain Technologies and Digital Currencies. *Energy Research and Social Science*, 44, 399–410.

10. Popplewell, B. 2008. Can Branson Globetrot on Reduced Carbon Diet? *The Star* (February 14).

11. Devinney, T., Auger, P., and Eckhardt, G. 2010. *The Myth of the Ethical Consumer.* Cambridge: Cambridge University Press.

12. Leonard, A. 2010. *The Story of Stuff: How Our Obsession with Stuff is Trashing the Planet, Our Communities, and Our Health – and a Vision for Change.* New York, NY: Free Press.

13. Willett, W. et al. 2019. *Food in the Anthropocene: the EAT-Lancet Commission on Healthy Diets from Sustainable Food Systems.* Lancet; Springmann, M. et al. 2016. Analysis and Valuation of the Health and Climate Change Cobenefits of Dietary Change. *Proceedings of the National Academy of Sciences.* 113 (15), 4146–4151.

14. McKibben, B. 2019. Glaciers and Arctic Ice Are Vanishing. Time to Get Radical before it's Too Late. *The Guardian* (April 10).

9 WE CAN BE CARBON NEUTRAL

1. Keith, D. et al. 2018. A Process for Capturing CO_2 from the Atmosphere. *Joule.* 2, 1573–1594; Carbon Engineering. 2019. *About Us.* https://carbonengineering.com/company-profile/.

2. IPCC. 2014. *Fifth Assessment Report.* Cambridge: Cambridge University Press.

3. Anderson, K. and Peters, G. 2016. The Trouble with Negative Emissions: Reliance on Negative-emission Concepts Locks in Humankind's Carbon Addiction. *Science*, 354 (6309), 182–183.

4. IPCC. 2005. *Special Report on Carbon Dioxide Capture and Storage.* Cambridge: Cambridge University Press.

5. Schapiro, M. 2010. Conning the Climate: Inside the Carbon-trading Shell Game. *Harper's* (February).

6. May, P. 2007. Offset Your Infidelity? *New Statesman America* (May 14).

7. Elsworth, C. 2007. Eco-trendy Hollywood Stars as Major Polluter. *The Telegraph* (October 2).

8. Rivers, N. and Jaccard, M. 2011. Electric Utility Demand Side Management in Canada. *The Energy Journal*, 32 (4), 93–116; Murphy, R., Gross, D., and Jaccard, M. 2018. Use of Revealed Preference Data to Estimate the Costs of Forest Carbon Sequestration in Canada. *Forest Policy and Economics*, 97, 41–50.

9. Loughran, D. and Kulick, J. 2004. Demand-side Management and Energy Efficiency in the United States. *The Energy Journal*, 25(1), 19–43.

10. Robalino, J., et al. 2008. *Deforestation Impacts of Environmental Services Payments: Costa Rica's PSA Program 2000–2005.* Washington, DC: Resources for the Future.

11. Kollmus, A., et al. 2015. *Has Joint Implementation Reduced GHG Emissions? Lessons Learned for the Design of Carbon Market Mechanisms.* Stockholm Environment Institute Policy Brief.

12. Cames, M., et al. 2016. *How Additional is the Clean Development Mechanism?* Berlin: Institute for Applied Ecology,

13. Song, L. 2019. An Even More Inconvenient Truth: Why Carbon Credits for Forest Preservation May Be Even Worse than Doing Nothing. *Propublica* (May).

14. Anderson, K. 2012. The Inconvenient Truth of Carbon Offsets. *Nature*, 484(7).

15. Kopp, R. 2010. Role of Offsets in Global and Domestic Climate Policy. *Resources for the Future.* Issue Brief 10–11.

10 ENERGY EFFICIENCY IS PROFITABLE

1. Chu, S. 2011. Energy Efficiency: Achieving the Potential, Realizing the Savings. *HuffPost* (May 25).

2. ExxonMobil. 2013. The Outlook for Energy: A View to 2040. *Energy Meetings* (June 11).

3. Creyts, J. et al. (eds.). 2007. Reducing US Greenhouse Gas Emissions: How Much at What Cost? *McKinsey and Company* (December).

4. Murphy, R. and Jaccard, M. 2011. Energy Efficiency and the Cost of GHG Abatement: A Comparison of Bottom-up and Hybrid Models for the US. *Energy Policy*, 39, 7146–7155.

5. Lovins, A. 1977. *Soft Energy Paths: Toward a Durable Peace.* Cambridge, MA: Ballinger.

6. Brockway, P. et al. 2017. Energy Rebound as a Potential Threat to a Low-carbon Future: Findings from a New Exergy-based National-level Rebound Approach. *Energies.* 10, 51–75.

7. Jevons, W. 1865. *The Coal Question: An Inquiry Concerning the Progress of the Nations and the Probable Exhaustion of our Coal Mines.* London: Macmillan & Co.

8. Fouquet, R. and Pearson, P. 2006. Seven Centuries of Energy Services: The Price and Use of Light in the United Kingdom (1300–2000). *The Energy Journal.* 27 (1), 139–177.

9. Edison, T. 1880. As quoted in the *New York Herald.* While this version of the quote is best known, the quote in the original article differed slightly.

10. O'Grady, M. 2018. Ed Begley Jr. Reflects on Boycott Lists and Riding a Bicycle to Make Toast. *The Globe and Mail* (October 21).

11. Talley, I. 2009. Americans Are Like 'Teenage Kids' When It Comes to Energy. *The Wall Street Journal* (September 21).

11 RENEWABLES HAVE WON

1. Lynn, J. and Jay, A. 1989. *Yes Minister.* London: BBC Books.

2. IPCC. 1990, 1995, 2001, 2007, 2014. *Assessment Reports.* Cambridge: Cambridge University Press.

3. Smil, V. 2017. *Energy Transitions: History, Requirements, Prospects.* (2nd edition) Santa Barbara, CA: Praeger.

4. Johansson, T. et al. (eds.). 2012. *The Global Energy Assessment: Towards a Sustainable Future.* Cambridge: Cambridge University Press; Sachs, J. et al. 2014. *Pathways to Deep Decarbonization.* Paris: Sustainable Development Solutions Network.

5. Jacobson, M. and Delucchi, M. 2009. A Path to Sustainable Energy by 2030. *Scientific American*, 301(5), 58–65; The Solutions Project. 2019. https://thesolutionsproject.org/.

6. Loftus, P., et al. 2014. A Critical Review of Global Decarbonization Scenarios: What Do They Tell Us about Feasibility? *Wiley Interdisciplinary Reviews: Climate Change*, 6(1), 93–112.

7. Clack, C. et al. 2017. Evaluation of a Proposal for Reliable Low-cost Grid Power with 100% Wind, Water and Solar. *Proceedings of the National Academy of Sciences*. 114(26), 6722–6727.

8. Jaccard, M. 2005. *Sustainable Fossil Fuels: The Unusual Suspect in the Quest for Clean and Enduring Energy*. Cambridge: Cambridge University Press.

9. Jaiswal, D., et al. 2017. Brazilian Sugarcane Ethanol as an Expandable Green Alternative to Crude Oil Use. *Nature Climate Change*. 7, 788–792.

10. United States Department of Energy. 2016. *Billion-ton Report: Advancing Domestic Resources for a Thriving Bioeconomy, Volume 1: Economic Availability of Feedstocks*. Oak Ridge, TN: Oak Ridge National Laboratory.

11. Joskow, P. 2011. Comparing the Costs of Intermittent and Dispatchable Electricity Generation Technologies. *American Economic Review: Papers & Proceedings*, 100(3), 238–241.

12. Smil, V. 2017. *Energy Transitions: History, Requirements, Prospects*. (2nd edition) Santa Barbara, CA: Praeger.

13. Gates, B. 2010. Bill Gates on Energy: Innovating to Zero! *TED Talk*. www.ted.com/talks/bill_gates.html.

14. Nordhaus, T. and Shellenberger, M. 2010. The End of Magical Climate Thinking. *Foreign Policy* (January 13).

15. Johansson, T. et al. (eds.). 2012. *The Global Energy Assessment: Towards a Sustainable Future*. Cambridge: Cambridge University Press.

16. Ericsson, K. 2009. *Introduction and Development of Swedish District Heat Systems: Critical Factors and Lessons Learned*. RES-H Policy Program, Lund University.

17. Shmelev, S. and Speck, S. 2018. Green Fiscal Reform in Sweden: Econometric Assessment of the Carbon and Energy Taxation Scheme. *Renewable and Sustainable Energy Reviews*. 90, 969–981.

18. Norsk elbilforening. 2019. *Norwegian EV Policy: Norway is Leading the Way for a Transition to Zero Emission in Transport*. https://elbil.no/english/norwegian-ev-policy/.

12 WE MUST ABOLISH CAPITALISM

1. Klein, N. 2014. *This Changes Everything: Capitalism vs the Climate*. New York: Simon and Schuster.

2. Jaccard, M. 2014. I Wish this Changed Everything: Review of This Changes Everything by Naomi Klein. *Literary Review of Canada*. 22(9), 3–4.

3. IPCC. 1990, 1995, 2001, 2007, 2014. *Assessment Reports*. Cambridge: Cambridge University Press.

4. IPCC. 2005. *Special Report on Carbon Dioxide Capture and Storage.* Cambridge: Cambridge University Press.

5. Jaccard, M. 2005. *Sustainable Fossil Fuels: The Unusual Suspect in the Quest for Clean and Enduring Energy.* Cambridge: Cambridge University Press.

6. Gardner, D. 2009. *Risk: The Science and Politics of Fear.* London: Virgin Books.

7. Krugman, P. 2014. Errors and Emissions. *NY Times* (September 18).

13 THE SIMPLE PATH TO SUCCESS WITH OUR CLIMATE-ENERGY CHALLENGE

1. Schwarzenegger, A. 2003. Public Announcement of Candidacy for California Governor.

2. Government of California. 2006. *Global Warming Solutions Act (Assembly Bill 32).*

3. California Air Resources Board. Numerous reports at: https://ww2.arb.ca.gov/homepage.

4. Fairbrother, M., 2016. Trust and Public Support for Environmental Protection in Diverse National Contexts. *Sociological Science.* 3, 359–382.

5. Bataille, C. et al. 2018. A Review of Technology and Policy Deep Decarbonization Pathway Options for Making Energy-intensive Industry Production Consistent with the Paris Agreement. *Journal of Cleaner Production.* 187, 960–973.

6. Rivers, N. and Jaccard, M. 2010. Intensity-based Climate Change Policies in Canada. *Canadian Public Policy.* 36(4), 409–428.

7. McKibbin, W., et al. 2018. The Role of Border Carbon Adjustments in a US Carbon Tax. *Climate Change Economics.* 9(1), 1840011.

8. Healey, S. and Jaccard, M. 2016. Abundant Low-cost Natural Gas and Deep GHG Emissions Reductions for the United States. *Energy Policy.* 98, 241–253.

9. Jaccard, M. 2019. Finally, Canada is a Global Example for Climate Action. *Globe and Mail* (April 15).

10. Saxifrage, C. 2012. Thirteen Arrested Blocking BNSF Coal Train in White Rock. *Vancouver Observer* (May 6).

11. Jaccard, M. 2013. The Accidental Activist: How an Energy Economist and Former Harper Government Advisor Found himself Blocking a Coal Train. *The Walrus* (March 28).

Bibliography

Achen, C. and Bartels, L. 2016. *Democracy for Realists: Why Elections Do Not Produce Responsive Government.* Princeton, NJ: Princeton University Press.

Aguilera, R. and Radetzki, M. 2016. *The Price of Oil.* Cambridge: Cambridge University Press.

Anderson, K. 2012. The Inconvenient Truth of Carbon Offsets. *Nature.* 484(7).

Anderson, K., and Peters, G. 2016. The Trouble with Negative Emissions: Reliance on Negative-Emission Concepts Locks in Humankind's Carbon Addiction. *Science,* 354 (6309), 182–183.

Arrhenius, S. 1896. On the Influence of Carbonic Acid in the Air upon the Temperature of the Ground. *London, Edinburgh and Dublin Philosophical Magazine and Journal of Science,* 41, 237–275.

Associated Press. 2006. Shell Oil Chief: US Needs Global Warming Plan (September 23).

Associated Press. 2012. Climate Change Fears Overblown, Says Exxon Mobil Boss. *The Guardian* (June 28).

Baron, N. 2010. *Escape from the Ivory Tower: A Guide to Making your Science Matter.* Washington, DC: Island Press.

Bataille, C. et al. 2016. The Need for National Deep Decarbonization Pathways for Effective Climate Policy. *Climate Policy.* 16, S7–S26.

Bataille, C. et al. 2018. A Review of Technology and Policy Deep Decarbonization Pathway Options for Making Energy-Intensive Industry Production Consistent with the Paris Agreement. *Journal of Cleaner Production.* 187, 960–973.

Beck, M. et al. 2015. Carbon Tax and Revenue Recycling: Impacts on Households in British Columbia. *Resource and Energy Economics.* 41, 40–69.

Beller, H. 1992. *The Restless Conscience: Resistance to Hitler inside Nazi Germany* [Documentary film].

Bernauer, T. and McGrath, L. 2016. Simple Reframing unlikely to Boost Public Support for Climate Policy. *Nature Climate Change.* 6, 680–683.

Berry, T. and Jaccard, M. 2001. The Renewable Portfolio Standard: Design Considerations and an Implementation Survey. *Energy Policy.* 29, 263–277.

Bertram, C. et al. 2015. Carbon Lock-in through Capital Stock Inertia Associated with Weak Near-term Climate Policies. *Technological forecasting and social change.* 90, 62–72.

Boustany, N. 1991. Iraqi Leader Remains Defiant Following US-led Air Attacks. *The Washington Post* (January 17).

Brandt, A. 2007. *The Cigarette Century: The Rise, Fall, and Deadly Persistence of the Product that Defined America.* New York, NY: Basic Books.

Brinkley, D. 2006. *The Great Deluge: Hurricane Katrina, New Orleans, and the Mississippi Gulf Coast.* New York, NY: Harper Collins.

British Columbia Government, 2008. *Climate Action Plan.* Victoria: Government of B.C.

British Columbia Government. 2008. News Release: Balanced Budget 2008 – Greener Future, Stronger Economy. www.bcbudget.gov.bc.ca/2008/newsrelease/.

British Petroleum. (annual report, all years) *Statistical Review of World Energy.*

Brockway, P. et al. 2017. Energy Rebound as a Potential Threat to a Low-Carbon Future: Findings from a New Exergy-Based National-Level Rebound Approach. *Energies.* 10, 51–75.

Broder, J. 2009. Obama to Toughen Rules on Emissions and Mileage. *The New York Times* (May 18).

California Air Resources Board. Numerous reports at: https://ww2.arb.ca.gov/homepage.

Callendar, G. S. 1938. The Artificial Production of Carbon Dioxide and its Influence on Temperature. *Quarterly Journal of the Royal Meteorological Society,* 64, 223–230.

Cames, M. et al. 2016. *How Additional is the Clean Development Mechanism?* Berlin: Institute for Applied Ecology,

Caplan, B. 2007. *The Myth of the Rational Voter: Why Democracies Choose Bad Policies.* Princeton, NJ: Princeton University Press.

Carbon Engineering. 2019. About Us. https://carbonengineering.com/company-profile/.

Charney, J. et al. 1979. *Carbon Dioxide and Climate: A Scientific Assessment.* Washington, DC: National Academy of Sciences Press.

Chu, S. 2011. Energy Efficiency: Achieving the Potential, Realizing the Savings. *HuffPost* (May 25).

Churchill, W. 2012. *The Power of Words,* ed. Gilbert, M. Boston, MA: Da Capo Press.

Clack, C. et al. 2017. Evaluation of a Proposal for Reliable Low-Cost Grid Power with 100% Wind, Water and Solar. *Proceedings of the National Academy of Sciences.* 114(26), 6722–6727.

The Colbert Report. 2012. Season 7, Episode 42.

Coll, S. 2012. *Private Empire: ExxonMobil and American Power.* New York, NY: Penguin.

Creyts, J. et al. (eds.). 2007. Reducing US Greenhouse Gas Emissions: How Much at What Cost? *McKinsey and Company.*

Devinney, T., Auger, P., and Eckhardt, G. 2010. *The Myth of the Ethical Consumer.* Cambridge: Cambridge University Press.

Diamond, J. M. 2005. *Collapse: How Societies Choose to Fail or Succeed.* London: Penguin.

Elliott, S. 2008. When Doctors, and even Santa, Endorsed Tobacco. *The New York Times* (October 6).

Elsworth, C. 2007. Eco-trendy Hollywood Stars as Major Polluter. *The Telegraph* (October 2).

Emanuel, K. 2005. *Divine Wind: The History and Science of Hurricanes.* New York, NY: Oxford University Press.

Ericsson, K. 2009. *Introduction and Development of Swedish District Heat Systems: Critical Factors and Lessons Learned.* RES-H Policy Program, Lund University.

European Commission. 2005. *EU Emissions Trading System.* https://ec.europa.eu/clima/policies/ets_en.

ExxonMobil. 2013. The Outlook for Energy – A View to 2040. *EnergyMeetings* (June 11).

Fairbrother, M., 2016. Trust and Public Support for Environmental Protection in Diverse National Contexts. *Sociological Science.* 3, 359–382.

Farrell, J., McConnell, K., and Brulle, R. 2019. Evidence-based Strategies to Combat Scientific Misinformation. *Nature Climate Change.* 9, 191–195.

Festinger, L., Riecken, H., and Schachter, S. 1956. *When Prophecy Fails: A Social and Psychological Study of a Modern Group that Predicted the Destruction of the World.* Minneapolis, MN: University of Minnesota Press.

Flannery, T. 2005. *The Weather Makers: How Man is Changing the Climate and What it Means for Life on Earth.* New York, NY: Grove Press.

Flannery, T. 2015. *Atmosphere of Hope: Searching for Solutions to the Climate Crisis.* New York, NY: Grove Press.

Fouquet, R., and Pearson, P. 2006. Seven Centuries of Energy Services: The Price and Use of Light in the United Kingdom (1300–2000). *The Energy Journal.* 27 (1), 139–177.

Fourier, J. 1824. Remarques générales sur les températures du globe terrestre et des espaces planétaires. *Annales de Chimie et de Physique, 27,* 136–67.

Frank, R. H. 2009. *The Economic Naturalist's Field Guide: Common Sense Principles for Troubled Times.* New York, NY: Basic Books.

Gardner, D. 2009. *Risk: The Science and Politics of Fear.* London: Virgin Books.

Gates, B. 2010. Bill Gates on Energy: Innovating to Zero! *TED Talk.* www.ted.com/talks/bill_gates.html.

Gilbert, D. 2006. *Stumbling on Happiness.* New York, NY: Alfred A. Knopf.

Girrbach, C. 2012. Three Ways IT Can Support Greener Behaviors. *GreenBiz* (March 20).

Gleick, P. H. et al. 2010. Climate Change and the Integrity of Science. *Science, 328,* 689–690.

Goodell, J. 2007. *Big Coal: The Dirty Secret behind America's Energy Future.* Boston, MA: Mariner Books.

Goodell, J. 2010. As the World Burns. *Rolling Stone* (January 7).

Gore, A. 2006. *An Inconvenient Truth: The Planetary Emergency of Global Warming and What We Can Do About It.* Emmaus, PA: Rodale Press. [Film. Hollywood. CA: Paramount.]

Government of California. 2006. *Global Warming Solutions Act (Assembly Bill 32).*

Groves, S. 2009. The Desire to Acquire: Forecasting the Evolution of Household Energy Services. Master's research project, Simon Fraser University.

Grubb, M. and Newberry, D., 2018. UK Electricity Market Reform and the Energy Transition: Emerging Lessons. *The Energy Journal.* 39 (6), 1–25.

Haidt, J. 2012. *The Righteous Mind: Why Good People are Divided by Politics and Religion.* New York: Pantheon.

Hamilton, C. 2010. *Requiem for a Species. Why We Resist the Truth about Climate Change.* Sydney, AU: Earthscan.

Hansen, J. 2009. *Storms of my Grandchildren: The Truth about the Coming Climate Catastrophe and our Last Chance to Save Humanity.* New York, NY: Bloomsbury.

Hastorf, A., and Cantril, H. 1954. They Saw a Game: A Case Study. *The Journal of Abnormal & Social Psychology, 49,* 129–134.

Healey, S. and Jaccard. M. 2016. Abundant Low-cost Natural Gas and Deep GHG Emissions Reductions for the United States. *Energy Policy.* 98, 241–253.

Hirsch, R. L., Bezdek, R., and Wendling, R. 2005. *Peaking of World Oil Production: Impacts, Mitigation, and Risk Management.* Washington, DC: U.S. Department of Energy.

Hite, S. 1976. *The Hite Report.* New York, NY: Macmillan.

Hitler, A. 1925. *Mein Kampf.* Munich: Eher-Verlag.

Hoffman, A. 2015. *How Culture Shapes the Climate Change Debate.* Palo Alto, CA: Stanford University Press.

Hoggan, J. 2016. *I'm Right and You're an Idiot: The Toxic State of Public Discourse and How to Clean it up.* Gabriola Island, British Columbia: New Society Publishers.

Hoggan, J. and Littlemore, R. 2009. *Climate Cover-up: The Crusade to Deny Global Warming.* Vancouver: BC: Greystone Books.

Holland, S., Hughes, J., and Knittle, C. 2009. Greenhouse Gas Reductions under Low Carbon Fuel Standards? *American Economic Journal: Economic Policy.* 1(1), 106–146.

Horne, J. 2006. *Breach of Faith: Hurricane Katrina and the Near Death of a Great American City.* New York, NY: Random House.

Hornsey, M. et al. 2016. Meta-analysis of the Determinants and Outcomes of Belief in Climate Change. *Nature Climate Change.* 6(6), 622–626.

Howden, D. 2007. World Oil Supplies Are Set to Run Out Faster than Expected, Warn Scientists. *The Independent* (June 14).

Hubbert, M. K. 1956. *Nuclear Energy and the Fossil Fuel.* In: Meeting of the Southern District, Division of Production, American Petroleum Institute. Shell Development Company, San Antonio, TX.

Hulme, M. 2009. *Why We Disagree about Climate Change: Understanding Controversy, Inaction and Opportunity.* Cambridge: Cambridge University Press.

IPCC. 1990, 1995, 2001, 2007, 2014. *Assessment Reports.* Cambridge: Cambridge University Press.

IPCC. 2005. *Special Report on Carbon Dioxide Capture and Storage.* Cambridge: Cambridge University Press.

IPCC. 2014. *Fifth Assessment Report.* Cambridge: Cambridge University Press.

IPCC. 2018. *Global Warming of 1.5°C. An IPCC Special Report.* Cambridge: Cambridge University Press.

Jaccard, M. 2005. *Sustainable Fossil Fuels: The Unusual Suspect in the Quest for Clean and Enduring Energy.* Cambridge: Cambridge University Press.

Jaccard, M. 2012. The Political Acceptability of Carbon Taxes: Lessons from British Columbia. In Milne, J. and Anderson, M. *Handbook of Research on Environmental Taxation.* 175–191. Cheltenham: Edward Elgar.

Jaccard, M. 2013. The Accidental Activist: How an Energy Economist and Former Harper Government Advisor Found himself Blocking a Coal Train. *The Walrus* (March 28).

Jaccard, M. 2014. I Wish this Changed Everything: Review of This Changes Everything by Naomi Klein. *Literary Review of Canada.* 22(9), 3–4.

Jaccard, M. 2019. Finally, Canada is a Global Example for Climate Action. *Globe and Mail* (April 15).

Jaccard, M., Hein, M., and Vass. T. 2016. *Is Win-Win Possible? Can Canada's Government Achieve its Paris Commitment ... and Get Re-elected?* Energy and Materials Research Group, Simon Fraser University.

Jaccard, M., Hoffele, J., and Jaccard, T. 2018. Global Carbon Budgets and the Viability of New Fossil Fuel Projects. *Climatic Change.* 150, 15–28.

Jaccard, M., Nyboer, J., and Sadownik, B. 2002. *The Cost of Climate Policy.* Vancouver: University of British Columbia Press.

Jaccard, M. and Wu, H. (co-chairs). 2009. *Report and Recommendations to Chinese Premier Wen on the Prospects and Policies for Sustainable Use of Coal in China.* Beijing: China Council for International Cooperation on Environment and Development.

Jacobson, M. and Delucchi, M. 2009. A Path to Sustainable Energy by 2030. *Scientific American,* 301(5), 58–65.

Jaiswal, D. et al. 2017. Brazilian Sugarcane Ethanol as an Expandable Green Alternative to Crude Oil Use. *Nature Climate Change.* 7, 788–792.

Jenkins, J. 2014. Political Economy Constraints on Carbon Pricing Policies: What Are the Implications for Economic Efficiency, Environmental Efficacy, and Climate Policy Design? *Energy Policy.* 69, 467–477.

Jevons, W. 1865. *The Coal Question: An inquiry Concerning the Progress of the Nations and the Probable Exhaustion of our Coal Mines.* London: Macmillan & Co.

Johansson, T. et al. (eds.) 2012. *The Global Energy Assessment: Towards a Sustainable Future.* Cambridge: Cambridge University Press.

Joskow, P. 2011. Comparing the Costs of Intermittent and Dispatchable Electricity Generation Technologies. *American Economic Review: Papers & Proceedings,* 100(3), 238–241.

Kahan, D. 2018. Why Smart People are Vulnerable to Putting Tribe before Truth. *Scientific American* (December 3).

Kahneman, D. 2011. *Thinking Fast and Slow.* New York, NY: Farrar, Straus and Giroux.

Kamiya, G., Axsen, J. and Crawford, C. 2019. Modeling the GHG Emissions Intensity of Plug-in Electric Vehicles Using Short-term and Long-term Perspectives. *Transportation Research Part D.* 96, 209–223.

Keith, D. et al. 2018. A Process for Capturing CO_2 from the Atmosphere. *Joule.* 2, 1573–1594.

Keys, D. 1982. *Earth at Omega: Passage to Planetization.* Wellesley, MA: Branden.

Kinsey, A. C. et al. 1953. *Sexual Behavior in the Human Female.* Philadelphia, PA: Saunders.

Klein, N. 2014. *This Changes Everything: Capitalism vs the Climate.* New York: Simon and Schuster.

Kluger, R. 1996. *Ashes to Ashes: America's Hundred-year Cigarette War, the Public Health, and the Unabashed Triumph of Philip Morris.* New York, NY: Knopf.

Kollmus, A. et al. 2015. *Has Joint Implementation Reduced GHG Emissions? Lessons Learned for the Design of Carbon Market Mechanisms.* Stockholm Environment Institute Policy Brief.

Kopp, R. 2010. Role of Offsets in Global and Domestic Climate Policy. *Resources for the Future.* Issue Brief 10–11.

Krey, V. et al. 2014. Getting from Here to There: Energy Technology Transformation Pathways in the EMF27 Scenarios. *Climatic Change,* 123, 369–382.

Krugman, P. 2008. *The Return of Depression Economics and the Crisis of 2008.* New York, NY: W. W. Norton & Company.

Krugman, P. 2014. Errors and Emissions. *New York Times* (September 18).

Last Week Tonight with John Oliver. 2019. (May)

Leonard, A. 2010. *The Story of Stuff: How Our Obsession with Stuff is Trashing the Planet, Our Communities, and Our Health – and a Vision for Change.* New York, NY: Free Press.

Le Quere, C. et al. 2019. Drivers of Declining CO_2 Emissions in 18 Developed Economies. *Nature Climate Change.* 9, 213–218.

Loftus, P. et al. 2014. A Critical Review of Global Decarbonization Scenarios: What Do they Tell us about Feasibility? *Wiley Interdisciplinary Reviews: Climate Change,* 6(1), 93–112.

Lomborg, B. 2001. *The Skeptical Environmentalist: Measuring the Real State of the World.* Cambridge: Cambridge University Press.

Lontzek, T. et al. 2015. Stochastic Integrated Assessment of Climate Tipping Points Indicates the Need for Strict Climate Policy. *Nature Climate Change.* 5 (5), 441.

Loughran, D. and Kulick, J. 2004. Demand-side Management and Energy Efficiency in the United States. *The Energy Journal.* 25(1), 19–43.

Lovins, A. 1977. *Soft Energy Paths: Toward a Durable Peace.* Cambridge, MA: Ballinger.

Lynn, J. and Jay, A. 1989. *Yes Minister.* London: BBC Books.

MacKay, D., Ockenfels, A., and Stoft, S. 2017. *Global Carbon Pricing: The Path to Climate Cooperation.* Cambridge, MA: MIT Press.

Mann, M. 2012. *The Hockey Stick and the Climate Wars: Dispatches from the Front Lines.* New York, NY: Columbia University Press.

Mann, M. and Toles, T. 2016. *The Madhouse Effect: How Climate Change Denial is Threatening our Planet, Destroying our Politics, and Driving us Crazy.* New York, NY: Columbia University Press.

Marshall, G. 2014. *Don't Even Think About It: Why our Brains are Wired to Ignore Climate Change.* New York, NY: Bloomsbury.

May, P. 2007. Offset your Infidelity? *New Statesman America* (May 14).

McAuley, J. 2019. Low Visibility. *New York Review of Books* (March 21).

McCollum, D. et al. 2014. Fossil Resource and Energy Security Dynamics in Conventional and Carbon-Constrained Worlds. *Climatic Change,* 123, 413–426.

McKibben, B. 1989. *The End of Nature.* New York, NY: Random House.

McKibben, B. 2010. *Eaarth: Making a Life on a Tough New Planet.* New York, NY: Holt.

McKibben, B. 2019. Glaciers and Arctic Ice Are Vanishing. Time to Get Radical before it's Too Late. *The Guardian* (April 10).

McKibbin, W. et al. 2018. The Role of Border Carbon Adjustments in a US Carbon Tax. *Climate Change Economics.* 9(1), 1840011.

Meadows, D. H. et al. 1972. *The Limits to Growth: A Report for the Club of Rome's Project on the Predicament of Mankind.* New York, NY: Universe Books.

Metcalf, G. 2018. *Paying for Pollution: Why a Carbon Tax is Good for America.* New York, NY: Oxford University Press.

Michaels, D. 2008. *Doubt is their Product.* Oxford: Oxford University Press.

M.K. Jaccard and Associates. 2008. A Quantitative Analysis of Selected Climate Policies in British Columbia. Prepared for the B.C. Climate Action Secretariat.

Mooney, C. 2011. The Science of Why We Don't Believe Science. *Mother Jones* (May/June).

Moses, M. 2018. What Drives Doomsday Preppers? *The New Yorker* (November).

Murphy, R., Gross, D., and Jaccard, M. 2018. Use of Revealed Preference Data to Estimate the Costs of Forest Carbon Sequestration in Canada. *Forest Policy and Economics.* 97, 41–50.

Murphy, R. and Jaccard, M. 2011. Energy Efficiency and the Cost of GHG Abatement: A Comparison of Bottom-up and Hybrid Models for the US. *Energy Policy.* 39, 7146–7155.

National Conference of State Legislatures. 2019. *State Renewable Portfolio Standards and Goals.* www.ncsl.org/research/energy/renewable-portfolio-standards.aspx.

Natural Resources Defense Council. 2010. Simple and Inexpensive Actions could Reduce Global Warming Emissions by One Billion Tons. *Energy Facts* (May).

National Survey on Energy and Environment. 2019. http://closup.umich.edu/national-surveys-on-energy-and-environment/.

Nordhaus, W. 2015. Climate Clubs: Overcoming Free-riding in International Climate Policy. *American Economic Review,* 105(4), 1339–1370.

Nordhaus, T. and Shellenberger, M. 2010. The End of Magical Climate Thinking. *Foreign Policy* (January 13).

Norsk elbilforening. 2019. *Norwegian EV policy: Norway is Leading the Way for a Transition to Zero Emission in Transport.* https://elbil.no/english/norwegian-ev-policy/.

O'Grady, M. 2018. Ed Begley Jr. Reflects on Boycott Lists and Riding a Bicycle to Make Toast. *The Globe and Mail* (October 21).

Olson, M. 1965. *The Logic of Collective Action: Public Goods and the Theory of Groups.* Cambridge, MA: Harvard University Press.

Olson, R. 2009. *Don't Be Such a Scientist.* Washington, DC: Island Press.

Oreskes, N. and Conway, E. 2010. *Merchants of Doubt.* New York, NY: Bloomsbury.

Real Time with Bill Maher. 2005. Season 3, Episode 15.

Orwell, G. 1949. *Nineteen Eighty-four.* London: Secker & Warburg.

Popplewell, B. 2008. Can Branson Globetrot on Reduced Carbon Diet? *The Star* (February 14).

Rabe, B. *Can We Price Carbon?* Cambridge, MA: MIT Press.

Rees, W. 2010. What's Blocking Sustainability? Human Nature, Cognition and Denial. *Sustainability: Science, Practice and Policy,* 6(2), 13–25.

Revkin, A. 2003. Politics Reasserts itself in the Debate over Climate Change and its Hazards. *The New York Times* (August 5).

Rhodes, K., Axsen, J. and Jaccard, M. 2014. Does Effective Climate Policy Require Well-informed Citizen Support? *Global Environmental Change*, 29, 92–104.

Rhodes, K., Axsen, J. and Jaccard, M. 2015. Gauging Citizen Support for a Low Carbon Fuel Standard. *Energy Policy*. 79, 104–114.

Rhodes, K. and Jaccard, M. 2013. A Tale of Two Climate Policies: Political-economy of British Columbia's Carbon Tax and Clean Electricity Standard. *Canadian Public Policy*. 39, S37–51.

Rich, N. 2019. Losing Earth: A Recent History. New York, NY: Farrar, Straus, & Giroux.

Ridley, M. 2010. *The Rational Optimist: How Prosperity Evolves*. New York, NY: Harper Collins.

Rivers, N. and Jaccard, M. 2010. Intensity-based Climate Change Policies in Canada. *Canadian Public Policy*. 36(4), 409–428.

Rivers, N. and Jaccard, M. 2011. Electric Utility Demand Side Management in Canada. *The Energy Journal*. 32 (4), 93–116.

Robalino, J., et al. 2008. *Deforestation Impacts of Environmental Services Payments: Costa Rica's PSA Program 2000–2005*. Washington, DC: Resources for the Future.

Rogelj, J. 2016. Paris Agreement Climate Proposals Need a Boost to Keep Warming Well Below 2°C. *Nature*. 534, 631–639.

Rolling Stone. 2006. Kurt Vonnegut Says this is the End of the World (August 24).

Rudd, S. 2012. Cost-effectiveness of Climate Change Policies for the United States. (Master's thesis) School of Resource and Environmental Management, Simon Fraser University.

Sachs, J. et al. 2014. *Pathways to Deep Decarbonization*. Paris: Sustainable Development Solutions Network.

Saxifrage, C. 2012. Thirteen Arrested Blocking BNSF Coal Train in White Rock. *Vancouver Observer* (May 6).

Schapiro, M. 2010. Conning the Climate: Inside the Carbon-trading Shell Game. *Harper's* (February).

Schmidt, C. 2006. *Workers of the World Relax*. Vancouver, BC: WLP Publishing.

Schwarzenegger, A. 2003. Public Announcement of Candidacy for California Governor.

Shmelev, S. and Speck, S. 2018. Green Fiscal Reform in Sweden: Econometric Assessment of the Carbon and Energy Taxation Scheme. *Renewable and Sustainable Energy Reviews*, 90, 969–981.

Shulman, S., et al. 2007. *Smoke, Mirrors, and Hot Air. How ExxonMobil Uses Big Tobacco's Tactics to Manufacture Uncertainty on Climate Science*. Cambridge, MA: Union of Concerned Scientists.

Simpson, J., Jaccard, M., and Rivers, N. 2007. *Hot Air: Meeting Canada's Climate Change Challenge*. Toronto: McLelland and Stewart (Doug Gibson books).

Smil, V. 2017. *Energy Transitions: History, Requirements, Prospects*. (2nd edition) Santa Barbara, CA: Praeger.

The Solutions Project. 2019. https://thesolutionsproject.org/.

Song, L. 2019. An Even More Inconvenient Truth: Why Carbon Credits for Forest Preservation May Be Even Worse than Doing Nothing. *Propublica* (May).

Springmann, M. et al. 2016. Analysis and Valuation of the Health and Climate Change Cobenefits of Dietary Change. *Proceedings of the National Academy of Sciences.* 113 (15), 4146–4151.

Stern, N. 2006. *The Economics of Climate Change.* Cambridge: Cambridge University Press.

Stiglitz, J. 2010. *Freefall: America, Free Markets, and the Sinking of the World Economy.* New York, NY: W. W. Norton & Company.

Talley, I. 2009. Americans Are Like 'Teenage Kids' When It Comes to Energy. *The Wall Street Journal* (September 21).

Tavris, C. and Aronson, E. 2007. *Mistakes Were Made (But Not by Me): Why We Justify Foolish Beliefs, Bad Decisions, and Hurtful Acts.* Orlando, FL: Harcourt.

Truby, J. 2018. Decarbonizing Bitcoin: Law and Policy Choices for Reducing the Energy Consumption of Blockchain Technologies and Digital Currencies. *Energy Research and Social Science,* 44, 399–410.

Tyndall, J. 1861. On the Absorption and Radiation of Heat by Gases and Vapours, and on the Physical Connexion of Radiation, Absorption and Conduction. *Philosophical Transactions of the Royal Society of London.* 151, 1–36.

United Nations Framework Convention on Climate Change. 2015. *Paris Agreement.*

United States Department of Energy. 2016. *Billion-ton Report: Advancing Domestic Resources for a Thriving Bioeconomy, Volume 1: Economic Availability of Feedstocks.* Oak Ridge, TN: Oak Ridge National Laboratory.

United States Environmental Protection Agency. 2015. *Clean Power Plan for Existing Power Plants.* https://web.archive.org/web/1920160325042337/ https://www .epa.gov/cleanpowerplan/clean-power-plan-existing-power-plants.

United States House of Representatives. 2009. *American Clean Energy and Security Act.*

Upton, G. and Snyder, B. 2017. Funding Renewable Energy: An Analysis of Renewable Portfolio Standards. *Energy Economics.* 66, 205–216.

Vass, T. and Jaccard, M. 2017. Driving Decarbonization: Pathways and Policies for Canadian Transport. *Energy and Materials Research Group: Simon Fraser University.*

Victor, D. 2001. *The Collapse of the Kyoto Protocol and the Struggle to Slow Global Warming.* Princeton, NJ: Princeton University Press.

Victor, D. 2011. *Global Warming Gridlock.* New York, NY: Cambridge University Press.

Wallace-Wells, D. 2019. *The Uninhabitable Earth: Life after Warming.* New York, NY: Tim Duggan Books.

Wexler, B. 2006. *Brain and Culture: Neurobiology, Ideology, and Social Change.* Cambridge, MA: MIT Press.

Weyant, J. and Kriegler, E. 2014. Preface and Introduction to EMF 27. *Climatic Change, 122,* 345–352.

Willett, W. et al. 2019. Food in the Anthropocene: The EAT-Lancet Commission on Healthy Diets from Sustainable Food Systems. *Lancet.*

Yergin, D. 2011. *The Quest: Energy, Security, and the Remaking of the Modern World.* London: Penguin.

Zito, S. 2016. Taking Trump Seriously, not Literally. *The Atlantic* (September 23).

Index